Grammar in Context
Proficiency Level English

Hugh Gethin

Collins ELT: London and Glasgow

Collins ELT
8 Grafton Street
London W1X 3LA

First published 1983
Reprinted 1984, 1985, 1986, 1987, 1988, 1989

Printed in Great Britain by
Bell and Bain Ltd., Glasgow

ISBN 0 00 370025 9

Acknowledgements

I should like to thank the Directors of the Anglo-Continental Educational Group, Bournemouth,
for facilities afforded me in the earlier stages of preparation of this book; and Arminio Ciumei
('Jimmy'), the Group's xeroxer, for his efficient and cheerful help. To my erstwhile colleague,
David Marchesi, goes my warm gratitude for a fruitful partnership of several years, during
which he shared with me the use of most of this book in draft form. The co-operation and
comments of a person of his mature judgement did much to encourage me to proceed with the
enterprise. This, in its later stages, came under the scrutiny of Rosalind Grant-Robertson, whose
knowledge of EFL is wide and deep. Any improvements I have latterly been able to make in the
text have in large measure been due to her careful and constructive criticism, for which I am
indeed grateful. I should also like to thank Christian Kay for her stimulating comments,
particularly those on the earlier sections; Caroline Egerton for her informed and penetrating
reading and sensible suggestions, which have contributed so much to the text's final form; and
Gordon Jarvie, whose lively professional interest in the book has led to its publication. To my
wife I am indebted as always, both for sustaining me and helping to resolve the various
problems of authorship.

HG

Contents

Introduction

For the learner

If you are the kind of learner for whom this book has been written, you will have learnt English intensively for months or less intensively for years. You will now be in contact with the language as it is used by British, American and other native speakers in conversation, on radio and television, in letters, books or newspapers. You yourself may be using the language socially or in your work; you may be studying it full- or part-time; you may be preparing for an examination such as the Cambridge Proficiency.

Whatever you are doing, you will have some academic background and some acquaintance, although it may be only slight, with grammatical concepts. With the help from time to time of a good dictionary or a teacher, you will be able to read this and the rest of the book with adequate understanding. In short, you will have reached an advanced level in English but you will still be learning it with a view to improving it as a means of communication, both written and spoken.

Apart from vocabulary, idiom and pronunciation, what you will still be learning is grammar, which is the way the vocabulary organises itself or, in other words, how the language works. A lot of grammar you will already know, such as the general order of words, basic tenses and verb forms, the making of questions and statements. Some of this, however, will have been imperfectly learnt, while there will be some grammar that you do not know at all. It is for this purpose, then, that the book has been written: to review the grammar that you may know imperfectly and to teach the grammar that you need to know but do not. (You may know it in the sense that you have heard or seen it used but not in the more important sense that you can recognise it and can use it yourself.) How does the book set out to achieve this?

Examples

The way a language works is best shown first by example, and so nearly every section of the book begins with examples of the grammar dealt with in that section. Since language is normally organised for intelligent communication, and is not a collection of unconnected utterances, the examples in each section are as far as possible connected to form a discourse or 'story' to show grammar in use and not just as 'naked' grammar lying about doing nothing. From these examples you should be able to get quite a good idea of how the language works.

Explanation

In order thoroughly to understand the examples, however, you will need some help in clarifying the way the language works; and to make understanding and learning easier you will probably feel the need for rules. To answer these needs as far as possible, an explanation follows the examples. It is linked for reference purposes to the examples by numbers and letters, so that you do not have to go through the whole explanation to clarify a certain example. This should be of particular advantage in review sections such as those on verb tenses (**1B**) and relatives (**8A**), where you may find that your existing knowledge makes some of the explanation unnecessary. In any explanation of grammar, descriptive terminology is unavoidable, and this is not introduced here for its own sake. Sometimes you will recognise the terms used through your own language, but in any case their meaning is illustrated in the examples and, if necessary, explained in a footnote.

Exercises

Having, through the examples and the explanation, understood the grammar involved, you now have to practise and test your knowledge. The exercises, like the examples, are as far as possible organised as discourse so that you can use the grammar you are learning in a meaningful context. It is important, therefore, to read out or to rewrite the whole text and not just the portion that needs changing. To help you prepare for some of the exercises, there are study lists towards the end of the book, placed there to make it easier for you not to refer to them while actually doing the exercises. If you find the exercises too difficult, you should return to examples, explanation or lists, and also if necessary to your dictionary, for better preparation.

Order of contents

The numbered sections of the book are in an order that can be followed to advantage, but are sufficiently independent of each other to be taken in the order that best answers your needs. However, the subsections **A**, **B** etc. build upon each other, and should be done in the order given.

Indexes

There are grammatical and word indexes that refer you by section number and letter to the relevant explanations, which, as mentioned above, are themselves linked with the examples.

Key to exercises

So that you can correct your answers to the exercises yourself, there is a key to them at the end of the book.

For the teacher

It is through what I have already said to the learner that I can best introduce the book to a teacher. In continuation I should like to add the following.

Rationale

This book has come into being, over many years of teaching and organising courses, in response to the need of post-intermediate students to feel bedrock beneath them. Learners at this level may be superficially fluent and able to cope socially in the language, but often flounder in a slough of words when more exact communication, written or spoken, is required of them. Those who meet the challenge and make further progress are usually those who not only need but actively demand a fuller understanding of grammar. At the stage we are talking about, this demand can best be met through the medium of English itself.

Although there are several EFL books dealing with grammar at this level, they have not all got exercises under the same cover. Also I have thought it to be very well worthwhile to try and put the grammar into more homogeneous contexts than are found in other books. The object thereby is not that learners should lose sight of the grammar as such (which happens in some books) but that they should see it used in examples in a contextual situation, and therefore in a more meaningful way, than they would in unconnected sentences. Where possible I have extended this treatment to the exercises. Thus the book, and thus its title.

Use

As already pointed out to the learner, the order followed by the main sections of this book is a recommended one only. The extensive cross-referencing that is provided should allow you to integrate the book into the rest of your teaching programme in any order required. Whichever section is selected for teaching, it is of course most important that you should thoroughly acquaint yourself beforehand with its examples, explanation and exercises.

Most of the grammatical categories that I have used will be familiar to you. I have departed from the traditional ones only where, after experiment and discussion, it has been apparent that there are better ways (at least at this level of teaching) of presenting the grammar of the language. Instances are the division of verb use into the categories of 'fact' and 'non-fact' and the incorporation into the passive of an auxiliary form. The examples and explanation of each section should soon put you in the picture regarding the categories used.

Depending on the time available and the depth of study required, the exercises may be done in class, orally or in writing, or as homework for later checking and comment.

Weighting

The book does not set out to be a comprehensive grammar of English. Some grammatical features, such as independent prepositions, have been considered familiar enough to the post-intermediate learner to be used in examples and exercises without grammatical comment. Others, such as verb tenses and relative pronouns, are not dealt with from scratch but are extensively reviewed and presented as a working unit.

The emphasis throughout is on the essential unit of discourse, which is the contextualised sentence; the relation between grammar and meaning is never forgotten. The aim is that serious learners should acquire, without the need for systematic structural analysis, a knowledge of the English sentence so that they can get its grammar **and** its meaning right not only in exercises but in their own connected speech and writing. In several years' use of this material, my colleagues and I have seen this aim achieved.

Style and usage

Closely connected with grammar is the question of style. Grammatical transformations and substitutions can involve changes between informal and more formal language. Where I have thought it necessary I have drawn attention to such changes by pointing out that certain uses are more formal than others, but have avoided extremes of style one way or the other and have generally embedded the grammar in moderately informal language identified by the use of colloquial contraction (*I'm, isn't* etc.). The absence of such contraction from the examples or exercises usually means either that the grammar requires the language to be more formal (as in some of the material on relative pronouns) or that contraction (as in the earlier sections on verb tenses) might obscure what was being exemplified.

Under this heading it is convenient to refer briefly to the question of British against American English. The grammar dealt with here is that of British English, but in saying that I am not aware of any differences sufficiently important to make it invalid as the grammar of an English speaker amongst Americans. Any problem caused by its use in the USA would be as nothing compared to its misuse there or in Britain, since in all important aspects the grammar of English is common to both 'languages'. Such uses as *like* for *as*, *than* after *different*, or *just* with the past tense are mentioned in this book, but not as linguistic differences because, although characteristic of American, they occur this side of the Atlantic as well.

1 Verb tenses

1A The past tense of certain verbs

Examples

1 What time did the sun *rise*? $\longrightarrow$ The sun *rose* just after
   Just after five o'clock.   five o'clock.

2 Did it *shine* into the room? $\longrightarrow$ Yes, it *shone* into the room.
   Yes, it did.

Note: Under 17A you will find a study list of the forty verbs used in the
following two Exercises. Although they are all quite common verbs their past
tenses often cause difficulty, and you are advised to familiarise yourself with
them first, so that you can do the Exercises with little hesitation and with
appreciation of their meaning.

Exercises

Combine the question and the answer to make a complete statement as shown
in the Examples above.

1

1 How far did the car skid?
  Nearly thirty metres.
2 Why did the driver tread on the accelerator?
  Because he thought it was the brake.
3 Did the accelerator stick wide open?
  Yes, it did.
4 What did the car hit?
  A lamp-post.
5 What did they bind the driver's wound with?
  A piece of shirt.
6 How long did the passenger's nose bleed for?
  Quite a long time.
7 Where did the passenger lie down?
  On the pavement.
8 Where did the driver wake up?
  In hospital.

9 Who did they lay the blame on?
   The other driver.
10 How much did they sue him for?
   Twenty thousand pounds.
11 When did he quit his job?
   Straight after the accident.
12 Why did he flee the country?
   To escape the law.
13 Did anyone shed any tears when he left?
   No, no one.
14 Where did he seek refuge?
   In Australia.
15 Did he dig for gold there?
   Yes, he did.
16 Did he strike any gold?
   Hardly any.
17 Did he grow rich?
   No, grass.
18 Where did he sow grass?
   Wherever he could.
19 Why did he saw down trees?
   To make a fence for sheep.
20 What did he feed the sheep on?
   Bananas, of course!

2

1 Why did Sheila's lip swell up?
   Because a wasp stung her.
2 How did Ken split his trousers?
   Climbing over a fence.
3 Did Toby bet that Ken could not sew them up himself?
   Yes, he did.
4 Did Ken sew them up himself?
   Yes, he did.
5 How did Helen slit the envelope open?
   With her enormously long fingernail.
6 How did Marilyn speed up her typing?
   By going to evening classes.
7 How much did Zena bid for the Chinese vase?
   A couple of hundred.
8 When did she fall?
   Going down the stairs.
9 How did she feel about breaking the vase?
   Terrible.

10   Did she hurt herself?
     Yes, her wrist.
11   Where did all the water flow?
     Downstairs.
12   Why did Helen fly out of the room in a rage?
     Because of what her father said.
13   What did her father forbid her to do?
     Go out with Denis.
14   How did her father deal with her?
     By stopping her monthly allowance.
15   Why did Denis stroke Helen's hand?
     To try and calm her down.
16   What rumour did Helen's friends spread?
     That she was going to get married.
17   What did Marilyn weave her rugs on?
     The looms over there.
18   How much did she raise her prices by?
     Fifteen per cent.
19   When did the question of a bank loan arise?
     At the directors' meeting.
20   When did they broadcast the news?
     Just now, on the BBC.

1B   Tense use for fact: review

Introductory note: Verb tenses in English fall into two main categories:
those used for FACT and those used for NON-FACT. By fact we mean what we
treat* as real or quite possible. Non-fact is what is supposed† or wished for,
which is either unreal or improbable. Here are some examples:

I became Managing Director five years ago.	FACT
I'll soon be sixty.	FACT
I wish I were Managing Director!	NON-FACT: WISH
Then I'd have an office on the top floor.	NON-FACT: SUPPOSITION

Fact is directly related to time, and so generally is the tense use. Non-fact has
no direct relationship with time and neither has the tense use. Non-fact tense
use is dealt with in sections 1D and 1E. Tense use for fact is reviewed in this
section and in 1C. In section 1F both kinds of use are compared and
summarised.

---

* 'Treat' as real, because fact in this sense includes fiction.
† Or HYPOTHETICAL, a term used in some grammar books together with HYPOTHESIS, which in this book is
called SUPPOSITION.

You should already be familiar with English tenses and to a large extent with their use, and so what follows immediately below is in the nature of revision so that you can refresh and exercise your knowledge. The Examples set out tenses for fact, together with their English names, divided into the SIMPLE and the PROGRESSIVE form (called CONTINUOUS in some books). The Explanation draws attention to the more important points regarding their use. The three Exercises deal first with the present and past tenses, then with tenses relating to future time, and finally with all tenses.

Examples

	TENSES (SIMPLE)	
I (1) *became* Managing Director five years ago. I (2) *had been* Personnel Manager for three years and	PAST	**a**
	PAST PERFECT	**b**
(3) *joined/had joined* the firm in 1970,	PAST/PAST PERFECT	**a, b**
so I (4) *have been* here for fifteen years.	PRESENT PERFECT	**c**
I (5) *work* in an office on the top floor.	PRESENT	**d**
I (6) *retire* in five years. I think I	PRESENT (FUTURE USE)	**e**
(7) *will/shall* go and live in the	FUTURE	**f, r**
country. I (8) *will/shall have been* with the firm for twenty years by then.	FUTURE PERFECT	**g, r**

	TENSES (PROGRESSIVE)	**s**
I (9) *was* still *working* at eight o'clock yesterday evening. I (10) *had been working* since early morning. We	PAST	**h**
	PAST PERFECT	**j**
(11) *have been working* very hard at the office lately as we (12) *are*	PRESENT PERFECT	**k**
negotiating an important contract.	PRESENT	**l**
Tomorrow I (13) *am flying* to Milan.	PRESENT (FUTURE USE)	**m**
(14) *Will* it still *be raining* like this when I get back, I wonder? I hope	FUTURE	**n, r**
not, because I (15) *am going to take* a	*going to*	**p**
few days off as soon as I can. I (16) *'ll have been working* non-stop for over three weeks.	FUTURE PERFECT	**q, r**

Explanation

a PAST SIMPLE refers (1, 3) to a definite time in the past or 'then' (*five years ago, in 1970*). The time itself is not always mentioned:

Thomas Edison invented the electric light bulb.
See also **c** below.

b PAST PERFECT SIMPLE refers (2) to indefinite time until (*for three years*) then or before* then. It may also refer (3) to a definite time (*in 1970*) before then.

c PRESENT PERFECT SIMPLE refers (4) to indefinite time before or until (*for fifteen years*) now. It can **not** refer to definite time or 'then' (**not** 'I've joined the firm in 1970'). But it may be used with several words to refer to 'before now':

He has *just* told me that he has *recently* been made Managing Director and has *already* been busier than he has ever been *before*.

Recently and *just (now)* also occur with the past tense:

The man you just spoke to/spoke to just now recently became our Managing Director.

d PRESENT SIMPLE refers principally (5) to what exists or occurs habitually (*I work*) in our present lives or nowadays. In this use it refers to repeated, not single, events:

When do you go to London? – (I go) On Fridays/Every Friday.

e PRESENT SIMPLE (FUTURE USE) refers (6) to a future that is planned, usually through regulations, programmes, timetables etc. (compare **m** below). In this use it may refer to single events:

When (according to your travel schedule) do you go to London? – (I go) On Friday/Next Friday.

f FUTURE SIMPLE is used for the future when there is no definite plan or intention (but see **p** below), or if there is a condition attached (1C). It often occurs with *think* (7), *expect, wonder, perhaps, probably* etc. But it is used for a planned future when the verb has no progressive form (see **s** below):

I'll have my new car next month.

g FUTURE PERFECT SIMPLE usually refers (8) to indefinite time (*for twenty years*) before or until then in the future (*by then*). But like the past perfect and unlike the present perfect, it may sometimes refer to definite time:

I'll be tired when I arrive, because I'll have had an exam the day before.

h PAST PROGRESSIVE refers to what was IN PROGRESS in the past. When this was over a PERIOD of time, either the progressive or the simple form may be used with no essential difference in meaning:

Yesterday I was working/worked from eight in the morning until nine at night.

But for what was in progress at a POINT in time (9) only the progressive form can be used. (See also **l** below.)

---

* As, for example, in 'I'd acted as Managing Director several times before (then).' *Several times before* and *for three years* are both indefinite because they do not answer the question *When . . . ?* Compare *five years ago, in 1970*.

j PAST PERFECT PROGRESSIVE refers (10) to what was in progress **until** then. If the activity itself did not last until then, its effect did:

> I couldn't shake hands as mine were dirty; I'd been working on my car.

k PRESENT PERFECT PROGRESSIVE refers (11) to what has been in progress **until** now. It may be used with *just, recently* or *already* (see **c** above), but not with *before* (*I've worked* (**not** have been working) *here before*).

l PRESENT PROGRESSIVE refers to what is in progress now (12) or at repeated time points nowadays:

> They're always/often/never watching television when I visit them.

Compare 'They always/often/never (= start to) watch television when I visit them.' *Always* or *continually* may be used with the present or past progressive without reference to time points:

> They're/They were always watching television.

This is for repeated activity that, usually because it annoys us, claims our attention to such an extent that it seems to be always in progress.

m PRESENT PROGRESSIVE (FUTURE USE) refers (13) to a future that is planned, usually as a particular arrangement rather than as part of a programme etc. (see **e, n**).

n FUTURE PROGRESSIVE refers (14) to what will be in progress at a future time point (*when I get back*). It is also used when we anticipate something without actually arranging it. Compare the following (with reference to **e, m**):

> (According to my travel schedule) I don't return until next week.
> I'm not returning until next week. (That's the particular arrangement.)
> I shan't be returning until next week. (That's what I anticipate.)

The distinction between these uses is not a strict one.

p *Going to* is used for intention (15), before we have made a definite plan. For sudden intention (when we make up our mind on the spur of the moment) it is usually replaced by the future simple. Compare with Example 15 the following:

> I'm taking a few days off next week. (I've already arranged it.)
> So you're going to Wales. What a good idea! I'll take a few days off and come too. (I've suddenly thought of it.)

(Again the distinction between the uses is not strict.) *Going to* is also used when we are convinced something is going to happen, either (**i**) because it has already started to happen or (**ii**) because of what we know of the circumstances. In the second use (**ii**), but not in the first, *going to* can alternate with the future simple tense:

i She's going to (**not** will) have a baby.
ii She's going to find/will find it difficult to carry on working.

To express the future from the point of view of the past, *going to* may be used with *was/were*:

> He was going to take a few days off; I hope he managed it.

q   FUTURE PERFECT PROGRESSIVE is similar in principle to **j** and **k** above, but with reference to what will have been in progress **until** then in the future (16).

r   *Will* AGAINST *shall* IN FUTURE TENSES: The question of which to use is not an important one. Apart from the fact that they are often contracted and therefore indistinguishable (16), it is seldom incorrect to use *will* with all persons (*I, we* as well as *she, you* etc.). For an exception, see **12Bb**.

s   NON-USE OF PROGRESSIVE FORMS: When there is nothing in progress or happening, such as when we **think** (= believe) or **have** (= possess) something, progressive forms are not used:

> i I think Ken has two cars. Am I right?

Compare:

> ii I'm having (= taking) a holiday next month. I'm thinking of
>   (= contemplating) going hang-gliding. Am I being rash?

In general, verbs such as *think/believe* or *have/possess* which describe states of mind, ownership etc. (how things **are**) do not have progressive forms (i), while verbs (the majority) such as *have/take* or *think/contemplate* which describe some sort of activity or process do have them (ii). The verb *be* commonly refers to states like that of *belief* and so is most often used in a simple form (i), but it may occur in the progressive to relate to something in progress like *contemplating* (ii). Verbs of perception like *see* and *hear* generally have no progressive forms either, but they too may have other meanings:

> Sheila's seeing (= consulting) a doctor about her cough.
>
> I've been hearing a lot (= getting a lot of news) about her lately.

Exercise 1

For each verb in brackets, choose one of the following tenses: the PRESENT, PRESENT PERFECT, PAST or PAST PERFECT, in either the SIMPLE or PROGRESSIVE form. If there is an adverb before the bracket, note the position it should have in a PERFECT or a PROGRESSIVE tense by referring to **c** and **l** in the preceding Explanation.

Brenda Pearl (**1** join) our firm ten years ago. She (**2** work) for the previous five years with an advertising company and (**3** acquire) much useful experience. For the first eight years with us she (**4** work) in the Sales Department, and (**5** work) there when I (**6** become) Managing Director. Since then she (**7** work) as my personal assistant, and (**8** prove) herself to be outstandingly capable on many occasions. She (**9** work) on the top floor, in an office next to mine, but at the moment (**10** work) in London on a special assignment.

When the North and South finally (**11** lay) down their arms in 1865 at the end of the American Civil War they (**12** fight) for over four years and the South, which (**13** win) several battles but (**14** lose) the war, (**15** be) economically exhausted. It (**16** be) a tragedy that Abraham Lincoln, who (**17** lead) the North to victory and (**18** be) now ready to be generous to the South, (**19** not|survive) to make the peace. Five days after General Lee (**20** surrender) at Appomattox, Lincoln (**21** be) assassinated.

Denis always (**22** ring) me up when I am in the shower or washing my hair. The last time it (**23** happen) I (**24** not|answer) the phone. I (**25** learn) afterwards that someone (**26** ring) me up that day to offer me a job which they then (**27** offer) to someone else. I just (**28** tell) Denis that he (**29** be) to blame for the fact that I (**30** miss) a golden opportunity.

'What (**31** do|you) with yourself lately? I (**32** not|see) you for over a month.'
'I (**33** be) in Stockholm since I last (**34** see) you.'
'Really? How long (**35** be|you) there and what (**36** do|you)?'
'Nearly three weeks. I (**37** do) some research at the Royal Library. I think I already (**38** tell) you that I (**39** work) on a book about Scandinavia.'
'Yes. How (**40** go|it)?'
'Not so bad. I (**41** hope) to have it in the hands of the publisher by the end of the year.'

Peter (**42** live) in Nodnol, the capital of Mercia. At least, that's where he (**43** live) when he last (**44** write). In his letter he (**45** invite) me to visit him, but as I (**46** have) no answer to my last two letters I (**47** wonder) whether I should go or not. I also (**48** have) no reply from the consulate about the Mercian visa I (**49** apply) for two weeks ago. Although I (**50** be) born in Mercia, I no longer (**51** have) a Mercian passport.

(On the telephone): Yes, I'm at Georgina's house this evening. What (**52** do|I) here? I (**53** babysit). She and her husband (**54** go) to a party. Four – four children. They (**55** be) usually rather wild. I (**56** babysit) here once when they all (**57** start) screaming. But they (**58** be) very good at the moment. I can see the youngest now in the room next door: she (**59** eat) a huge box of chocolates that Georgina (**60** give) me before she (**61** leave). The others (**62** find) a tin of paint and happily (**63** paint) the walls of the kitchen. They (**64** assure) me that they (**65** do) this before and that their mother and father (**66** have) no objection then. I only (**67** hope) they (**68** tell) me the truth. One of them (**69** get) himself in a bit of a mess. I (**70** try) to clean him up with paint remover, but so far without much success.

Exercise 2

This exercise covers the tenses and forms used for future time, namely the SIMPLE or PROGRESSIVE FUTURE, FUTURE PERFECT and PRESENT tenses, and the *going to* form. For each verb in brackets use one of these. Instructions for any adverb in front of the bracket are in principle the same as for Exercise 1.

I hope Brenda still (**1** work) for me when I retire in six years' time. She (**2** retire) herself a few years afterwards, because she then (**3** be) sixty. She (**4** work) for the firm for twenty years by then and (**5** qualify) for the firm's full pension. She says that when she retires she (**6** work) as a business consultant. She probably (**7** earn) more money doing that than she does now. At the moment she is in London on a special assignment, but she (**8** come) back tomorrow, so if you look in then I (**9** introduce) you to her. (**10** tell|I) her you may come?

I (**11** see) Willie tomorrow at our weekly Japanese class, so I (**12** tell) him what you have just told me. He (**13** be) very pleased to know that you have passed your music exam. What (**14** do|you) next? (**15** prepare|you) for the higher grade?

According to this timetable for my business trip to Brazil for the firm, I (**16** be) due in Rio on the fourteenth and (**17** leave) for São Paulo on the seventeenth. That (**18** not|give) me enough time to visit the three factories that are listed: they (**19** need) at least a day each. Incidentally, when (**20** meet|I) our representative in São Paulo? There's no mention of that here. And I see that I (**21** be) due back in Britain on the twenty-second, which (**22** mean) only forty-eight hours in Brasilia, which in my opinion (**23** not|be) enough. (**24** be|you) free any time this afternoon? Three-thirty? Good. So (**25** be|I). Could I discuss my Brazilian programme with you then?

'I hear that Marilyn (**26** go) to the States shortly. What (**27** do|she) there?'
'She (**28** promote) her firm's products.'
'How (**29** do|she) that?'
'She (**30** demonstrate) them to selected retail outlets. I am sure she (**31** do) extremely well.'

Sir James and Lady Blenkinsop (**32** be) married for thirty years next March. They (**33** celebrate) their wedding anniversary with a dinner party at Blenkinsop Hall on the seventeenth. I don't think it (**34** be) a particularly stylish affair, but I am sure a lot of good food (**35** be) served. Sheila, Ken and Willie have been invited and (**36** go). Marilyn was invited too, but can't go because she (**37** leave) for the States by then. Helen and Denis say they (**38** go) – if they're invited! I haven't been invited yet, but I can't go anyway, as I (**39** work) on a job in Glasgow at the time. (**40** go|you)?

'Do you think there (**41** be) an election next month?'
'There definitely (**42** be) one; they've just announced it on the radio. They haven't given a date, but it probably (**43** be) on the second Thursday.'
'Who do you think (**44** win)?'
'I don't know who (**45** win). But the Government (**46** lose).'

'This time tomorrow I (**47** take) my driving test. Wish me luck!'

'I (48 do) better than that; I (49 give) you some last-minute instruction.'
'Thank you, but I (50 not|go) out this evening. I (51 stay) in and (52 go) to
bed early. That (53 be) the best way to prepare for the test.'

'I've just heard the weather forecast. It (54 snow). And that reminds me that
Christmas soon (55 be) here. Have you any plans for a holiday?'
'I (56 fly) to Mercia to stay with a friend, but as I probably (57 not|get) a visa
in time I've decided to cancel the trip. So it looks as if I (58 spend) Christmas
at home as usual. (59 do|you) the same?'
'No, I (60 go) to Sweden.'
'Really? What (61 do|you) there?'
'I (62 do) some research for my book on Scandinavia. Then, if I have time, I
(63 visit) friends in Dalarna, about three hundred kilometers from
Stockholm.'
'So when (64 be|you) back in England?'
'I (65 fly) back on the eighth of January.'

'Have you heard the latest? I expect it (66 surprise) you. Helen and Denis
(67 get) married!'
'I (68 believe) that when it happens. I'm sure their engagement or whatever
you like to call it (69 not|last) long; they soon (70 start) quarrelling again.'

Exercise 3

This Exercise covers all the tenses dealt with in this section. Choose a suitable
tense for each verb in brackets. The position of any adverb before a bracket
will be the same as that in the previous two Exercises.

Ken (1 drive) along yesterday when a stone (2 go) clean through the
windscreen. As he (3 pass) another car at the time it (4 be) lucky he
(5 not|have) a nasty accident. He says that lorries from the quarry still (6 use)
that road and that stones often (7 fall) off them. I (8 not|drive) that way into
town in future if I can possibly avoid it.

Next month I (9 be) married for ten years. We (10 live) in this house for ten
years too. We (11 celebrate) the two anniversaries with a party to which we
(12 invite) some friends and neighbours. Most of our neighbours (13 be) also
our friends, and already (14 say) they (15 come). The family next door,
however, (16 not|be) very friendly at the moment and (17 decline) the
invitation, presumably because of a dispute about the fence between their
garden and ours. We (18 have) the fence repaired last week, since it (19 be)
broken for several months, with the result that dogs (20 get) in on several
occasions and (21 do) quite a lot of damage. It is our neighbours who (22 be)
responsible for the maintenance of this particular fence, and so we naturally
(23 send) them the bill, which they so far (24 refuse) to pay.

'It (25 not|be) so very long ago that man first (26 land) on the moon. What an astonishing achievement that (27 be)! I remember how one evening at nine o'clock Armstrong and Aldrin (28 walk) about and (29 chat) 400,000 kilometers away, and you and I (30 watch) and (31 listen) to them. Nothing like it ever (32 happen) before and I sometimes (33 think) that nothing like it ever (34 happen) again.'
'Why (35 say|you) that nothing like it ever (36 happen) before? Astronauts from other planets (37 visit) our solar system ever since it (38 begin). At this very moment spaceships (39 hover) overhead and (40 watch) what you and I (41 do). As I (42 walk) home the other evening I (43 see) something in the sky which definitely (44 not|come) from anywhere on this planet. And if you (45 think) I (46 drink) you are wrong. That (47 not|be) the only time I (48 see) strange objects in the sky. I (49 see) quite a few over the years and (50 report) them all to the UFO club. One day I (51 write) a book about them. Tomorrow, though, I (52 go) to Manchester to buy the latest UFO literature.'

'I (53 think) about our plans for next week. What (54 do|you) next Thursday evening? (55 be|you) on duty at the hospital?'
'I (56 be) on duty, but I (57 change) with a friend who (58 want) Friday off. What (59 have|you) in mind?'
'How about going to see *Macbeth*? It (60 be) on for the whole of next week. (61 ever|see|you) it?'
'I (62 see) a film of it once. But I never (63 see) the play. Yes, that's a good idea: we (64 go) and see *Macbeth*,'
'I (65 book) the seats. (66 ask|I) Willie to come too?'
'He (67 work), I bet. He always (68 work). He (69 work) too much. He (70 have) a nervous breakdown if he's not careful.'

1C   Use of present for future tenses

Introductory note: We have seen in section **1B** that, with the exception of the future uses of the present tense forms, tenses generally relate to time when they are used for fact. There is, however, another important exception: verbs that refer to future time are **not** used in the future or future perfect tenses directly after CONDITIONAL links or TIME links;* instead they are used in the present or present perfect tenses:

I'll tell her more on Monday *if* she <u>comes</u>. (Compare: She'<u>ll</u> *probably* <u>come</u> on Monday; I'll tell her more then.)
When I'<u>ve read</u> the book I'll lend it to him. (Compare: I'll lend him the book next week; I'<u>ll have read</u> it *by then*.)
The principal conditional and time links are as follows:

---

* Called LINKS because they link or join two parts of a sentence together. As you will see from the Examples, either part may come first.

CONDITIONAL LINKS

if
providing, provided (that), as/so long as
even if
unless
supposing
whether . . . or (not)
however, no matter how
whoever, wherever, whenever etc.
no matter who/where/when etc.

TIME LINKS

after	*while*
before	*until, till*
when	*as soon as, immediately*
as	*by the time*

There are one or two other instances of the use of present for future tenses which, although not so important as the above, should be mentioned. They are included in the Examples and Explanation below.

Examples

1 *Providing* you're back by eight o'clock you can go to the airport to welcome the group.   **a**
2 You must come back then *even if* they haven't arrived.   **b, j**
3 They'll drive to the concert hall in an open car *unless* it's raining.   **c**
4 *Whether* the plane's late *or* not, they'll get a terrific welcome.   **d**
5 I'm not going to miss the chance of seeing them *however* late they are.   **e**
6 There'll be a lot of fans at the airport *whenever* the group arrives.   **f**
7 What will the police do, *supposing* the crowd gets out of hand?   **g**
8 Some of the fans will be pretty impatient *by the time* the plane lands.   **h**
9 Here they are! Don't worry – I'll give you your camera back *when/after/as soon as/immediately* I've taken a photo!   **j**
10 The police will stop people *who* try to get too close to them.   **k**
11 I *don't care* what the police do: I'm going to get their autographs.   **l**
12 It'll be the first *time* I've spoken to a pop star.   **m**
13 (Police officer): Now *if* you girls and boys will all stop pushing and shoving, we'll be a lot more comfortable, won't we? (Exception!)   **n**

Explanation

a *Providing* (1), *provided (that), as/so long as* are approximately equivalent. They are all emphatic forms of *if*, emphasising a condition.

b *Even if* (2) introduces an extreme condition. Emphasis is on *even*, not *if*.

c *Unless* (3) can generally be replaced by *if . . . not* (*if it's not raining*) or *providing* etc. . . . *not*, but sometimes more suitably by *except when*:

> I won't ever use the car for work unless/except when it's raining.

d *Whether . . . or* (4) used conditionally must be distinguished from the interrogative link used in indirect questions, after which the future tense may be used:
> I wonder whether they'll come (or not).

Unlike conditional *whether*, the interrogative link can usually be replaced by *if* (*I wonder if . . .*).* Here again it is important to distinguish between this interrogative use of *if* and its conditional use.

e *However* as a conditional link (5) must be distinguished from the adverb *however* (**2Bm, 5e**). Conditional *however* can be replaced by the more formal *no matter how*.

f Similarly, *whenever* (6) and other *-ever* forms can often be replaced by *no matter when* etc. But *whenever* can also mean *(at) any time (that)*:
> Come whenever/(at) any time (that) you want.

Here, although it is still followed by a present and not a future tense, it cannot be replaced by *no matter when*. The other *-ever* forms may be used in a similar way:
> The police will stop whoever/anyone who tries to get too close.

The two different uses can occur in the same sentence:
> Come any time (= whenever) you want, whenever (= no matter when) it is.
> The police will stop anyone who (= whoever) tries to get too close, whoever (= no matter who) it is.

g *Supposing* (7) may, like other conditional links, be used at the beginning of a sentence. But then it often does not act as a link, and so one sentence is turned into two. In this position *supposing* can alternate with *suppose*:
> Supposing/Suppose the crowd gets out of hand. What will the police do?

h *By the time* (8) is used when we do not wish to refer to a definite time (see **1Bb, c, g**): *by the time the plane lands* = some time not later than when it lands. Note that *by eight o'clock* (1) = not later than eight o'clock.

j *When, after* etc. (9) are followed by the present perfect to indicate completion of an action. Note also a similar use after *even if* (2).

k A DEFINING RELATIVE (**8Ab**) like *who* (10) is used with a present tense to refer to future time when the relative itself follows a future tense (*will stop*). Compare:
> There's no one here who'll stop you.

l *Don't care* (11) is always used with a present instead of a future tense. With *hope* we can use either:
> I hope the police won't/don't stop you.

*It cannot be replaced by *if* when it is directly followed by an infinitive: 'I don't know whether to go or not.'

m After *it will/won't be the first/second* etc. *time* (12) we always use the present perfect tense. Note carefully the corresponding uses for present and past time:

> It'*s* the first time I'*ve spoken* to a pop star.
> It *was* the first time I'*d spoken* to a pop star.

You will see that for future time we use the same tense (*have spoken*) as for present time; we do not use the tense one might expect, namely the future perfect (**1Bg**).

n The more important exceptions to the non-use of *will* after conditional links are as follows:

   i When we request or hope that people will do something (13).

   ii When we use *will not* to mean *refuse* (**11Bf**): '*If* Sheila <u>won't</u> do it, I'll ask Helen.'

   iii When a future condition can be satisfied (at least as far as we are concerned) in the present:

> Shopper: *Provided* this sleeping bag <u>will</u> keep me warmer than the others I'll buy it, although it's the most expensive.
> Assistant: It definitely will.
> Shopper: OK, I'll buy it.

Exercise

Choose a correct tense for each verb in brackets. Where there is no verb (_____), give the correct auxiliary such as *does* or *has*. The position of any adverb immediately before the bracket will be the same as it was in the Exercises in section **1B**.

Zena (**1** go) to Paris to work in a fashion show and (**2** not|be) back until next week. When I (**3** see) her off at the airport this morning she (**4** look) forward to it very much. Although she (**5** go) there once as a very small girl she (**6** not| remember) it, and so in a sense this (**7** be) the first time she (**8** be) there.

Deni̇s continually (**9** urge) me to lend him money for a business venture which he says (**10** pay) his creditors back handsomely. I always (**11** refuse) his request as politely as I can. He (**12** not|yet|show) any talent for business and until he (**13** _____) I (**14** not|lend) him a penny.

Marilyn (**15** go) to the States on business in a few days. I am told that while she (**16** be) away, Georgina's brother (**17** keep) an eye on her firm for her. He (**18** help) Marilyn with her business before, and she (**19** trust) him implicitly. As long as she (**20** not|be) away for too long, it should be a satisfactory arrangement.

Robert (**21** go) around recently saying that he (**22** think) people who (**23** go) to university (**24** have) a great advantage over those who (**25** _____ not). (**26** mean|this) that he (**27** think) of going to university himself? If it

(28 _____) and if he actually (29 succeed) in getting there, he (30 do) what his father always (31 want) him to do, partly because he never (32 have) the chance of doing it himself. But I (33 doubt) if Robert (34 get) a university place all that easily if he (35 not|improve) his academic qualifications. He (36 leave) school over a year ago with poor grades, and unless he now (37 go) to a college and (38 work) hard to get better ones, few universities (39 accept) him. The trouble is that Robert is not the sort of person who (40 find) it easy to start studying again.

Robert (41 prefer) sport to books, and since leaving school (42 continue) to play a lot of football. In fact the manager of the local team says he (43 consider) Robert for a place in it provided he (44 train) hard. And here (45 lie) another of Robert's problems: he is a sociable, easy-going sort of chap with a strong streak of laziness in his character, whether we (46 talk) of study or sport. Unless he (47 take) regular exercise – which he seldom (48 _____) – he (49 tend) to run to fat, even at his age. Until he (50 spend) less time eating and chatting idly with friends, he (51 not|become) the professional footballer he sometimes (52 dream) of being. Whichever he (53 choose), university or football, he clearly (54 have) to discipline himself. However, a self-disciplined Robert is someone I (55 find) hard to imagine; I (56 feel) that even if it (57 cost) him a career he (58 go) on being the same Robert, which (59 mean) that by the time he (60 be) thirty he (61 be) really fat!

My son (62 study) medicine for six years and (63 take) his final examinations in two months' time. Provided he (64 pass) them, he then (65 specialise) in psychiatry, which (66 take) another two years' study at least. So he (67 not|be) ready to practise full time until he (68 be) nearly thirty. He then (69 study) for a total of eight or nine years and (70 earn) practically nothing. Until now his wife (71 work) and (72 support) him, but she (73 expect) a baby in four months' time. So she soon (74 give up) her job. What on earth they (75 live) on when she no longer (76 work) I do not know. But they (77 not|worry) about it. My daughter-in-law says that she never (78 feel) better in her life, while my son says simply that he (79 qualify) as a psychiatrist however long it (80 take).

Retired people quite rightly think that if they (81 work) hard for most of their lives they (82 earn) the right to a bit of comfort in their old age. Unfortunately, unless they (83 qualify) for pensions indexed to the cost of living, they will be among those who (84 suffer) most if there (85 be) bad inflation.

'So long as political leaders (86 keep) their heads a third world war certainly (87 not|be) inevitable.'
'But supposing they (88 lose) their heads already! Many people think that unless this ludicrous arms race (89 cease) we (90 be) bound to have another war.'
'My prediction is that providing a nuclear holocaust (91 not|occur) by the end of the century, mankind (92 pass) the danger point.'

'You're too complacent. Even if your prediction (**93** prove) correct, there always (**94** be) the danger of man destroying himself.'

'I (**95** come) with you only if you (**96** drive) more slowly than you usually (**97** _____).'
'Of course I (**98** _____)! Jump in! You can put the handbrake on immediately you (**99** think) I (**100** go) too fast.'

1D   Tense use for non-fact: supposition

Introductory note: For supposition we use the same conditional links as in 1C and the sentences in which we use them are, like those in 1C, called conditional sentences. But tense use for supposition is different, as the following examples show:

> She always *waited* for me if I *was* late.   FACT: PAST TIME
> I'm sure she *would* always *wait* for me if I *was* late.
> > SUPPOSITION: FUTURE REFERENCE

The obvious difference, then, between conditional sentences for fact and for supposition is the use in the latter of a CONDITIONAL tense. Conditional tenses are formed by the substitution of *would/should* for *will/shall* in the future tenses (**1Bf, g, n, q**), so that we get the following:

	CONDITIONAL	CONDITIONAL PERFECT
SIMPLE FORM	*would wait*	*would have waited*
PROGRESSIVE FORM	*would be waiting*	*would have been waiting*

In the rest of the sentence (that is to say, after a link such as *if*), we use one of the past tenses already dealt with in **1B**, with the important difference that for supposition a past tense does **not** relate directly to time; as we see from the example above (*was*), it may have a future reference. Sometimes the subjunctive *were* is used instead of *was*; and *could* or *might* may be used instead of a conditional tense. Possible combinations of these tenses and verbs are given below.

Thus we see that conditional sentences consist of two parts. These are called CLAUSES. The one beginning with the link is the CONDITIONAL CLAUSE (since it expresses the condition), while the other is the MAIN CLAUSE.* As the Examples here and in **1C** show, either clause may come first in a sentence, but under tense use (see below) the main-clause tense is listed first.

---

* In some grammar books, what is called a dependent or subordinate clause (for example, a conditional clause) is defined as part of a main clause. In this book main and dependent clauses are separate parts of a sentence.

To remind you of the conditional links mentioned in 1C, these are as follows:

if, providing, provided (that), as/so long as, unless, supposing, even if, whether . . . or (not), however, no matter how, whoever etc., no matter who etc., any . . . (that) etc.

Examples

	TIME REFERENCE	TENSE USE
1 *If* Brenda <u>was/were</u> here she <u>would be working</u> in the office next door. **a**	PRESENT	CONDITIONAL + PAST or SUBJUNCTIVE *were*
2 *If* she <u>left</u> her job tomorrow she <u>would</u> <u>get</u> some pension. **b**	FUTURE	
3 *However* long Brenda <u>had</u> stayed in her last job she <u>would</u> not have got a pension. **c**	PAST	CONDITIONAL PERFECT + PAST PERFECT
4 But she <u>would</u> now <u>be</u> <u>earning</u> a good salary *if* she <u>had</u> not <u>left</u>. **d**	MIXED: PRESENT–PAST	CONDITIONAL + PAST PERFECT
5 Brenda <u>would have told</u> me *if* she <u>did</u> not <u>like</u> her present job. **d**	MIXED: PAST–PRESENT	CONDITIONAL PERFECT + PAST
6 She <u>might</u> now be a director *if* she <u>had stayed</u> in her last job. **e**	MIXED: PRESENT–PAST	*might* WITH INFINITIVE + PAST PERFECT
7 Brenda <u>could have made</u> a success of *any* career (*that*) she <u>had chosen</u>. **f,g**	PAST	*could* WITH PERFECT INFINITIVE + PAST PERFECT

Explanation

a Reference (1) is to a supposed or hypothetical present, that is to say, to one which does not exist. Note the tense use:

Main clause:	CONDITIONAL (*would be working*)
Conditional clause:	PAST (*was*)

The use of the progressive form (*would be working*) corresponds to its use for FACT:

Brenda is here; she is working in the office next door.

After *if, even if* or *unless* the subjunctive *were* is a common alternative to *was*, and in the expression

If I was/were you I would/should . . .

is probably the more common of the two. However, *were* is seldom used after the other conditional links.

b Reference (2) is to a future that is supposed or hypothetical for one of several reasons:

  i We do not think it probable or do not consider it seriously (Example 2). Compare the following, where the tense use (see **1C**) shows that the same future possibility is either considered probable or, if improbable, is taken seriously as something that **may** happen:

    If she leaves her job tomorrow she will get some pension.

  ii We consider future possibilities seriously, but have not yet made up our minds what to do:

    Why not ask her now? She would still be at home if we phoned straight away.

  iii We want to be polite, and therefore approach the future cautiously, as supposition rather than possible fact:

    Would it be all right if I used your phone?*

This is more polite than 'Will it be all right if I use your phone?'
Tense use for the supposed future is the same as for the supposed present, except that as alternatives we can use *was to/were to* or *should* in the conditional clause after *if, even if* or *unless*. These alternative uses are generally more formal than the standard use:

  If she was to/were to leave her job tomorrow she would ...

  If she should leave her job tomorrow she would ...

Should can also be used in a conditional sentence like that in **i** above:

  If she should leave her job tomorrow she *will* ...

The probable effect of *should* here is to make the sentence less 'factual' and more 'suppositional' like Example 2. But whether it is used with *will* or *would* in the main clause, *should* after *if* has nothing to do with *ought* or the conditional tense; it can **not** be replaced by *would* (**not** 'If she would leave her job tomorrow she will/would ...') and it can **not** be contracted to *'d* (see **11Fe**).

c Reference (3) is to a supposed or hypothetical past which never existed. Note the tense use:

    Main clause: CONDITIONAL PERFECT (*would have got*)
    Conditional clause: PAST PERFECT (*had stayed*)

For the conditional link *however*, see **1Ce**.

d Mixed reference (4,5) occurs in many conditional sentences. The main clause may have one reference, for example to the supposed present, and the conditional clause another reference, perhaps to the supposed past (4); or the references may be reversed (5). Tenses are used accordingly. Here are mixed future–past references:

* Note a variation using the infinitive instead of a clause: 'Would it be possible (for me etc.) to use your phone?' (See **1Fd**.)

I would come with you tomorrow if I hadn't already promised to go out with Denis.

I would have accepted your invitation if I wasn't going out with Denis tomorrow.

Sometimes the conditional or past tense is downgraded to the conditional perfect or past perfect to give a sentence with uniform tense use:

I would have come with you tomorrow if I hadn't already promised . . .

I would have accepted your invitation if I hadn't been going out . . . tomorrow.

e *Might* (6) is often used instead of *would perhaps* to express possibility (= She would perhaps now be a director if . . .). *Might* with a perfect infinitive (*have been*) is used instead of the conditional perfect tense:

She might have been (= would perhaps have been) a director by now if . . .

f *Could* normally replaces *would be able to*, expressing ability: *could make* = *would be able to make*. With the perfect infinitive (7) it replaces the conditional perfect tense (*would have been able to make*).

g We have already seen (1Cf) that links like *any time (that)* can be the equivalent of conditional links like *whenever*. Similarly, *any career (that)* (7) can be the equivalent of *whatever career* and act as a conditional link in a supposition (= If she had chosen any career at all she could have made a success of it). Here are some more examples:

I'd give a reward to anyone who (= to whoever) found my necklace.

They'd have done anything (= whatever) she'd asked.

These links are DEFINING RELATIVES (see 8Ab). Sometimes they are more precise in meaning than *-ever* forms:

I'd punish any child of mine who (**not** whoever) did a thing like that.

For my holiday I'd choose a nice seaside resort that (**not** wherever) promised some sun.

NON-DEFINING RELATIVES (8Aa) cannot act as conditional links.

h *Would* against *should*. Like *shall* (1Br), conditional *should* may be used with the first persons (*I, we*), but as it can be confused with *should* in its other uses (11C,E,F) it is generally better to use *would* for the conditional tense. In either case the distinction between conditional *would* and *should* often disappears, since contraction to *'d* is normal in colloquial English (see 1F, Examples).

Exercise

Use correct tenses for the verbs in brackets. These include tenses for fact (1B,C) as well as for supposition. Where there is no verb (_____), give the correct auxiliary like *could* or *did*. For the possible position of an adverb in front of a bracket, see Example 4 above.

'As long as you (1 be) sure it (2 be) perfectly convenient, 1 (3 call) round tomorrow to see Miss Pearl as you just (4 suggest).'
'I (5 not|suggest) it unless it (6 be) convenient. If you (7 want) to come on Friday it (8 be) a different matter; Brenda (9 be) too busy to see you.'

Sheila teaches only the younger children at her school, but I think she (10 be) equally successful no matter who she (11 teach). I hear that however ill-behaved and uncooperative her classes (12 be) in the beginning, she always (13 win) them round in the end.

'If I (14 be) a successful doctor like you I never (15 do) what you've done: I (16 not|go) and live in a town I (17 not|like), however much the people (18 need) me.'
'If I (19 not|be) a doctor I (20 agree) with you. I (21 live) near my family and friends, not where my fellow citizens (22 need) me most. But I *am* a doctor, and if I (23 do) that my skills would be wasted. And if I felt that was happening, how (24 justify|I) my choice of career?'

I don't keep a dog or a cat because if I (25 _____) I (26 have to) find someone to look after it whenever I (27 go) away, and as I travel a lot on business that (28 be) a nuisance. However, when I (29 get) married, which I (30 expect) to do quite soon, I (31 keep) one.

Even if I (32 have) all the money in the world I (33 not|be) happier than I am now. Providing one (34 have) reasonably good health, it (35 be) possible to be happy with very few material possessions. I hope I (36 continue) to think as I do however rich I (37 get).

'Do you think pigs (38 fly) if they (39 have) wings?'
'I don't think they (40 _____); their weight (41 be) all in the wrong place.*
But what a silly question! If pigs (42 have) wings they (43 not|be) pigs!'

If we (44 live) on grass we (45 need) a special stomach like a cow's and teeth that (46 chew) vegetable matter more efficiently than ours. We also (47 need) to spend a great deal more time eating than we (48 _____) now.

'If we (49 fit) ourselves with an extra heart, (50 not|do|we) a lot more work?'
'I don't know. We (51 be|able) to do more physical work. But whether we (52 have) an extra heart or not, we (53 not|do) more mental work without an extra brain. The trouble is that some people (54 use) an extra brain to avoid doing extra work.'

If it (55 not|be) for Napoleon Bonaparte, who (56 make) his cavalry ride on the right side of the road, the whole world now (57 drive) on the left, as they (58 _____) in Japan, India, Australia and Britain. The left, after all, (59 be) the right side to drive for right-handed people.

* Note that a conditional sentence may consist only of one or more main clauses when the conditional clause is understood from the context, and is therefore not stated. Such sentences occur here and later in the Exercise.

The Frenchman Pascal writes somewhere that if Queen Cleopatra of Egypt (60 have) a shorter nose, the face of the world now (61 be) different. He means, presumably, that Julius Caesar and Mark Antony (62 not|fall) in love with her, and so (63 spend) their energies on other conquests.

'Unless you (64 leave) by the time I (65 count) ten,' he shouted, 'I (66 call) the police!'
'I (67 have) no intention of leaving, whatever you (68 count) and whoever you (69 call),' I replied. 'If you (70 know) anything about the law, which you clearly don't, you (71 realise) I have as much right here as you have. Why (72 not|mind|you) your own business? If you (73 _____), the world (74 be) a better place.'

'I (75 take) some of my pupils to Oxford tomorrow on a sightseeing tour.'
'Really? (76 be|it) possible for my daughter to join the party? You (77 show) her so much more than if she (78 go) with us, as we (79 not|know) Oxford very well.'
'Certainly. The coach (80 leave) at eight-thirty from outside the school. So if she (81 be) there in good time it (82 be) a pleasure to have her with us. There (83 be) several spare seats.'
'In that case, (84 mind|you) if we (85 come) too?'
'I'm very sorry, but this is strictly an outing for the children. If I (86 allow) you to come I (87 have to) allow the other parents to come as well.'

'My colleague Brenda Pearl nearly (88 get) married a few years ago. I doubt whether she now (89 work) with me if she (90 _____). I almost certainly (91 lose) a wonderful assistant.'
'You (92 _____), but on the other hand you (93 _____|not). Even if she (94 get) married, I am sure she now (95 work) somewhere.'

'Someone (96 break) the calculator again.'
'I (97 not|be) a bit surprised if it (98 be) Denis. It (99 not|be) the first time he (100 do) it.'

1E   Tense use for non-fact: wish

Introductory note: There are four different phrases* that may be used to introduce a fanciful or unfulfilled wish:

If only Brenda was/were here!
I *wish* (that) she was/were here.
It is time she was here.
I *would rather* she was/were here (than in London).

---

* In this book the word PHRASE is used loosely to mean a group of related words.

The first three are in descending order of strength of feeling; *if only*, the strongest, is often used with an exclamation mark. *Would rather* expresses a wish in the form of a comparison or preference, although the phrase introduced by *than* may be left out if the comparison is understood from the context.

You will see that they are used with a past tense (*was*) or (with the exception of *it is time*) the subjunctive *were* to express a wish that is unfulfilled in the present. They may also be used to express wishes for the future that may or may not be fulfilled:

> *If only* Brenda would come back!
> I *wish* (that) she would come back.
> *It is time* she came back.
> I *would rather* she came back (than stayed in London).

Here the tense used with the first two and the last two phrases is different. The first two phrases, *if only* and *wish*, but not the last two (*it is time* and *would rather*), often introduce wishes unfulfilled in the past:

> *If only* Brenda hadn't gone to London!
> I *wish* (that) she hadn't gone to London.

These various tense uses are amplified and explained below.

Examples

		TIME REFERENCE	TENSE USE
1	I *wish* Brenda <u>was/were</u> here. *If only* she <u>was/were</u> <u>working</u> in the office next door! **a**	PRESENT	PAST **or** SUBJUNCTIVE *were*
2	*If only* I <u>could</u> (= <u>was/</u> <u>were able to</u>) telephone her! **b**	PRESENT	*could* WITH INFINITIVE
3	I *wish* Brenda <u>would get</u> in touch! *If only* she <u>would phone</u> me! **c**	FUTURE	CONDITIONAL
4	I *wish* Brenda <u>hadn't gone</u> to London. *If only* she <u>had stayed</u> here! **d**	PAST	PAST PERFECT
5	I *wish* we <u>could have</u> <u>postponed</u> (= <u>had been</u> <u>able to postpone</u>) her trip to London **e**	PAST	*could* WITH PERFECT INFINITIVE
6	(On phone): Brenda, *it is time* you <u>were</u> back. I *would rather* you <u>were</u> <u>helping</u> me here than working in London. **f, g**	PRESENT	PAST

7 Yes, *it is* high *time* you   FUTURE   PAST
  came back. There is an
  important matter I *would*
  much *rather* you <u>dealt</u> with
  than anyone else.   f, g

Explanation

a Where we would use a present tense for fact ('Brenda is here; she is working in the office next door'), we use (1) *wish* or *if only* with the PAST tense or subjunctive *were* for an unfulfilled wish.

b *Could* (2) usually replaces *was/were able to* (see e below).

c Where we might use the future tense for possible fact ('I expect Brenda will get in touch; she'll probably phone me'), we use (3) *wish* or *if only* with the CONDITIONAL tense for a wish that we **hope** will be fulfilled. Compare the use of *wish* or *want* with the infinitive (*wish* being the more formal and the less common of the two):
     I wish/want Brenda to phone me.
Here we have what is almost a command, which we **expect** to be fulfilled.

d Where we would use the present perfect or past tense for fact ('Brenda hasn't gone to London; she stayed here'), we use (4) *wish* or *if only* with the PAST PERFECT tense.

e After *wish* or *if only*, *could have* (5) usually replaces *had been able to*. Compare 1Df, where we have seen that *could* and *could have* replace *would be able to* and *would have been able to* respectively.

f *It is time* is followed only by the PAST tense to express a wish. This may be a wish unfulfilled in the present (6) or that may or may not be fulfilled in the future (7). Compare the use of *it is time* with the infinitive to express a fact that is in the nature of a command:
     It is time (for you) to come back.

g *Would rather* (6,7) is essentially similar regarding tense use to *it is time*. However, although uncommon, its use with the past perfect tense to express a wish unfulfilled in the past can occur:
     I would rather Brenda had gone to London last week (than this week).
For the use of *would rather* with the plain infinitive, see **9g**.

Exercise

Choose a correct tense for the verbs in brackets. As well as tenses used to express wish, some of the tenses required are those used for fact or for supposition (1D). Where there is no verb (_____), give the correct auxiliary, such as *can* or *would*.

Sheila, whose mother is ill, wishes she (1 get) better so that they could go on holiday together next month. She says she (2 _____) rather go with her than with anyone else.

'If only,' some people say, 'the world (3 be) a kinder place than it is!' It's time such people (4 realise) that charity begins at home and (5 act) accordingly.

'If only,' thinks Georgina's husband, 'I (6 get) Georgina to sew or read a book! I wish she (7 learn) to enjoy domestic life a bit more and (8 not|want) to go out every evening.'

I would always rather people (9 think) me a rogue than a fool. Rogues are quite popular at parties and other social gatherings, whereas if people (10 think) you are stupid they never (11 ask) you anywhere.

I wish I (12 call) round to see you tomorrow, but I don't think I (13 _____). I (14 let) you know, though, if there is any change of plan.

'Don't you wish your late aunt (15 leave) you some money when she died?' 'Not really. If she (16 _____) I expect I (17 give) it away. I (18 _____) rather any money of mine (19 be) earned than inherited.'

'I wish I (20 be) as artistic as you. Then* I (21 spend) all my time painting beautiful scenery.'
'If you think art is just painting beautiful scenery, it's time you (22 learn) something about it!'

'It's high time someone (23 tell) Denis how objectionable he is.'
'I wish you always (24 not|criticise) Denis behind his back the way you do. He's not so bad. I'd rather he (25 become) my son-in-law than Ken, for example.'
'What's wrong with Ken? If you (26 know) him as well as I do, you (27 realise) he's worth ten Denises.'
'Oh, I wish you (28 stop) weighing people up like lumps of meat!'

Sir James thinks it's time his son Toby (29 get) a proper job and (30 begin) to think seriously about a career. Of course Sir James would rather Toby (31 work) in his own firm than anywhere else, but in any case he wishes he (32 adopt) a more positive attitude towards life.

People often wish they (33 choose) a different career when they were young. 'If only,' they say, 'I (34 do) what I really wanted to do!' Or: 'I wish I (35 listen) to so-and-so's advice.' Well, the truth of the matter often is that if they (36 have) their lives over again they (37 choose) the same.

'I must say I wish I (38 be) born a bird and not a human. Then* I (39 not|have

---

* The adverb *then* here replaces a missing conditional clause *If* . . . (see footnote on p. 27).

to) come in to work this morning. And I (**40** have) more freedom to go where I pleased when I pleased. I (**41** migrate) last autumn if I (**42** want) to!'
'You do talk a lot of nonsense. It's time you (**43** come) to terms with life as it is. If you (**44** be) born a bird, you (**45** be) dead at your age.'

1F   Fact and non-fact: summary of tense use

Introductory note: The following Examples summarise in dialogue form tense use for supposition (**1D**) and wish (**1E**) as non-fact and compare it with tense use for fact (**1B,C**). The Examples show how use can vary between non-fact and fact, even within the same sentence (B3, A5, B5, A6). As this is a dialogue, colloquial abbreviations are used, *had* being distinguished as *'(ha)d* from *would/should* (= *'d*). The small letters (**a**, **b** etc.) refer to the Explanation below.

Examples

A1 I*'d like* to learn to play the piano. I wish
I *knew* a good teacher who *lived* near
here and who*'d give/could give*
me lessons.

B1 Suppose I *gave* you lessons. What *would*
you *say*?   NON-FACT   **a, d**

A2 Oh, if only you *would/could*! I*'d* rather
you *taught* me than any other teacher.

B2 I*'d* teach you only if you *practised*.

I*'ll* never teach anyone who *is* not
prepared to practise, no matter who   FACT   **b**
she *is*.

A3 I*'d have asked* you before if I*'(ha)d*   NON-FACT   **a**
thought you*'d have* the time.

B3 It sounds as if you*'re* keen and as if   FACT   **b, c**
you*'d practise*.

A4 I*'d practise* as if it *was/were* a matter of
life and death.   NON-FACT   **a,c**

B4 Good. What *would* you *pay* me?

A5 I*'d pay* you what you *wanted*, even if
it *was/were* more than
you *are getting* at the music
school, however much that *is*.   FACT   **b**

B5 It's time we *started* the first lesson,   NON-FACT   **a, f**
then. I*'d be* grateful if you*'d put*
what you*'ve* just *said* in writing!   FACT   **b**

A6 I'*d have liked* to start/to have started
today, but I *can't*. Also we'*(ha)d better*
settle the price before we *start, hadn't*
we? If I *started* before we *settled* it, it
wouldn't be businesslike.

NON-FACT   **a, d**

FACT   **b, e**

NON-FACT   **a**

Explanation

a The dialogue consists largely of wishes and suppositions (NON-FACT), since the speakers are feeling their way towards an agreement. Therefore most verbs are in conditional and past tenses or the subjunctive (*were*).

b Sometimes, however, the speakers deal in FACT, and then tenses relate to time except:
  i after conditional links like *anyone who, no matter who* in B2 or time links like *before* in A6 (see1C);
  ii in the case of the idiom *had better* in A6 (see **e** below).

c Note in particular how the tense varies in B3 and A4 after *as if*, which is not a true conditional link (it may be followed by a future tense), but a link for condition (*if*) + similarity (*as*):

It sounds as if you*'re* keen (= I believe you are).   FACT
It sounds as if you*'d* practise (*if* I taught you, but I may not).   NON-FACT
I'd practise as if it *was/were* a matter of life and death (but it wouldn't actually be as serious as all that).   NON-FACT

Compare:

It sounds as if you *were* keen (but I doubt if you are).   NON-FACT
It sounds as if you*'ll* practise (*when* I teach you, which I've decided to do).   FACT

The past perfect tense may also be used after *as if*:

The town looks as if it *had been struck* by a tornado (but I know it hasn't/wasn't).   NON-FACT

Compare:

The town looks as if it *has bĕen/was struck* by a tornado (= I believe it has/was).

As though is an alternative to *as if*.

d *Would/should like* + infinitive may express a wish that is entirely fanciful (see 1E):

I should like to be the most beautiful woman in the world (= I wish I were ...)!

Usually, however, it expresses a reasonable wish that we hope to realise

(A1). If we decide we cannot or may not realise it (A6), we can use either
would/should like + perfect infinitive (*to have started*) or *would/should have liked* + infinitive/perfect infinitive (the choice of infinitive is in this case not important). We then have what is in effect a conditional sentence with past reference (1Dc):

I should have liked (it if we had been able) to start today.

This use of a conditional tense + infinitive as a replacement for a full conditional sentence is common with adjectives (*nice, better*):

It would have been nice to start/to have started today (= if we had started today).

It would be better to settle the price before we start (= if we settled the price before we start).

e   The idiom *had better* (A6) + plain infinitive (*settle*) expresses fact rather than non-fact, although the past tense is used with a future reference. In strength and meaning it comes between *would be better to* (see d above) and *should/ought to (*11C, E).

f   Just as *will* is not normally used after conditional or time links (1C), so *would* is not generally used after *if* etc. An important exception is the common formula (B5) for polite requests:

I (etc.) would/should be grateful if you (etc.) would/could . . .

Compare the use of *will* in **1Cn(i)**.

Exercise

Put the verbs in brackets into a correct tense and fill any blanks (_____) with a suitable auxiliary verb like *would/could* in Example A2.

'If only we (**1** have) a car! Life (**2** be) much more pleasant. Today, for instance, I (**3** like) to have driven into the country to see and hear the spring. Don't you think it's time you (**4** buy) a car and I (**5** learn) to drive it?'
'It (**6** be) nice to have a car if it (**7** not|be) so expensive. The trouble is that I (**8** have to) give up a lot of things I now (**9** enjoy).'

Denis is only a junior employee in this firm, but he behaves as if he (**10** run) it. It's time someone (**11** put) him in his proper place. I (**12** do) it myself, but the trouble is that he probably (**13** not|pay) any attention to what I (**14** say).

If we stayed here until we (**15** finish) all this work, we (**16** be) here until midnight. Suppose we then (**17** discover) that we (**18** be) all alone in this huge building. (**19** _____ n't) you be frightened? I (**20** leave) before it (**21** get) dark.

If only you (**22** stop) worrying about what is going to happen! It's almost as if you (**23** think) you (**24** can) change things by worrying. But you (**25** can|not). Suppose I (**26** worry) like that when my husband (**27** be) so ill last year. It (**28** not|do) any good, (**29** _____) it?

Would you please pay a little more attention when I (**30** speak)? You behave as if everything I say (**31** be) rubbish, which I can assure you it (**32** not|be). I would rather you (**33** leave) the lecture room altogether than (**34** have) you sitting there yawning your head off.

It's about time Denis (**35** learn) some table manners. I would never get up from the table before others (**36** finish), would you? And would you stick your finger in the soup to see if it (**37** be) warm enough? And supposing we all (**38** help) ourselves to everything we (**39** want) without offering it to others first. What (**40** happen)? The table (**41** become) a feeding trough.

It looks as if we (**42** have) a long, difficult committee meeting tomorrow. I am sorry your boss (**43** come). It (**44** be) easier if he (**45** _____ n't). Then we (**46** finish) by six o'clock, but as it is we (**47** be) there until nine. I gladly (**48** give) a prize to anyone who managed to stop your boss talking so much!

I wish you (**49** not|laugh) about the accident. Suppose you (**50** hit) the other car. You (**51** not|sit) here now. Even if you (**52** not|be) killed, you (**53** be) badly injured.

'(**54** _____) you rather I (**55** take) my holiday in June next year instead of later? If I (**56** _____) you (**57** have) your holiday in July or August, when your children always (**58** have) their school holidays.'
'I (**59** be) most grateful if you (**60** _____). It (**61** be) very nice if the whole family (**62** spend) its holidays together for once. It (**63** be) a long time since we (**64** _____) so.'

Listen, children! I (**65** punish) whoever (**66** be) late for class tomorrow, whatever excuse they (**67** have). It's not as if I (**68** not|warn) you many times before about unpunctuality, and so if anyone (**69** be) late again they (**70** know) what to expect.

'Good heavens! Is anything wrong? You look as though you (**71** see) a ghost!'
'If I (**72** _____) to tell you that I have, (**73** believe|you) me?'
'No, I (**74** _____ n't). I (**75** not|believe) in ghosts. If anyone told me he (**76** see) a ghost, I (**77** tell) him he only (**78** think) he (**79** see) one and that he (**80** _____) better pull himself together.'

'I wish you (**81** warn) me about Helen before I (**82** meet) her.'
'Even if I (**83** _____), I doubt whether you (**84** take) any notice of what I (**85** say). She always looks as if butter (**86** not|melt) in her mouth.'
'Exactly! If only she (**87** not|look) so innocent!'

My friend Zena is a very hard-working model, but to hear her talk one (**88** think) she (**89** do) nothing but enjoy herself. I often think she (**90** do) better to give herself a less pleasure-loving image.

2 Adverbials

2A   Adverbs against adjectives

Examples

NOUN WITH ADJECTIVE	VERB WITH ADJECTIVE

1 That cheese has a *terrible smell*. $\longrightarrow$ That cheese *smells terrible*.

	VERB WITH ADVERB

2 Take a *cautious smell* at it and $\longrightarrow$ *Smell* it *cautiously* and see if you
see if you agree.   agree.

3 Those men are pretty *hard* $\longrightarrow$ Those men *work* pretty *hard* on
workers on the whole.   the whole.

	VERB WITH ADVERB PHRASE

4 One of them gave us a *friendly* $\longrightarrow$ One of them *waved* at us *in a
wave*.   friendly way/manner*.

Explanation

a **General rule**: An ADJECTIVE is used with a VERB to describe the STATE
   (nature, condition, appearance etc.) of someone or something (1).*
   Otherwise verbs are used with ADVERBS (2). Words that are difficult to deal
   with under this general rule are reserved for the explanations preceding
   Exercise 2 on p. 38–39 (f–h).

b Adjectives normally form their corresponding adverbs by the addition of
   -*ly* (2).† Exceptions are:
   i   *good* $\longrightarrow$ *well*
   ii adjectives ending in -*ic*, which add -*ally*: *basic* $\longrightarrow$ *basically*
   iii adjectives ending in -*able*/-*ible*, in which final -*e* becomes -*y*: *comfortable*
        $\longrightarrow$ *comfortably*; *possible* $\longrightarrow$ *possibly*
   iv adjectives with adverbs of the same form: *hard* $\longrightarrow$ *hard* (3).

c Adjectives that themselves end in -*ly* do not form adverbs by the addition
   of a further -*ly*. Some of them, such as *early*, *monthly*, have adverbs of the

---

* Activity is sometimes needed to maintain a state; or a state may be in the process of change. Therefore
adjectives sometimes occur with verbs that themselves refer to activity in progress (1Bs): 'The children are
being naughty/The sky is getting lighter.'
† Adjectives ending in -*y* [I] have -*i*- in the adverb: *clumsy* $\longrightarrow$ *clumsily*.

same form. Others, like *friendly* (4), have no corresponding adverbs and can be used with verbs only in an adverb phrase.

d Sometimes, although a corresponding adverb exists, an adverb phrase may be more common: I pay a monthly rent ⟶ I pay rent every month/by the month (instead of 'I pay rent monthly').

e The adjective *sly* [slaɪ] does not end in *-ly* [lɪ], and so forms an adverb in the normal way (see **b** above).

Exercise 1

Transform the following sentences as shown in the Examples, namely by changing the nouns with adjectives into their corresponding verbs with adjectives, adverbs or adverb phrases, as required. In each sentence the adjective, adverb or adverb phrase will come last.

1 He gave a bitter smile.
2 There has been a drastic fall in the dollar.
3 The Stock Exchange's reaction was quite calm.
4 To a European, Chinese has a strange sound.
5 These almonds have a bitter taste.
6 Why did she give me a stern look?
7 Try and give an intelligent answer.
8 Your action was a cowardly one.
9 The boy had a slight limp.
10 The little girl had rather a sad look.
11 Her mother had given her a hard slap.
12 Her movements were clumsy.
13 She has an ugly walk.
14 But she's a good tennis player.
15 The sports committee has monthly meetings.
16 What they said had a deep effect upon me.
17 The room had a nice, cosy look.
18 The flowers had a fragrant smell.
19 I gave her a fatherly talk.
20 I said that her behaviour had been extremely silly.
21 She gave me a sly glance.
22 An early start would be advisable. (Begin *It* . . . .)
23 I'm sure her parents will give me a warm welcome.
24 Your argument isn't logical.

Examples and Explanation

Sometimes verbs which we might expect to be used with adverbs according to the general rule (**2Aa**) are apparently used with adjectives. Such phrases fall into three categories (see under **f**, **g** and **h**):

f   Phrases like *run deep* (referring to a river), *travel light, shut it tight, come closer* are, if we think about them, not describing an action itself but the STATE (see **2Aa**) in which things are, either when they are happening (first two) or have finished happening (last two). It is therefore not surprising that here in fact the verbs are being used with adjectives. (Compare *affect deeply, tread lightly, squeeze tightly, examine more closely*.) However, the adjectives come **after** the verb; before a verb or participle an adverb is used: 'The windows have all been *tightly* shut/shut *tight*.'

g   Some adverbs which have the same form as their corresponding adjective have a different meaning from the form ending in -*ly*:

clean	completely
cleanly	in a clean way, neatly
direct	by the shortest way, without intermediary
directly	closely, intimately; immediately
hard	adverb of *hard* (worker, blow etc.): *work hard, hit hard*
hardly	scarcely, barely
high	at/to a high level/altitude
highly	very (much), favourably: *highly appreciated, think highly* (of somebody)
(a)loud	not to oneself, openly: *read aloud, laugh out loud*
loudly	opposite of quietly, faintly
right	correctly; favourably; completely (*turn right round*)
rightly	sensibly, wisely; justly, lawfully, rightfully
short	before finishing: *stop short, fall short* (of target)
shortly	soon
wrong	incorrectly; unfavourably
wrongly	incorrectly; unjustly, unlawfully, wrongfully

As in f above, it is normally only the -*ly* forms that can come before a verb ('It directly concerns us/concerns us directly'), but there are exceptions ('I've clean forgotten what she said'). Although either *wrong* or *wrongly* can mean *incorrectly*, only *wrongly* precedes verbs, while after verbs it is generally *wrong* that is used in everyday English ('You've done it wrong again'); but *wrongly* does occur ('You've added the figures up wrong/wrongly'). As the opposite of *right* meaning *favourably*, it is of course *wrong* that is always used ('Our plans have gone wrong, I'm afraid'); while *wrongly* is used as the opposite of *rightly* ('He wrongly accused her/He acted wrongly'). In the sentence 'He did wrong/right', *wrong* and *right* may be considered as nouns rather than as adjectives or adverbs.

h MISCELLANEOUS: There are a few idioms such as *go slow* (= avoid strain or excess) and *going strong* (= thriving, flourishing) which do not fall into the above two categories. In the pair *bad/badly*, *bad* is an adjective which may be used with *go* to describe a state: 'The food went (= became) bad.' The adverb *badly* is the opposite of the adverb* *well*: 'Things went (= progressed) badly.' Note also 'turn *sharp* left/right' (= at right angles) but 'turn *sharply*' (= quickly, abruptly).

Exercise 2

With the above notes and examples in mind, read or write out the following, choosing from each pair of words the one you think should be used. Remember that before a verb or participle it is the *-ly* form that is used.

I remarked that it was better to approach Ken (**1**) *direct/directly* and not through his secretary. His secretary laughed out (**2**) *loud/loudly* at my remark. I think really she was (**3**) *deep/deeply* offended by what I'd said.

Old Mr Elkins is still going (**4**) *strong/strongly* although he's over ninety. He says he'd like to reach a hundred, but admits he may be aiming a bit (**5**) *high/highly*. However, there's a (**6**) *wide/widely* held belief in the village that he'll get there.

Marilyn's eyes opened (**7**) *wide/widely* with amazement. She was about to say something but stopped (**8**) *short/shortly*. Somewhere in the house a trumpet had sounded (**9**) *loud/loudly*.

'He told me to turn (**10**) *sharp/sharply* left just past the station.'
'If he told you that he told you (**11**) *wrong/wrongly*. But you got here in the end even though you were (**12**) *wrong/wrongly* directed.'

(**13**) *Faint/Faintly* in the distance we heard the noise of thunder. Then the radio went (**14**) *faint/faintly* and we could (**15**) *hard/hardly* hear the news. We shut all the windows (**16**) *tight/tightly* and waited for the storm.

Marilyn's leaving (**17**) *short/shortly* for the United States on a business trip. As she (**18**) *right/rightly* says, there's nothing like personal contact for promoting one's products. Her suitcase is so (**19**) *tight/tightly* packed with samples there's not even room for a toothbrush. She refuses to take two suitcases because she wants to travel (**20**) *light/lightly*.

Ken was driving along at about eighty miles an hour when a stone went (**21**) *clean/cleanly* through the windscreen and hit him in the face. Afterwards he talked (**22**) *light/lightly* of the affair, but he was lucky to escape with his life.

There's a lot more to Willie than one would think: still waters run (**23**) *deep/*

---

* The adjective *well* is the opposite of *ill*.

deeply, as they say. I've been following his career **(24)** *close/closely*, and think **(25)** *high/highly* of his ability as an architect. But he's inclined to work too **(26)** *hard/hardly*, and the doctor has recently advised him to go **(27)** *slow/ slowly*.

When I took my driving test, the examiner said I did everything **(28)** *right/ rightly* except reversing, when I turned too **(29)** *sharp/sharply* and mounted the pavement. He **(30)** *strong/strongly* recommended me to practise in a smaller car than the one I've been using.

Denis thinks up the most ludicrous schemes, which all fall **(31)** *flat/flatly*. Helen's parents are **(32)** *flat/flatly* opposed to any idea of her marrying him. They say he was **(33)** *direct/directly* involved in the recent financial scandal at the Town Hall.

The struggles my parents had in the early years of their marriage brought them **(34)** *closer/more closely* together. Things often went **(35)** *bad/badly* for them in those days, but look at them now! Things turned out **(36)** *right/rightly* in the end.

2B   Position

Introductory note: In the Examples below, the adverbials are in *italics*. You will see that they consist of both single-word adverbs like *yesterday*, *unfortunately*, *eagerly*, *clearly* and adverb phrases like *in the Thames*, *the other day*. Adverb phrases are usually placed after the verb and (if it has one) its object in END position; or at the beginning of a sentence in FRONT position. Adverbs may occur in these two positions or elsewhere in the sentence, and in particular before a verb (but after *is*, *are*, *was*, *were*) in MID position. The following are the **common** positions of adverbials according to their meaning and function:

MANNER (*eagerly*, *rapidly*)	END or MID
PLACE (*in the Thames*, *there*)	END
DEFINITE TIME (*yesterday*, *the other day*)	END or FRONT
INDEFINITE TIME (*already*) OR FREQUENCY (*always*)	MID
COMMENT (*clearly*, *unfortunately*)*	FRONT or MID
CONNECTOR (*therefore*, *however*)	FRONT or MID
DEGREE (*nearly*, *very*)	before the words they qualify (but see *enough*, 3Bh)
ADDITION (*too*) AND RESTRICTION (*only*)	various

* Many adverbs of comment are alternatives to introductory phrases like 'It's obvious that' (= *clearly*) or 'I'm afraid that' (= *unfortunately*).

Since there is some choice of position for most of these groups, and since adverbials may have other positions besides the common ones, it is important to know where **not** to put adverbials, and this, as well as their right positions, is what the Examples show.

Examples

ADVERBIALS			WRONG (X) AND RIGHT (√) POSITIONS
1 *with his new rod*	a	⟶	Charles's cousin David caught (X) *nearly two dozen fish* (√) *in the Thames last week.*
2 *eagerly*	b	⟶	He *therefore* (√) went (X) *back* (X) *there* (√) *yesterday.*
3 *very quickly*	c	⟶	*Unfortunately* he fell in the river and (√) got (X) *very* wet (√).
4 *rapidly*	d	⟶	His uncle Harry, *though*, says that's the best way of (√) becoming (X) a true fisherman (√).
5 *already*	f	⟶	Harry, an expert angler, (X) has (√) taken David under his wing (√).
6 *clearly*	e	⟶	(√) He (X) is (√) delighted at David's enthusiasm.
7 *wisely*	h	⟶	Fishermen, says Harry, are people who (X) spend their spare time (√).
8 *wisely*	h	⟶	His wife Mary does not *always* agree, but (√) says nothing (X).
9 *too*	k	⟶	*The other day* Charles (√) went fishing (√).
10 *only*	l	⟶	*However*, he (√) fished (√) for an hour (√); his real interest is his model railway and pop music.

Explanation

a Do **not** (1) put an adverbial between a verb (*caught*) and its object (*nearly two dozen fish*).* The normal order for adverbials after a verb/object is MPT or manner (*with his new rod*), place (*in the Thames*), time (*last week*).

b **But** do **not** (2) put an adverbial between a verb of motion (*went*) and common adverbials of place like *here, there, home, to work*. Also, if it is a phrasal verb (**16Aa**) like *go back*, do **not** put an adverbial between the verb itself and its particle (*back*). The order may therefore be P(*there*), M (*eagerly*), T (*yesterday*).

---

* The main exception to this rule occurs when we wish to avoid ambiguity or double meaning: 'David *caught in a few hours* more fish than he had ever caught *before* (**not** David caught more fish than he had ever caught before in a few hours).'

c Do **not** (3), in the case of verbs used with adjectives (**2Aa**), put an adverbial between the verb and the adjective (*very wet*).

d Do **not** (4) put an adverbial between *become* and a following noun (*a true fisherman*).

e These rules (**c, d**) do **not** (6) apply to *is, are, was, were*. Mid-position adverbs come **after** these forms of the verb *to be* except when the verb is stressed, as in argument ('I disagree: Harry clearly **is** delighted'), or when commas are used (see **m** below).

f Do **not** put a mid-position adverb in front of the **whole** verb. It should go **after** the auxiliary part of it: *is, was* etc. in progressive forms, *will, have* etc. in future and perfect tenses (5). In tenses with two auxiliaries such as the conditional perfect (**1D**), position varies, although adverbs of manner usually come after the second auxiliary:

$$\text{If I'd fallen in} \begin{cases} \text{I'd } \textit{soon} \text{ have/have } \textit{soon} \\ \text{I'd have } \textit{rapidly} \end{cases} \text{lost my enthusiasm for}$$

fishing.
In the passive, manner adverbs generally come after *been*, other mid-position adverbs before it:

    If Harry had fallen in he'd *probably* have/have *probably* been *severely* scolded by Mary.

The position of adverbs is the same in relation to modal auxiliaries (**11**) like *can/could*. Instead of the conditional perfect we might have (see **11Af**):

    David could *easily* have/have *easily* been drowned.

(Note that here *easily* is not an adverb of manner but of comment, like *probably*.)

g The above rule (**f**) does **not** apply when auxiliaries are stressed ('Yes, I probably **would** have lost my enthusiasm') or when they are on their own: 'Do you think you would have lost your enthusiasm? – Yes, I probably would have.'

h Do **not** (7) put an adverb of manner in front of a verb if it can also be an adverb of comment. Conversely, do **not** (8) mistake an adverb of comment for an adverb of manner and put it after the verb. In 7, *wisely* tells us **how** fishermen spend their time; in 8, *wisely* is the writer's **comment** on Mary's behaviour. Here is another example: 'She treated me kindly' refers to someone's kind behaviour towards me; 'she kindly treated me' must refer to my good opinion of a doctor or dentist who accepted me as her patient.

j All the above rules do **not** apply to adverbs of degree like *nearly* (1) and *very* (3), which come directly before the words they qualify.

k The adverb of addition *too* (9) comes after the words it qualifies. It should come directly after them, and should be used with a comma, if there is possible ambiguity (double meaning). Thus in the given context, Example 9 can have only one meaning in whichever position we put *too*:

i Charles went fishing as well as David.

But in another context 'Charles went fishing too' might mean:

ii Charles went fishing as well as sailing (etc.).

In the spoken language, stress removes the ambiguity:

i **Charles** went fishing **too**.

ii Charles went **fishing too**.

In the written language ambiguity can be removed (for the sensitive reader!) with a comma: (**ii**) Charles went fishing, too. (For *too* as an adverb of degree, see **3B**.)

l The adverb of restriction *only* (10) comes before or, less commonly, after the words it qualifies; it should come **directly before them** if there is any ambiguity. In 10 the meaning is clear in whichever of the three positions we put *only*. But look at the following:

   Charles only listens to pop music.

This might mean that Charles, unlike David, does not himself play music; or that he does not listen to any other sort of music (= 'Charles listens only to pop music'). Again, in spoken English stress makes the distinction: '**Charles** only **listens** to pop music/**Charles** only listens to **pop** music.'

m Adverbials of connection and comment like *therefore* (2), *unfortunately* (3), *clearly* (6) or *wisely* (8) that are not in their common positions should be used with commas:

   He went back there yesterday, therefore.

   He fell in the river, unfortunately.

   Harry, quite clearly, is delighted at David's enthusiasm.

   Mary says nothing, wisely enough.

However (10) and *though* (4) are always used with commas. (For the links *however* and *though*, which are not used with commas, see **1Ce** and **5b**.)

Exercise 1

Read or write out the sentences with the adverbials in suitable positions, of which there may be more than one. (Some of the sentences do not make sense without the adverbials.)

1 *by car*	Ken goes to work on most days.
2 *though*	Sometimes he leaves his car behind and goes by bus.
3 *never*	He says he would drive to work if there was a better bus service.
4 *too*	Sheila usually drives to work.
5 *only*	She has to drive a few miles.
6 *quicker**	In the rush hours she can get there and back by bicycle.

* Although grammatically irregular, this normally replaces *more quickly* in everyday English.

7 *seriously*	Are Sir James and Lady Blenkinsop still considering selling the Hall?
8 *recently*	No, they have changed their minds.
9 *probably*	Lady Blenkinsop will join her daughter in the USA in the spring.
10 *then*	Blenkinsop Hall may be closed.
11 *only*	But it will be closed temporarily.
12 *unfortunately*	Lady B's son Toby hasn't found a job yet.
13 *no longer*	Luckily she considers he's a genius.
14 *slowly*	Actually Toby seems to be getting more sensible.
15 *easily*	No doubt Sir James will win the by-election at Doncaster in October.
16 *always*	I do not entirely agree with what he says in his speeches.
17 *however*	I quite agree with what he said in his Manchester speech on Friday.
18 *entirely*	Did Marilyn set up her business by herself last year?
19 *eventually*	No, she didn't because her father rather unwillingly lent her some money.
20 *too*	Apparently Sheila invested a little money in Marilyn's business.
21 *already*	Marilyn is on good terms with her father again.
22 *in the beginning/in the end*	She nearly went bankrupt, but she succeeded.
23 *very sensibly*	Marilyn behaves in business matters.
24 *very sensibly*	She leaves her work behind in the office at weekends.
25 *quietly*	She spends some weekends with her parents in the country.
26 *almost certainly*	Marilyn would have succeeded without her father's help.
27 *clearly*	She has great strength of character.
28 *at present*	She is in the USA.
29 *very hospitably*	Marilyn is being treated over there.
30 *strangely enough*	She ran into Lady B's daughter in Dallas the other day.

Exercise 2

In this Exercise, which is an extension of Exercise 1, you have more adverbials to deal with.

1 The car skidded, missed a lamp-post, and came to a halt. *(badly/finally/in the butcher's/just/only)*

2 My car was damaged. *(also/badly/in an accident/the other day/ unfortunately)*

3 It was not my fault. *(definitely/in any way)*

4 The other driver jammed on his brakes. *(in front of me/right/stupidly/ very)*

5 He thought the traffic lights had changed. *(from green to red/just/ possibly)*

6 Willie was with me and confirmed everything I said. *(at the time/enough/ fully/luckily)*

7 He had returned. *(apparently/from an architects' conference/in the States/ only/the day before)*

8 Did you know that Willie can estimate the height of a building? *(accurately/alone/by eye/sometimes)*

9 I had got home when it started to snow. *(hardly/in my car/last night/ suddenly)*

10 It is snowing. *(hard/quite/still/today)*

11 It is lying. *(already/at least/twenty centimetres deep)*

12 If it is snowing I shall stay. *(at home/at six o'clock/by the television/ comfortably/probably/still/the whole evening)*

13 Transport has been affected. *(already/seriously/throughout the country)*

14 It has been brought to a standstill. *(in fact/practically)*

15 The local authorities are not equipped to deal with heavy falls. *(adequately/clearly/efficiently/such)*

16 It will snow. *(as well/likely/tomorrow/very)*

17 I have liked snow. *(frankly/much/never)*

18 Children adore it because they rush out. *(evidently/however/immediately/ into it)*

19 You would rather stay. *(at your age/indoors/presumably/snugly)*

20 I would prefer to run about. *(energetically/enough/much/outside/ surprisingly)*

21 I want to do the things I couldn't do. *(luckily/obviously/only/rarely)*

22 My age prevents me from doing what I want to do. *(exactly/in fact/ seldom)*

23 I go for long walks. *(alone/occasionally/still/through the woods)*

24 I like to row. *(about the lake in the park/also/gently/in the early autumn/ sometimes)*

25 The leaves are turning and the grapes are ripe. *(fully/just/then)*

26 We used to take a trip. *(at that time of year/in the old days/often/up into the mountains/very)*

27 Things have changed. *(of course/since then/unbelievably)*

28 They have not changed. *(for the worse/in this part of the world/on the whole/though)*

3 Linking: result, cause

Introductory note: LINKING has already been touched upon in relation to tense use with conditional and time links (**1C, D**). Conditional sentences were shown (see **1D**, Introductory note) to consist of two parts or clauses, joined by such words as *if* to express their conditional relationship. Other sentences too are structured in this way, but with different methods of joining to express different relationships, for example RESULT or CAUSE.

    The linking or joining used in these various relationships between clauses involves special link words like *and, because, so . . . that, although, in spite of, as* or *who*; verb participles like *being* or *warned*; or the infinitive that expresses purpose. The following seven sections (**3–9**) deal with these links and also with adverbs like *therefore, then* or *however* which, although they cannot link clauses within sentences, can indicate corresponding relationships between one sentence and another.

3A Relation between result and cause

LINKS FOR RESULT	*and* *so (that)* *so . . . that* *such . . . that*
LINKS FOR CAUSE	*because* *as* *since* *for* *-ing* (present) ⎫ *-ed* etc. (past) ⎬ verb participles
ADVERBS OF RESULT	*consequently* *therefore* *so*

Examples

RESULT   CAUSE

1 The trains weren't running on ⟶ *As* the trains weren't running
  Monday, *so (that)* many   ⟵ on Monday (,) many commuters
  commuters had trouble getting   had trouble getting to work.   **f**
  to work.   **a**

2 I'm an incorrigible optimist (,) ⟶ *Being* an incorrigible optimist (,)
  and (so) (I) thought I'd be able to ⟵ I thought I'd be able to get to
  get to work by bus.   **a**   work by bus.   **b**

3 But the queues were *so* long *that* ⟶ But I couldn't get on a bus (,)
  I couldn't get on a bus.   **c, e** ⟵ *because* the queues were too
                                       long.   **f**

4 I realised I'd never get on a bus, ⟶ *Realising* I'd never get on a bus
  so (I) decided to thumb a lift.   **a** ⟵ (,) I decided to thumb a lift.   **b**

5 There were *so* few cars with a ⟶ *Since* there were very few cars
  spare seat *that* it took me a long ⟵ with a spare seat (,) it took me a
  time to get a lift.   **c, e**   long time to get a lift.   **f**

6 I was warned by my colleagues ⟶ *(Having been) Warned* by my
  it might be worse in the   ⟵ colleagues it might be worse in
  evening. I was *therefore* careful   the evening (,) I was careful to
  to leave for home early.   **a**   leave for home early.   **b**

7 Even so, the journey home was ⟶ Even so, I went to bed
  such a (tremendous) struggle ⟵ exhausted, *for* the journey home
  that I went to bed   was a tremendous struggle.   **f**
  exhausted.   **d, e**

Explanation

a There are two kinds of RESULT, namely material or physical (1, 3, 5, 7) and
   mental or psychological (2, 4, 6). The link *so* can be used for either kind (1,
   4), but the full link *so that* can be used only for the first, **not** (4): 'I realised
   I'd never get on a bus, so that I decided. . . .' Both links are used with a
   comma, and, in spoken English, with a tone change; neither can begin a
   sentence (compare *so that* for purpose, **4Ac**).

b The two kinds of result (see **a** above) correspond to the two kinds of CAUSE:
   material or physical causes (1, 3, 5, 7) and psychological causes or reasons
   (2, 4, 6). Normally it is only for reasons that we use verb participles (*being,
   realising, warned*) as links. We can also use adjectives: '*Aware* that it might
   be worse in the evening, I was careful . . . .'

c The link *so . . . that* (3, 5) is used with adverbs and adjectives when they are
   not (3) followed by a noun. However, it is also used with the quantitative
   adjectives *much, little, many* and *few* whether they are followed by a noun
   (5) or not. In addition, it is sometimes used with an adjective + noun instead
   of *such . . . that* (see **d** below).

d The link *such . . . that* (7) is used with an adjective + noun, although adjectives of abstract magnitude like *great* or *tremendous* are superfluous and often left out in the phrases *such a struggle/nuisance/fool/comfort/help* etc. *So . . . that* sometimes replaces *such . . . that* in literary English, but only with an ADJECTIVE + SINGULAR COUNTABLE NOUN and with the word order **reversed**: 'The journey home was so *tremendous a* struggle that . . . .' It could **not** replace *such . . . that* in 'The journey home was such hard work that . . . .'

e Both the links *so . . . that* and *such . . . that* often drop *that* in colloquial English: 'The queues were so long I couldn't get on a bus/The journey home was such a struggle I went to bed exhausted.'

f Of the four causal link words, *as* (1) and *since* (5) are the two which commonly begin sentences. *Because* (3) does so less often, while *for* does so only with reference to what goes before, to which it can always be linked:

> It was lucky I started home early. For (= early, for) if I hadn't I'd have been terribly late.

Otherwise there is little difference between them **except** when we are responding to the question *Why . . .?* Then only *because* can be used:

> He didn't marry her because she had money; he married her because he loved her.

Here the question in our minds or actually asked is 'Why did he marry her?' Note there are no commas, and no corresponding tone change, before *because*. Compare the following, where there is an optional comma and always a tone change:

> He didn't marry her(,) *as/because/for/since* she had no money.

Here we may be answering the question 'Did he marry her?', but we are **not** answering the question **why** he did not marry her (although we have given the answer to an unasked question!).

g For the causal link *because of*, see **6a**.

Exercise

Transform the following by using the words in *italics*. Most of the transformations required are as shown in the Examples, that is to say from result to cause and vice versa, but some are within either category (*such . . . that* ——→ *so that*, or *as* ——→ *being*).

1	*so . . . that*	As the lecturer spoke very fast I found it difficult to **make** any notes.
2	*as*	He also spoke with a strong accent, so that I didn't understand all he said.
3	*so*	Since he's a very keen fisherman, Mr McArthur spends a lot of time by the river.

4 *knowing*	Mrs McArthur knows that fishing is in his blood, and so doesn't try to stop him.
5 *because*	There was a lot of rain last night and many of the roads are flooded.
6 *so*	As the weather forecast is for more rain, I think we should postpone our trip.
7 *so that*	Two years ago there was such a bad drought that the wells in our village began to dry up.
8 *such . . . that*	Soon there was a great shortage of water and we had to ration it.
9 *since*	The next plane didn't leave until the evening, and so they decided to spend the afternoon sightseeing.
10 *so . . . that*	However, they soon returned to the airport, as there was very little to see.
11 *for*	I'd never talked to a film star before, so felt rather nervous.
12 *knowing*	She knew how I felt and soon put me at my ease.
13 *and so*	As my car wouldn't start I had to take a taxi.
14 *realising*	I realised I'd be late for an appointment and phoned my secretary.
15 *having*	I was getting rather worried, as I had heard nothing from my husband for over a week.
16 *being*	Ken is a friend of his and was getting worried too.
17 *because*	Willie had sprained his ankle, so found walking painful.
18 *such . . . that*	However, being a very reticent sort of fellow he said nothing about it.
19 *so*	My father retired early because his health was poor.
20 *finding*	He found himself short of money, and consequently gave up smoking.
21 *for*	The city was a vital communications centre, and so the Reds were determined to capture it.
22 *fully aware*	The Whites were equally determined not to surrender it, as they were fully aware of its importance.
23 *so . . . that*	Many children have very little leisure during the week since they have a great deal of homework to do.
24 *since*	This being the case, many families have to confine all their recreational activities to the weekend.
25 *such . . . that*	I kept my son home from school this morning as he had a very bad cough.

26 *so . . . that*   Very few of the children are well enough to perform in the school concert and so they've cancelled it.

27 *so*   Deprived of parental love, young David naturally sought affection elsewhere.

28 *since*   Mrs McArthur was able to provide that affection, and so David became more attached to her than to his own mother.

29 *as*   I'll be out quite late tonight, so I'm going to take a front-door key with me.·

30 *therefore*   My father made such a fuss about my coming in late last night that I told him I'd go and look for somewhere else to live.

3B   Result expressed with *too* or *enough*

Introductory note: When result involves degree (*thin/thick* etc.) or quantity (*little/much*) we can often express it by the use of neat constructions with *too* or *enough*. These are dealt with below in separate Examples and Exercises. Exercise 3 deals with how they are related.

Use of *too*

Examples

RESULT WITH *and, such* ETC.		RESULT WITH *too*
1 Sheila's a sensible driver *and* doesn't take risks.	⟶	Sheila's *too* sensible a driver *to* take risks. **a**
2 Helen's *such* a spendthrift (*that*) she never saves a penny.	⟶	Helen's *too* much of a spendthrift ever *to* save a penny. **b**
3 The ice is rather thin *and* one couldn't skate on it.	⟶	The ice is *too* thin *to* skate on/*for* skating. **c, d, e**
4 Those logs are very heavy; one man couldn't possibly lift them.	⟶	Those logs are much *too* heavy for one man *to* lift. **c, f, g**
5 There's an awful lot of violence in this film; I don't like it.	⟶	There's far *too* much violence in this film *for* my liking/my taste. **d, g**

Explanation

a *Too* (1) + adjective (*sensible*) can come in front of a SINGULAR COUNTABLE NOUN (*a driver*) in the same way as *so* (see **3Ad**). Again, note the word order: **not** 'a too sensible driver'. This construction with *too* is more common than the one with *so*.

b The equivalent of *such a* + noun (see **3Ad, e**) is *too much of a* + noun (2).

c *Too* (3, 4) + adjective comes **after** uncountable and plural nouns: **not** 'It's too thin ice/Those are too heavy logs . . . .' The exceptions, as in the case of *so* (see **3Ac**), are the quantitative adjectives *much, little, many* and *few*: 'There are too many logs . . . .'

d *Too* is used either with a full infinitive (1–4) or with *for* + noun (3, 5). Its use with a verb-noun or gerund should generally be avoided: **not** in 4 'too heavy for lifting.' (For the grammatical difference between nouns ending in -*ing* such as *skating*, which is a sport, and gerunds such as *lifting*, which unlike *weightlifting* is not a special activity or sport, see **10Bj**.)

e The infinitive is followed if necessary by a preposition (*on*) which relates it correctly to the noun at the beginning of the sentence (3): **not** 'The *ice* is too thin to skate' (compare '*He*'s too fat to skate').

f When, as in 4 (but not in 3), there is a significant change of grammatical subject (*Those logs* ⟶ *one man*), the second subject is introduced into the *too* construction by *for*.

g For emphasis (4, 5), either *much* or *far* can precede *too*.

Use of *enough*

Examples

RESULT WITH *and, such* ETC.		RESULT WITH *enough*
1 Sheila's a sensible driver *and* doesn't take risks.	⟶	Sheila's a sensible *enough* driver not *to* take risks. **h, j**
2 Do you think Denis would be *such* a fool/*so* foolish *as* to marry Helen? **p**	⟶	Do you think Denis would be fool/foolish *enough to* marry Helen? **h, k**
3 The fruit isn't very ripe yet *and* one couldn't make jam from it.	⟶	The fruit isn't ripe *enough* yet *to* make jam from/*for* jam-making. **h, l, m, n**
4 Now there's quite a lot of ripe fruit about, *so* my mother can start her jam-making.	⟶	Now there's *enough* ripe fruit about for my mother *to* start her jam-making. **h, n**

Explanation

h *Enough* can be either an ADVERB OF DEGREE (1, 2, 3) or an ADJECTIVE OF QUANTITY (4). As an adverb it comes **after** the words it qualifies; as an adjective it comes **before** the words it qualifies.

j An adjective (*sensible*) + *enough* (1) can, like *too* + adjective, come before a SINGULAR COUNTABLE NOUN (*driver*). But note the difference in word order: *a sensible enough* against *too sensible a*.

k The equivalent of *such a* + noun (3Ad) is sometimes *enough of a* + noun (like *too much of a* + noun). However, when (2) the noun has a corresponding adjective (*fool/foolish*) the equivalent is more commonly noun + *enough*. (There are some phrases where the reverse is true: *enough of a realist* is more common than *realist enough*.) If there is no corresponding adjective, a noun + *enough* or *enough of a* + noun construction is seldom used: **not** 'spendthrift enough' or 'enough of a spendthrift' as the equivalent of *such a/too much of a spendthrift*.

l An adjective (*ripe*) + *enough* (3) comes, like *too* + adjective, **after** uncountable or plural nouns: **not** 'There isn't ripe enough fruit . . . .'

m *Enough*, like *too*, is used either with the infinitive (1–4) or with *for* + noun (3). Once again (see **d** above), the distinction must be made between nouns and gerunds. Thus (compare Example 2) we could say 'old enough to marry' or 'old enough for marriage' but **not** 'old enough for marrying', since *marrying*, unlike *jam-making* (3, 4), is not a noun but a verb-noun or gerund.

n What is said above under *too* (**e, f**) about prepositions after the infinitive and the use of *for* to introduce a second subject applies equally to *enough* (3, 4).

p Note (2) that in asking questions about people's intentions it is normal to use *such/so . . . as* + infinitive instead of *so . . . that* (see 3Ac) as a link for result. Its most common use is in the request 'Would you be so kind as to . . .?'

Exercise 1

Express the following using *too* as shown in the Examples.

1 The lecturer spoke so fast I couldn't take any notes.
2 My dictionaries are very heavy, so I don't bring them to class.
3 It's a difficult subject, and we can't go into it now.
4 He said that no one was so old that they couldn't work.
5 Sir James is an intelligent politician and wouldn't have made a remark like that.
6 The coffee Zena served at her party was rather strong. I can't say I liked it.

7 The swimming-pool was so shallow you couldn't dive into it.
8 Those are very valuable antique chairs and no one should sit on them.
9 Do you mean they're so valuable they can't be used?
10 If razors are blunt and you can't shave with them, they have to be thrown away.
11 As an architect, Willie's such a perfectionist he couldn't possibly be responsible for the error on the plan.
12 It's a very important matter, so don't leave it to anyone but him.
13 The lighting in the room was so dim you couldn't read by it.
14 The woman was sitting rather a long way away and we couldn't see who it was. (Use *far*.)
15 She looked quite plump, so could hardly have been Zena.
16 There's a lot of difference in our ages, so I'm wondering whether our marriage will be a success. (Begin *I'm wondering* ....)
17 It's a good opportunity; Marilyn shouldn't miss it.
18 She's a smart businesswoman, and wouldn't miss a chance like that.
19 Ken's a terrible Philistine and doesn't like classical music.
20 Helen's very outspoken, and most people don't like that.

Exercise 2

Express the following using *enough* as shown in the Examples.

1 He was quite old and could have been her father.
2 She was very stupid and went and married him.
3 He wasn't much of a man; he didn't speak up in his own defence.
4 He didn't have much sense and didn't even realise what his rights were.
5 She was honest, and did not try to deny all responsibility for the accident.
6 She was also lucky, and had the services of a very good lawyer.
7 Don't you think she sang very well? Couldn't she have become a professional?
8 Her husband was undoubtedly a good guitarist and could have become a professional.
9 I was such an idiot that I threw away an opportunity of going to university.
10 I had no patience and would not even consider staying at school for the extra study required.
11 I haven't much time so won't be able to make a hotel reservation before I leave.
12 Would you be so kind as to book a room for me?
13 There are not many experienced political figures left, so the President will not be able to form an effective government.
14 Ken has a lot of athletic talent and could be very good indeed if he was well trained.
15 Marilyn didn't have much money of her own, so couldn't start a business by herself.

16 Sheila did quite well in the oral, and so made up for rather a poor paper in the written examination.

17 The country has considerable natural resources, so could be practically self-sufficient in the event of war.

18 There's not much of the green paint left; we won't be able to finish the wall with it.

19 My place of work isn't very far from my home, and so I don't qualify for a travel allowance.

20 These people are so fanatical in their cause that they would stop at nothing to gain their ends.

Exercise 3

The first Examples under *too* and *enough* above will have shown you that it is sometimes possible to express the same result with either of them:

> Sheila's *too* sensible a driver to ⟶ Sheila's a sensible *enough* driver
> take risks. ⟵ not to take risks.

This is because *enough*, unlike *too*, can be used with *not*. However, a negative infinitive (*not to*) as used in the example above often cannot be used. Usually the *not* goes with the main verb, and we can then often express the same result with *too* or *enough* by using contrasting adverbs or adjectives:

> The ice was just a bit too *thin* to ⟶ The ice wasn't quite *thick*
> skate on. ⟵ enough to skate on.

Occasionally contrasting adjectives make it possible to use either form of negative with *enough* to obtain the same meaning, although with slightly different emphasis:

> Surely she's sensible enough *not* ⟶ Surely she's *not* fool(ish) enough
> *to* marry the man? ⟵ to marry the man?

With the above in mind, express the following using *enough*. You will have to find a contrasting adverb or adjective for most of them.

1 The lecturer spoke so fast I couldn't take any notes.

2 The swimming-pool was so shallow you couldn't dive into it.

3 If razors are blunt and you can't shave with them, they have to be thrown away.

4 The lighting in the room was so dim you couldn't read by it.

5 The woman was sitting rather a long way away and we couldn't see who it was.

6 She looked quite plump, so could hardly have been Zena.

7 Although it's an hour after sunset, it's still too hot for comfort, isn't it?

8 The coffee was just a little too strong for my liking.

9 Some people are foolish and don't realise it is to their own advantage that others should not starve. (Two possibilities!)

10 However, there are very few who are so mean that they won't give at least a little of their money to charity. (Two possibilities!)

4 Linking: purpose

4A Standard constructions

LINKS

(in order/so as)
in order not/so as not
so that
in case

ADVERBS

then
otherwise

Introductory note: The Examples will show that, just as there is a relation between result and cause (**3A**), so there is a relation between purpose on the one hand and result and cause on the other when links for the latter are used with verbs like *want* and with *may/might*. (For an introductory note on linking, see **3A**.)

Examples

RESULT, CAUSE; *then, otherwise*		PURPOSE
1 We want to catch the seven o'clock train, *and so* we're getting up early tomorrow.	⟶	We're getting up early tomorrow (*in order/so as*) to catch the seven o'clock train. **a**
2 We're leaving early *because* we don't want to be late for work.	⟶	We're leaving early *so as not/(in order not)* to be late for work. **b**
3 I'll lend you Sheila's alarm clock. *Then* you can be sure of waking up in time.	⟶	I'll lend you Sheila's alarm clock *so that/(in order that)* you can be sure of waking up in time. **c**
4 Sheila may think someone has pinched her clock, *so* I'll leave a note for her.	⟶	I'll leave a note for Sheila { *in case* she thinks / *so that* she won't think } someone has pinched her clock. **d**
5 I left her a note last time. *Otherwise* she might have thought someone had pinched her clock.	⟶	I left her a note last time { *in case* she thought / *so that* she wouldn't think } someone had pinched her clock. **d**

6 Personally I always use two   ⟶ Personally I always use two
   alarm clocks, *because* one of   alarm clocks *in case* one of them
   them mightn't go off.   doesn't go off.   **e**
7 I shan't take Sheila's clock   ⟶ I shan't take Sheila's clock
   without asking, *because* I might   without asking *in case* I annoy
   annoy her.   her.   **f**

Explanation

a The link for purpose where there is **no** change of grammatical subject is *in order* or *so as*. However, this link is very often left out (1), so that purpose is commonly expressed just with the full infinitive (*to catch*).

b The negative link (2) when there is **no** change of subject is *so as not* or, less commonly, *in order not*. This link cannot be left out.

c The link (3) when there **is** a change of subject is *so that* (less commonly, *in order that*). It is normally distinguished from *so that* for result (**3Aa**) by its use without comma or tone change and by its use with *can/could* (3) or *will/would* (4, 5). (In more formal English you will sometimes see it used with *shall/should* or *may/might*.) Although *that* is often dropped in spoken English ('I'll lend you Sheila's alarm clock *so* you can be sure . . .'), the full link *so that* is normal in written English. Either *so (that)* or, more formally, *in order that* can begin a sentence: 'So you can be sure of waking up in time, I'll . . .' This is another difference between *so (that)* used for purpose and *so (that)* used for result.

d When our purpose (4, 5) is to PREVENT what **may** or **might** happen (see left-hand Examples), we very often use *in case* instead of *so as not/so that . . . not*. *In case*, like *if* (**1C**), is used with present or past (including perfect) tenses, **not** with future tenses; and it is sometimes used with *should* (**11Fe**): 'I'll leave/I left a note for Sheila in case she should think. . . .'

e When our purpose (6) is to PREPARE for what **may** or **might** happen (because we cannot prevent it), we use only *in case*, not *so as not/so that . . . not*.

f When our expression of purpose (7) begins negatively ('I shan't . . .'), we must use *in case* for PREVENTION as well as for PREPARATION.

g Occasional alternatives to *in case* are *lest* and *for fear that*, but as these are somewhat formal or literary they have not been included in the Examples. They are normally used with *should*.

h Although you may see in some dictionaries that *if* is given as one of the meanings of *in case*, you are recommended to keep the uses and meanings of these two links **quite distinct**, as indeed they generally are; *if* instead of *in case* in Examples 4–7 above would make no sense at all. Neither should you confuse *in case* with *in case of*, a prepositional phrase which **does** have the meaning of *if*: 'If you have any difficulty, ring for the attendant ——→ In case of difficulty, ring for the attendant.'

Exercise

Transform the following into sentences expressing purpose, giving alternative links where possible as shown in Examples 4 and 5.

1 We're going to the coast because we want to get some photos of sea birds.
2 Don't go climbing up the cliff as you may fall.
3 We want to get good photos, so we'll have to climb the cliff.

4 We're leaving early. Then we won't have to hurry.
5 We don't want to skid on the wet roads, so we're going to drive slowly.
6 We're taking food with us, because we may be home late.

7 It may rain and so we'd better take our waterproofs with us.
8 And leave the heating on. Then the house won't get cold while we're out.
9 And put the food away. Otherwise the cat may get it.

10 I won't shut the front door as the cat may want to come in.
11 We're going to cut a hole in the back door, because we want the cat to be able to get in and out as it likes.
12 Hadn't you better cut a hole in the front door? It may want to get in and out that way as well.

13 I'm not taking my holiday next week after all, as I may have to fly to Milan on business.
14 I'd better come into the office on Sunday, as I'll need to prepare the necessary papers.
15 My assistant Brenda will keep in touch with you; then you'll know where I am.

16 I thought it might freeze tonight, so I've drained the water out of my car.
17 Why don't you put antifreeze in it? Then you wouldn't have to bother about such things.

18 Please talk quietly. Otherwise you may wake the baby.
19 Personally I always keep my baby up late. Then he's really tired by the time I put him to bed.

20 I'm sure Denis is marrying Helen only because he wants to have an influential father-in-law.
21 Yes, and Helen's trying to get a job as a teacher just because she wants to impress Denis.

22 When I'm away I shall telephone my husband every evening. Otherwise he may think I'm having too good a time.
23 Let me know when you're going. Then I can keep your husband company if he's lonely.

24 Sir James tried to persuade his son Toby to enter the family business because he wanted him eventually to take it over.

25 He would also have liked him to learn Arabic and Chinese, for then he would have been a real asset to the firm.

26 Zena wanted me to feed her alligator while she was away, so she gave me the key to her flat.

27 I shouldn't have gone near it if I'd been you, as I would have been afraid of its snapping my hand off.

28 Where can I find Harry McArthur? I must give him an important message.
29 You'd better go down to the river. He may be fishing.
30 He sometimes goes straight there from work. He saves time that way.

4B   Shortened constructions

Introductory note: It is common in some contexts to express purpose by means of constructions that are shorter than the standard ones (shown below in the left-hand Examples) and which are exceptions to the rule (**4Ac**); that is to say, they use only the full infinitive in spite of the fact that there is a change of grammatical subject (from *you* to *I* etc.). The Examples cover the several forms these constructions take. They usually describe some sort of transaction or arrangement, and contain verbs like *lend*, *give*, *leave* or *send*.

Examples

STANDARD CONSTRUCTION	SHORTENED CONSTRUCTION
1 Could you lend me that book *so that* I could show it to my dad?	⟶ Could you lend me that book *to show* (to) my dad? **b**
2 Yes, and I'll give you this paper *so that* you can wrap the book up (in it).	⟶ Yes, and I'll give you this paper *to wrap* the book up *in*. **c**
3 I'll leave the book here *so that* you can pick it up on your way home.	⟶ I'll leave the book here (*for* you) *to pick up* on your way home. **d**
4 Mary McArthur sent her son shopping *so that* he would be out of the way.	⟶ Mary McArthur sent her son shopping *to be* out of the way. **e**
5 Yes, she sent him out *so that* she could get some peace.	⟶ Yes, she sent him out *so as to get* some peace. **e**

Explanation

a You will see (1–5) that the main clauses (*Could you lend me that book?* etc.) in both standard and shortened constructions are the same.

b If in the standard construction (1) the subject (*I*) and object (*it*) in the *so that* clause occur as objects (*me, that book*) in the main clause, they are left out of the shortened construction.

c If in the standard construction (2) the object (*the book*) in the *so that* clause does not occur as an object in the main clause, it occurs in the shortened construction. Sometimes a preposition (*in*) is necessary to relate it to an object (*the paper*) in the main clause (= 'so that *you* can wrap the book up *in* it' **not** 'so that *it* can wrap the book up'). Compare 'I'll lend you my secretary to type your letters' and 'I'll lend you my typewriter to type your letters *with.*'

d If in the standard construction (3) the subject (*you*) in the *so that* clause does not occur as an object in the main clause, it is usually necessary to introduce it into the shortened construction by the use of *for*. It is not **always** necessary, since the context ('on *your* way home') may make the meaning clear.

e Examples 4 and 5 show us that, since we may use only the full infinitive in the shortened construction when the SUBJECTS in the standard construction are **different** (*Mary McArthur, he*), we may have to add *so as* (or *in order*) to the full infinitive when the SUBJECTS are the **same** (*she*) in order to avoid being misunderstood. Without *so as* the shortened construction in 5 would mean 'She sent him out so that **he** could get some peace.'

Exercise

Transform the following standard constructions with *so that* into shortened constructions with the full infinitive, using *so as* (or *in order*) only where necessary, as shown in the Examples.

1 Please send me some samples of your firm's products so that I can show them to my customers.
2 When we go out we always leave our dog at home so that he can guard it for us.
3 Sheila lent her sister a skirt so that she could wear it at Helen's party.
4 Marilyn is bringing some magazines with her this afternoon so that I can take them to my aunt in hospital.
5 If you're going out, buy some postcards so that we can send them off before we leave Rome tomorrow.
6 I'll get you a basket so that you can carry all those things.
7 Give me a nail so that I can hang this picture up.
8 Put the salmon in the freezer so that we can eat it next weekend.

9 I'm going to put this notice here so that everyone'll see it as they walk in.
10 We're gathering our old toys together so that Sheila can give them to orphan children next Christmas.
11 As I'm arriving at the airport in the early hours of the morning, my wife's leaving our car there so that I can drive home.
12 I didn't put that book there so you could pinch it but so that Willie could have a look at it during lunch.

13 When we go to town we always leave our children in the municipal playground so that they can amuse themselves on the swings and roundabouts.
14 We also leave them there so that we can do the shopping undisturbed.

15 I've asked my secretary to stay at the office so that she can cope with visitors while I see to the arrangements for the banquet over here.
16 I'll get her over here later so that she can help me with the arrangements.
17 In the meanwhile I'm leaving her there so that I can be free to concentrate on things over here.

18 Our parents sent us all to Britain when we were quite young so that we could learn English.
19 They sent us so that they could learn English from us afterwards.
20 Personally I think they sent us there so that we'd learn to stand on our own feet.

5 Linking: concession

LINKS		
	although	
	even though	
	though	
	as	
	much as	
ADVERBS ETC.	*however*	*but*
	nevertheless	*(and) yet*
	though	
	even so	

Introductory note: The Examples show how the adverbs listed above, together with *but* and *yet*, are related to links of concession such as *although*. You will see that, as with result and cause (**3A**), the transformation of one use into the other involves changes in the relative positions of links and adverbs. This needs to be particularly noticed in the case of *though*, which can be link or adverb according to position. (For the concessional links *in spite of* and *despite* see **6**.)

Examples

But, *yet* AND ADVERBS	CONCESSION
1 A strike of all transport workers was called for Monday, *but* the bus drivers did not join it.	⟶ ⟵ *Although* a strike of all transport workers was called for Monday, the bus drivers did not join it. **a**
2 There were no trains that morning, *(and) yet* most people managed to get to work.	⟶ ⟵ *Even though* there were no trains that morning, most people managed to get to work. **a, f, g**
3 Quite a lot of commuters used the extra buses that ran in some areas. The majority, *though*, got lifts in private cars.	⟶ ⟵ *Though* quite a lot of commuters used the extra buses that ran in some areas, the majority got lifts in private cars. **b**
4 We should very much like to see an end to the strike. *However*, we do not think the Government should give way to the strikers.	⟶ ⟵ *Much as* we should like to see an end to the strike, we do not think the Government should give way to the strikers. **c**

5 Their claims may be justified.   ⟶ Justified *as/though* their claims
   Even so/Nevertheless they   ⟵   may be, they should not have
   should not have gone on strike.   gone on strike.   **d**
   Their claims may be justified,
   but (even so/nevertheless) they
   should not have gone on
   strike.   **e**

Explanation

a *Although* (1) and *even though* (2) are approximate equivalents, but *even though* is more emphatic. Similarly, *yet* (2) is more emphatic than *but* (1). Both *but* and *yet* are used not only as links (1, 2) but as adverbs at the beginning of sentences: 'A strike ... was called for Monday. But/Yet the (= However, the) bus drivers ....' (This use of *but* in written English, although common, may still be thought of as incorrect by some people.)

b *Though* (3) as a LINK is equivalent to *although* (but see **d** below). It must be carefully distinguished from *though* as ADVERB, which (i) cannot link clauses (see **3A** Introductory note), (ii) cannot begin a clause or sentence, and (iii) is always used with commas.

c *Much as* (4) can be used only with verbs expressing one's inclinations, such as *like, dislike, admire, approve, disapprove, sympathise, enjoy*.

d *As* (5) or *though* (but **not** *although*) may be used after an introductory adjective (*justified*) in a special form of inversion (= '*Although/Though* their claim may be justified ...').

e Of the adverbs (3, 4, 5), *even so* and *nevertheless* are more emphatic than *however* and *though*, and would be unsuitable in 3. You will see (5) that they can be used on their own or to reinforce *but. However*, like *though*, is always used with commas, which help to distinguish it from the conditional link (**1Ce**).

f *Even though* and *even if* are sometimes given as equivalents in dictionaries and elsewhere. However, it is better to keep them separate, the first for concession, the second as a conditional link (**1Cb**). Thus 'He wouldn't* give up motor-racing even though his wife begged him to' should refer to past fact, whereas 'He wouldn't give up motor-racing even if his wife begged him to' is future supposition (**1Db**).

g In the Examples the concessional clauses have all been placed first but, like causal clauses (**3A**), may often come second in a sentence (2): 'Most people managed to get to work, even though. ...'

* *Wouldn't* here means *refused to* (see **11Bf**).

Exercise

Transform the following by the use of the words in *italics*. The transformations required are not only as shown in the Examples, that is to say from left
to right and vice versa, but also within either category, for example from
though to *much as* or *even so* to *yet*.

1 *although*	I've been without a car for most of my life, but I've always managed to get about as much as I've wanted.
2 *yet*	Even though cars are increasingly dangerous to life and limb, advertisers are still allowed to boast of their speed and acceleration.
3 *much as*	Though Topal would have very much liked to visit Cambridge during his trip to Britain, his tight schedule will make it impossible.
4 *but*	He really should find time to visit the university where so much is being done in his own field of research, tight as his schedule may be.
5 *even though*	There is considerable difference in my parents' ages, and yet it has been a successful marriage.
6 *though* (adverb)	Although what you say may be true in your parents' case, I think it's more the exception than the rule.
7 *though* (link)	Sheila's pupils have been learning Spanish for only a year. Some of them are already up to examination standard, though.
8 *even so*	Sheila hasn't spent more than three or four months in Spain, yet she has acquired a pretty sound knowledge of the language.
9 *much as*	Although I like Willie very much, I cannot honestly say I'd back him in a business venture.
10 *but*	Unbusinesslike though he may be, you must admit he's a damned good architect.
11 *however*	We've never met Helen. We've heard a lot about her, though!
12 *though* (adverb)	Much as we'd have liked to go to her party, I'm afraid we can't, because we'll be in London that day.
13 *yet*	Ken has a rather light-hearted approach to life. Even so, he's no fool.

14	*as*	Although he's fond of Sheila, he's not going to rush into marriage.
15	*though* (adverb)	I suppose that Sir James is hardly a brilliant politician, but he makes a splendid country gentleman.
16	*nevertheless*	Though he has had financial difficulties for a long time now, he has managed to avoid selling Blenkinsop Hall.
17	*even though*	Denis is only a junior employee, yet he has direct access to the boss.
18	*although*	Don't you realise that, junior as he is to you, he's engaged to the boss's daughter Helen?
19	*however*	Helen's father refused at one time to have anything to do with Denis, but now they're as thick as thieves.
20	*though* (link)	Mr Elkins is ninety-three. He's still going strong, though.
21	*as*	He still manages to enjoy life, although he's old.
22	*even so*	He's very quick on the uptake even though he is a little hard of hearing.
23	*much as*	I admire him very much, but I'd never want to be his age.
24	*nevertheless*	Much as you may dislike the idea of growing old, the chances are that you will find yourself old one day.

6 Linking: cause, purpose, concession (alternative)

Examples

CAUSE ALTERNATIVE

1 *As* my cousin Georgina believes   ⟶   *Because of* her *belief* in complete
in complete freedom of ex- freedom of expression, my
pression, she lets her children cousin Georgina lets her chil-
do exactly as they like. dren do exactly as they like.

PURPOSE

2 I think personally that some   ⟶   I think personally that some dis-
discipline is absolutely neces- cipline is absolutely necessary
sary *so that* children will not *to prevent* children (from) *devel-*
develop into hooligans. *oping* into hooligans.

CONCESSION

3 I must admit they're quite nice   ⟶   I must admit they're quite nice
youngsters *although* they are so youngsters *in spite of/despite*
undisciplined. their indiscipline/(their) *lack of*
discipline/(their) *being* so
undisciplined.

Explanation

a For cause (1) we can often, when a suitable noun (*belief*) exists, use the preposition *because of* as a link instead of *because* etc. (**3A**). *Owing to* and *on account of* are more formal alternatives. *Due to* is also used as an alternative to
because of, but incorrectly according to some authorities, who say that it is
equivalent to *caused by* and that therefore it should be used only in relation
to a preceding noun,* such as *lack* in the following:
> The children's lack of discipline is due to/caused by their mother's
> strange beliefs.

On the basis of this argument the use in the following example of *due to*
would be as incorrect as the use of *caused by* (which would definitely be
wrong):
> The children are completely undisciplined, because of their mother's
> strange beliefs.

You have been warned!

---

* Or pronoun like *this* or *which*.

b For purpose (2) we can sometimes avoid a change of grammatical subject and use of *so that* (4Ac) by substituting verbs such as *prevent* (see Example 2 and 17D for its use with *-ing*, with or without *from*), *allow*, *enable* (see 17C), *let*, *make* (see 17B) or *give*.

c For concession (3), instead of *although* etc. (5) we can often use *in spite of* or *despite* with:
   i a suitable noun (*indiscipline*) or pronoun
   ii *lack of* + noun (*discipline*) or pronoun
   iii the *-ing* form or gerund (*being*).
   With pronouns like *what* (8Am) or *everything* we can use *in spite of/despite* when the use of *although* etc. would be difficult or impossible: 'Despite what people say, Georgina refuses to change her habits.'

Exercise

Transform the following into alternative constructions like those shown above. Where possible use *in spite of/despite* in more than one way (see Example 3).

1 Although Harry McArthur was very well qualified for the job, he didn't get it.
2 Perhaps he didn't get it because he looks a bit scruffy.
3 No, I think it was because he fails to do justice to himself at interviews.

4 Some people are refused driving licences because they're short-sighted.
5 What can I do so that the examiner will give me my licence?
6 I can no longer read a number plate at the required distance for the test, although I've tried very hard to take care of my eyes.

7 Helen always locks up her favourite chocolates so that no one else will eat them.
8 Although I'm partial to good chocolates, I wouldn't dream of touching hers.
9 Because she suspects people like this, she always counts what are left in the box.

10 They are fitting the plane with extra fuel tanks so that it will have a greater range.
11 They are doing this so that it will be a better commercial proposition.
12 However, as it will weigh more, it will now need a longer take-off.

13 My cousin Georgina doesn't like where she lives because there's not enough social life.
14 Her husband often comes home early so that she can get out and about more.
15 Although he's trying to help her, she continues to grumble about the life she leads.

16 The flight was postponed because someone telephoned, warning about a bomb on board.
17 They took the plane out of service so that the security personnel could search it.
18 Because I was delayed like this, I did not get to my destination in time.

19 We won't get promoted because we haven't any technical qualifications.
20 Ah, but the management is going to rearrange your work programme so that you can attend training courses.
21 They're establishing these courses so that the staff can have the chance of becoming better qualified.

22 Exports should do better now, because the currency has just been devalued.
23 However, business generally is bad, because the economic situation is basically unstable.

24 We had a most pleasant day in the country, although there was no sun.
25 Willie, although he doesn't look it, is quite a handyman, and took charge of the barbecue.

7 Linking: time

LINKS	after	-ing (present participle or
	as	gerund)
	as soon as	
	before	
	immediately	
	(up)on	
	once	and (used in a general, rather
	when	than a special temporal,
	while	sense)

ADVERBS	then
	finally
	immediately

Introductory note: RELATIONSHIPS IN TIME between two events are very often, particularly in spoken English, expressed loosely with *and* with or without adverbs like *then* (see left-hand Examples below). However, particularly in written and more formal English, they are also expressed with appropriate time links that give greater variety and precision (see right-hand Examples). The purpose of this section is to show how these are used for past* events and how they relate to *and* and adverbs.

Examples

and, ADVERBS   TIME LINKS

Marilyn had been told by a
business client that she would
be met in Los Angeles.

1 She waited at the airport for ⟶ She (had) waited at the airport
   over an hour, *and (then) finally*   for over an hour *before* (finally)
   received a message telling her to   receiving/she (finally) received
   go direct to her hotel.   a message telling her to go direct
                                             to her hotel.   **a, b**

2 She made sure no one was wait- ⟶ ⎰ *After* making/she (had) made ⎱
   ing for her in the hotel lobby,   ⎱ *(After) Having* made   ⎰

---

*For the use of time links for the future, see 1C. The links listed in that section and in this are not exactly the same because of their different relevance to the respective sections.

and then collected her key at the reception desk.

sure no one was waiting for her in the hotel lobby, she collected her key at the reception desk.   **a, b, c**

3 She took the key *and* went up to her room.   ⟶   *Taking* the key, she went up to her room.   **d**

4 She opened the door ... *and* saw a man lying on the floor!   ⟶   *(Up)On* opening/*When* she opened the door, she saw a man lying on the floor!   **c, e**

5 She saw there was blood on his shirt *and immediately* knew she had to do something.   ⟶   *As soon as*/*Immediately* she saw there was blood on his shirt, she knew she had to do something.   **f**

6 She phoned reception *and* told them what had happened.   ⟶   She phoned reception, *telling* them what had happened.   **g**

7 She was waiting for someone to come up *when* suddenly the man gave a groan.   ⟶   *While* she was waiting for someone to come up, the man suddenly gave a groan.   **h**

8 She stood staring at him. He slowly opened his eyes and stared back.   ⟶   *While*/*As* she stood staring at him, he slowly opened his eyes and stared back.   **j**

Explanation

a **Examples 1 and 2:** The first event is **completed** before the second begins, this clear distinction between the two events often being indicated by the use after *and* of *then*. When using time links we can, depending on the relative importance of the events, either

  i emphasise the **first** event by using *before* (1), or

  ii emphasise the **second** event by using *after* or *having* (2).

If the subject of both verbs in the sentence is the same (*she*), we normally link with *-ing* as shown (*before receiving, after making, having made*). We should not do this, however, when the subject changes, because if we did we would have an unrelated participle (*Having waited* etc.):

> After *she* (had) waited (**not** Having waited/After waiting) at the airport for over an hour, *a message* came through telling her to go direct to her hotel.

Grammar would conflict with meaning if we used *-ing* here, because grammatically this would relate to *a message* but in meaning it would relate to *her*.

b *When* may be used instead of *before* (1) or *after* (2):

> She *had waited* at the airport for over an hour when she received a message.

> When she *had made* sure no one was waiting for her, she collected her key.

But note carefully that the past perfect tense must be used where, with *before* or *after*, there is a choice of tenses.* This is to make clear that the first event is completed before the second begins; use of the past tense (*she waited*) in 1 would indicate that she waited **after** receiving a message.

c   *Once* can replace *after* or *when* in Example 2 (see **b** above), because here someone (*she*) regards the completion of the first event as a necessary condition for passing on to the second:

> Once she had made sure no one was waiting for her, she collected her key.

But **not**, in Example 4: 'Once she opened the door, she saw a man lying on the floor.' Compare 'Once she opened the door, she was able to escape.'

d   **Example 3**: The first event is an introduction to the second, into which it **changes** without a break. In this kind of relationship between events, the subjects of the verbs are normally the same (*she*), and the appropriate time link is introductory *-ing* (*Taking*).

e   **Example 4**: The first event is **not** completed before the second begins, but **overlaps** it, so that the two events occur partly at the same time. Note that *when* is used here with the PAST, not past perfect, tense (compare **b** above). Similar use of *when* may occur with past states or repeated events: 'When Marilyn was at university she shared a room with a Lebanese girl/When Marilyn stayed at hotels strange things sometimes happened to her.'

f   **Example 5**: The first event is followed **urgently** by the second. As with *when* (see **b**, **e** above), we use the past tense when there is overlapping (5), but the past perfect tense when the first event is completed before the second begins:

> As soon as she*'d phoned* reception she returned to the injured man's side.

g   **Example 6**: The second event takes place only as **part of** the first event; that is to say, telling reception what she had seen was part of the act of telephoning. In this relationship as well (see **d** above), the subjects are normally the same, and we can use *-ing*; but now it is in second, not introductory, position.

h   **Example 7**: The first event is longer than the second, being **in progress** (1Bh) when the second occurs. The tense forms are accordingly **different** (progressive against simple). *(Just) as* or *when* commonly replaces *while* if the first event, although longer than the second, is of short duration:

> (Just) As/When she was picking up the phone, she saw the man move.

Both *while* and *when*, like *after*, *before* and *(up)on*, but unlike *as*, can be used

---

* You may come across the following tense use with *before*: 'We *got* to the airport before the plane *had arrived*.' The possible reason for this apparently illogical usage is that it echoes the logical tense use of the corresponding interrogative or negative: '*Had* the plane *arrived* before you *got* to the airport? – No, we *got* there before it *had arrived* (= It *hadn't arrived* before we *got* there).'

directly with -*ing* when subjects are the same:
> She fell when/while going downstairs.

(Note that *when* in the left-hand column is the equivalent of *and* (suddenly) *during this time*; it does not have the same function as the time link *when* that we have been discussing.)

j   Example 8: The two events are of approximately equal duration and **in progress at the same time**. (The use of *and* to link the two events is impossible.) The tense forms are accordingly **the same**, whether simple (8) or progressive:

> While she was staring at him, he was staring at her.

There is often little difference between *as* and *while*, although *as* rather than *while* can give the idea of gradual, simultaneous change:

> As she quietly approached him, he slowly opened his eyes.

But we must be careful in our use of *as* for time because of its possible causal meaning (3A): 'As she stared at him, he stared back at her' (with spoken stress on *she*, *him*, *he*, *her*) would probably mean that he stared at her **because** she stared at him.

Exercise

Transform the following by using the time links shown above. Where possible give alternatives, as in Examples 2 and 4.

1 I paid at the cash desk in the normal way and then left the supermarket.
2 I checked my change outside and found I was a pound short.
3 I checked it again very carefully and went back into the supermarket.

4 Harry was getting into bed the other night when his wife said she heard a strange noise.
5 He put on his dressing gown and went downstairs.
6 He went into every room and had a good look round, but could see nothing unusual.

7 Sheila went through her handbag three times and finally found the key to her flat.
8 She put the key in the lock and found it did not fit very well.
9 She tried again and again to unlock the door. She thought she could hear voices inside the flat.
10 She chanced to look up at the door number and realised at once what she was trying to do.

11 I touched the handle of the fridge and got an electric shock.
12 I called out to my husband in the garage and told him what had happened.
13 He heard me and came into the house straight away.
14 He made sure all the current was switched off and then carefully checked the wiring.

15 He examined one of the connections and discovered that the insulation was faulty.

16 He uttered a startled exclamation and rushed off to telephone the suppliers.

17 Georgina's brother was driving to the airport when he suddenly remembered his passport.

18 He drew up at the side of the road and emptied his briefcase on to his lap.

19 He seized his jacket off the back seat and searched all the pockets.

20 He got to the airport and immediately dashed off to the nearest phone.

21 He spoke to his secretary at the office and told her to look in the right-hand drawer of his desk.

22 He was waiting for her reply when he happened to feel his hip pocket.

23 'Eureka!' he shouted into the phone, and waved his passport in the air.

24 They heard him at the other end and thought he was mad.

25 He told them what had happened and they thought he was madder still.

8 Linking: relatives

8A Links and clause types: review

LINKS

RELATIVE PRONOUNS: *who, whom, which, whose, that, what*

RELATIVE ADVERBS: *where, when*

CLAUSE TYPES

NON-DEFINING and DEFINING

Examples

LINKS AND CLAUSE TYPES:

1 Sir James Blenkinsop, *who* is a Radical Member of Parliament, is sometimes advised by those of his fellow MPs *who/that* are socialists to give up Blenkinsop Hall, *which* was left him by his father, and live in something *which/that* would have a less aristocratic image.

NON-DEFINING	**a**
DEFINING	**b**
NON-DEFINING	**a**
DEFINING	**b**

2 Sir James, *whom* I have discussed politics with several times, is a man (*whom/that*) I respect despite the apparent discrepancy between his life style and the social philosophy of the political party (*which/that*) he belongs to. People criticise him without knowing his views, *which* is foolish.

RELATIVE WITH PREPOSITION **d**

{ CLAUSE TYPE AFTER *a(n)* **e**

OMISSION OF *whom* ETC. **c**

{ CLAUSE TYPE AFTER *the* **f**

OMISSION OF *whom* ETC. **c**

RELATIVE WITH PREPOSITION **d**

CLAUSE TYPE AFTER STATEMENTS **g**

3 Blenkinsop Hall, the garden *of which* is open to the public in summer, is a considerable attraction to tourists, *whose* money naturally finds its way into the pockets of the

POSSESSIVE RELATIVE **j**

POSSESSIVE RELATIVE **h**

local shopkeepers. This is a
fact *which/that* escapes many
people's notice and *which* Sir   SECOND RELATIVE   **k**
James should point out.

4 I told Sir James about the
manor house in my village,
which is now a college of   CLAUSE TYPE AFTER *the*   **f**
education(,) with *which* the   CLAUSE TYPE AFTER *a(n)*   **e**
local inhabitants feel they   RELATIVE WITH PREPOSITION   **d**
have absolutely no social or
historical connection. The
worst thing *that* could hap-   *that* AFTER SUPERLATIVES   **l**
pen is for Blenkinsop Hall to
go the same way.

5 The advantage of a supermar-
ket is that you can buy *what*   RELATIVE *what*   **m**
you want at a place *where*   RELATIVE *where*   **n**
you can park your car. Be-
sides, it is often open after six
o'clock, *when* other shops are   RELATIVE *when*   **n**
shut. It is then *that* I like to   *that* AFTER INTRODUCTORY *it*   **p**
do my shopping. It is also at a
supermarket *that* you get the   *that* AFTER INTRODUCTORY *it*   **p**
best value for money.

Explanation

a NON-DEFINING CLAUSES (1) differ from defining clauses in that they
   i   follow words (*Sir James Blenkinsop, Blenkinsop Hall*) of precise meaning
         which need no further definition;
   ii are additions to a sentence, which makes complete sense without them:
         'Sir James Blenkinsop . . . is sometimes advised by those of his fellow
         MPs who are socialists to give up Blenkinsop Hall . . . and live in some-
         thing that would have a less aristocratic image';
   iii cannot be used with *that*;
   iv are used with commas before and following;
   v   are spoken after a pause and with a tone change;
   vi are less common in spoken than in written English, which is the style of
         the Examples (note the absence of colloquial contraction).

b DEFINING CLAUSES (1) differ from non-defining clauses in that they
   i   follow words (*those of his fellow MPs, something*) of imprecise meaning
         which need further definition;
   ii are essential parts of a sentence, which makes incomplete sense without
         them: 'Sir James Blenkinsop, who is a Radical Member of Parliament, is

sometimes advised by those of his fellow MPs . . . to give up Blenkinsop Hall, which was left him by his father, and live in something . . .';

   iii can be used with *that*;

   iv are not used with commas;

    v are spoken without a pause or a tone change;

   vi are as common in spoken as in written English.

c OMISSION OF *whom* ETC.: Relative pronouns, like the pronouns *he/him, they/them* etc., may be grammatical subjects or grammatical objects. The form of either is the same (*which, that*) except in the case of *who* (subject)/*whom* (object). Relative pronouns (2) that are grammatical objects (*whom, which, that*) can be left out in defining clauses, but not in non-defining (*Sir James, whom* . . .). Relative pronouns (1) that are grammatical subjects (*who, which, that*) cannot be left out in either type of clause.

d RELATIVES WITH PREPOSITIONS (2, 4): Except in more formal English and in other cases mentioned in **8Bc**, a preposition used with a relative often remains in the same position in a sentence that it would occupy with a noun (2): 'I have discussed politics *with* Sir James several times ⟶ Sir James, whom I have discussed politics *with* several times. . . .' It must remain in this position if *that* is used or omitted (2): 'the political party (*that*) he belongs *to*.' However, a preposition at the end of a long clause becomes isolated from the relative pronoun, and to avoid this it is better to put it at the beginning with *whom* or *which* (4) than to write 'a college of education (that) the local inhabitants . . . with.' In the case of phrasal verbs (**16Aa, b**) like *point out* (3) or *look into* (**17Gii**), the particle *out* or *into* must always follow the verb itself: 'This is an important matter, which we must look into' **not** 'into which we must look.' Compare 'The party of scientists eventually reached the edge of the crater, into which they were now able to look.'

e CLAUSE TYPE AFTER INDEFINITE ARTICLE *a(n)*: When, by our use of *a*, we say something general or obvious, such as 'Sir James . . . is *a* man' (2) or 'This is *a* fact' (3), the clause that follows limits our general use of *a* to something particular, and is defining. When our use of *a* is not so general but is limited to something of which there are not so very many, like (4) 'a college of education', we are free to make the clause that follows defining or non-defining as we wish, without altering the meaning.

f CLAUSE TYPE AFTER DEFINITE ARTICLE *the*: When *the* (2) refers to something of which there is more than one (we know that there is more than one political party in the world) the clause that follows tells us which one it is, namely 'the (one) . . . he belongs to', and is defining. However, *the* (4) may refer to the **only** one ('the manor house in my village'), and then the clause that follows is non-defining and with a comma. If we removed the comma we would imply that there is more than one 'manor house in my village', and that we are referring to the one that has become a college of education.

g CLAUSE TYPE AFTER STATEMENTS (2): Relative clauses ('which is foolish') may refer back not to nouns or pronouns but to statements ('People criticise him without knowing his views'). In this case they are always non-defining clauses introduced by *which*.

h THE POSSESSIVE RELATIVE *whose* (3) is used for people, and corresponds to *her*, *his* or *their* ('. . . a considerable attraction to tourists. *Their* money finds its way . . .'). But it is also used for things, especially when these are a collection of people like a country, a firm or an office: 'The United Nations Organisation, whose headquarters are in New York, is . . . .' Here, of course, *whose* corresponds to *its*: 'Its headquarters are in New York.'

j THE POSSESSIVE RELATIVE *of which* (3), corresponding to *its/their*, is used for inanimate things, for which *whose* is not normally suitable: **not** 'Blenkinsop Hall, whose garden . . . .' Unlike *whose*, *of which* comes after the noun: **not** 'of which the garden' (compare *of which* corresponding to *of it/of them*, **8Bb**).

k A SECOND RELATIVE introduced by *and* or *but* (3) is generally a *wh-* relative and not *that*, in defining as well as in non-defining clauses.

l DEFINING CLAUSES AFTER SUPERLATIVES such as *worst* (4) are introduced by *that* and not by a *wh-* relative. The same is true after *all*, *everything*, *nothing*: 'All that glitters is not gold.' When *that* is the grammatical object (see **c** above) it is, of course, often left out: 'All I could see was a blank screen.'

m THE RELATIVE *what* (5) stands for 'the thing(s) that' and therefore, as it carries its own noun ('thing'), **cannot follow a noun** and **always introduces a defining clause**. This, unlike the other relative clauses so far considered, may come at the beginning of a sentence: '*What you say* is quite true.'

n THE RELATIVES *when* AND *where* (5) can be used in either non-defining or defining clauses. In the latter, the preceding noun may be left out, so that *when* and *where*, like *what*, can directly follow a verb: 'It is (the time) *when* I like to do my shopping/It is (the place) *where* you get the best value for money.' Note that *who*, *which* and *that*, unlike *what*, *when* and *where*, cannot carry their own nouns or pronouns in modern English: 'He who laughs last laughs longest' **not** 'Who laughs last . . . .'

p *That* AFTER INTRODUCTORY *it* (5): In the examples just given (**n**), *it* is not introductory but is a pronoun standing for something previously mentioned: 'It (= after six o'clock) is when . . ./It (= a supermarket) is where . . . .' Introductory *it*, on the other hand, does not stand for anything but introduces or reintroduces words that may or may not have been mentioned before, and in this way gives them emphasis: 'It is **then** (= after six o'clock) . . ./It is **at a supermarket** (= there) . . .' When these emphasised words are adverbials of time or place (**2B**) like those shown here, they are followed not by *when* or *where* but by *that*. Although this is not a true relative, it is always used without commas like relative *that*.

q Note that when introductory *it* introduces nouns these, in contrast to adverbials (see **p** above), **are** followed by a true relative, which is defining: 'It was *Sir James* who first had the idea of opening the gardens of Blenkinsop Hall to the public.' Compare the use of *it* as a pronoun with a non-defining relative in 'Who's that on the phone?' 'It's Sir James, who wants to speak to you.'

Exercise

Put in the relatives and the commas that are missing from the following. Give alternatives where possible (see Examples 1–4).

1 Our neighbours include Sir James and Lady Blenkinsop _____ live at Blenkinsop Hall _____ stands in grounds _____ are open to the public in summer.
2 Last Saturday we went to the Blenkinsops' party _____ I met Denis Chambers _____ I decided I did not like very much.
3 Willie _____ works for that firm of architects _____ I was telling you about the other day was there too.
4 It was also at the Blenkinsops' party _____ I was introduced to Sheila _____ I had heard a lot about but had never met before.
5 I told her that _____ I had heard about her was nearly all good _____ was true.
6 Sheila is one of the very few teachers _____ I know _____ can control their classes without ever raising their voices _____ is an ability _____ children appreciate highly.
7 The blond fellow _____ you saw her talking to was Ken _____ I must have mentioned before in connection with our athletic club.
8 Incidentally, our athletic club _____ present premises are being taken over by the local council are looking for someone like the Blenkinsops _____ might have some ground to spare for a running track.
9 At the stroke of midnight Toby Blenkinsop _____ can always be relied on at parties to do something bizarre rode a bicycle down the main staircase, a feat _____ drew loud applause.
10 It was one of those rare occasions _____ Toby's exuberance did not result in any damage _____ must have pleased his parents.
11 The time _____ I shall never forget was _____ Toby hung from a chandelier the chain _____ parted company with the ceiling, precipitating Toby onto a table _____ broke beneath him.
12 All _____ happened this time was that he tore his trousers _____ was hardly _____ you would call a calamity.

13 _____ surprises me most about Helen _____ was also at the party is that
she does not seem to worry at all about _____ others may think of her.

14 Marilyn _____ several people at the party asked about is now in the States
doing business for the little firm _____ she is head of.

15 I myself am not going abroad until October _____ the weather is cooler
and _____ it will be easier for me to chase business contracts _____ is the
whole purpose of my trip.

16 The first country on my itinerary is India _____ High Commission in
London has given me a list of those people _____ would be most interested in my line of business _____ is refrigeration equipment.

17 How lucky you are! India is _____ I have always wanted to go on that
dream holiday _____ I have always been promising myself but _____ I
have never been able to afford.

18 I am told I could renew my passport _____ is out of date at the nearest
consulate _____ address I could get from the embassy.

19 My grandmother _____ was Hungarian by birth was the youngest of three
sisters _____ might lead you to suppose that she was the last to marry.

20 Actually she was the one _____ got married first _____ is hardly surprising when you consider her looks _____ dazzled any man _____ came near
her.

21 It is three years ago today _____ I first met my wife and so yesterday
_____ I had little to do at the office I left early to buy something _____ I
thought would please her.

22 I bought _____ I wanted and hurried home _____ who should I find* but
the decorators _____ I had not expected until the following week. These
men had not only convinced my wife it was I _____ had mistaken the date
but had reduced the apartment to chaos.

23 It was on 6th August 1945 _____ man committed _____ is still his most
destructive single act: he dropped an atomic bomb on Hiroshima _____ is
estimated to have killed 200,000 people. That _____ fell on Nagasaki three
days later is estimated to have killed some 140,000 people.†

24 The difference in the casualty figures between the two cities is partly explained by the nature of the terrain _____ in Nagasaki is hilly and by the
position of the bomb _____ in Nagasaki was three kilometres from the city
centre.

25 The atomic bombs _____ were dropped on Hiroshima and Nagasaki had a
power of twenty kilotons _____ is equal to that of 20,000 tons of TNT,
whereas some of the bombs _____ have been developed since then are said
to have a power as great as forty-five megatons _____ equals that of
45,000,000 tons of TNT.

* For the use of *should* here, see 11Fd.
† These figures are from a Japanese report published in 1981, and include long-term causes of death such as
radiation sickness.

26 These more powerful bombs _____ are now included in the arsenals of all countries _____ call themselves nuclear powers are known as hydrogen or thermonuclear bombs.

27 A hydrogen bomb depends for its operation not only on the process of nuclear fission or splitting _____ is the basis of the atomic bomb, but on nuclear fusion _____ two nuclei _____ in this case are nuclei of 'heavy' hydrogen come together to form a larger nucleus.

28 Nuclear fission _____ is the source of energy of atomic power stations results in the accumulation of harmful residues _____ are difficult to dispose of, whereas nuclear fusion _____ is the source of energy of the sun has no such residues.

29 The problem _____ scientists are faced with in trying to harness nuclear fusion as a peaceful source of energy is that it requires for its operation the very high temperatures _____ are found in the sun but _____ so far have been produced artificially only by the nuclear fission _____ provides the 'trigger' mechanism of the hydrogen bomb.

30 Our greatest benefit would come not from our ability to control nuclear fusion and other processes of nature _____ we seem increasingly able to do but to control ourselves _____ we seem unable to do as witnessed by _____ occurred at Hiroshima and Nagasaki in August 1945.

8B   Sentence building with relatives

Introductory note: In written, and particularly in more formal, English the use of relative links to make sentences is common, and this section gives some practice in it. Of course it is not suggested that you should try and build up all your sentences in this way, since your style would then become rather heavy. There should be a balance between this kind of linking and that dealt with in other sections.

Examples

SEPARATE SENTENCES

SINGLE SENTENCE

1 Shakespeare was born in 1564 and died in April 1616. *His* name is universally known but most of *his* life is lost in obscurity. Cervantes,

⟶ Shakespeare, *whose* name is universally known but most of *whose* life is lost in obscur- **b** ity, was born in 1564 and died in April 1616, *when*

79

Spain's greatest literary figure, also died *in April 1616. This* coincidence has often been remarked on.

Cervantes, Spain's greatest literary figure, also died, a coincidence *that* has often been remarked on. **d, e**

2 So far as we know, Shakespeare lived a fairly uneventful life. During *it* he apparently wrote thirty-three plays. Two of *them* consist of more than one part, making thirty-six full-length stage plays in all. 'Hamlet' is probably by general consent the greatest among *these*.

⟶ So far as we know, Shakespeare lived a fairly uneventful life (,) during *which* he apparently wrote thirty-three plays, two of *which*/of *which* two consist of more than one part, making thirty-six full-length stage plays in all, among *which* 'Hamlet' is probably by general consent the greatest. **c**

b

3 The obscurity surrounding Shakespeare's life led at one time to the advancement of the Baconian theory. According to *this* the plays were not written by Shakespeare but by a nobleman and philosopher, Francis Bacon. It was said that *he* would have had the necessary erudition. Shakespeare, a merchant's son, must have lacked *it*. And *Bacon* would have wished to disguise the fact that he was a playwright.

⟶ The obscurity surrounding Shakespeare's life led at one time to the advancement of the Baconian theory, according to *which* the plays were not written by Shakespeare but by a nobleman and philosopher, Francis Bacon, *who*, it was said, would have had the necessary erudition *that* Shakespeare, a merchant's son, must have lacked, and *who* would have wished to disguise the fact that he was a playwright. **c**

e

Explanation

a Note the correspondence between the italicised words (PRONOUNS etc.) in the left-hand Examples with those on the right (RELATIVES).

b You will see (2) that one can write either *two of which* or *of which two* to correspond with *two of them*. Similarly, one could write either *most (many, part* etc.) *of which/whom* or *of which/whom most*. However, with *whose* (1), the first, not the second, word order is normal.

c As already mentioned (8Ad), the placing of prepositions in front of relatives is usual in more formal English, and in these Examples and the Exercise below, which are fairly formal in style, one could expect it. There are also prepositions that must come in front of a relative because they are part of an adverb phrase of time or place (**2B**): *During it* (2) ⟶ *during which* (**not** 'which . . . during'). There are also phrases like *According to this* (3) where the word order must clearly remain as it is when *this* becomes relative *which*.

d It is possible but not very common in modern English to use relative *which* as an adjective, in other words to turn *This coincidence* (1) into *which coincidence*. Instead we generally put the noun (*a coincidence*) into what is called apposition with what goes before (*when Cervantes . . . also died*) and follow it with a defining relative as shown.

e When building sentences with relatives it is a good idea, for the sake of variety, to use *that* instead of a *wh-* relative wherever possible. This may be not only where the relative clause **must** be defining (1) but also where (3) it **can** be defining (see **8Af**).

Exercise

By replacing the words in *italics* with relatives, combine each group of sentences into one sentence, as shown in the Examples. Put all prepositions in front of their relatives (see **c** above).

1 New Zealand consists principally of two islands. The southern is the larger of *these* but the northern is the more highly populated. *New Zealand* is situated between latitudes 34°S and 47°S.
2 The Maoris were the dominant inhabitants of New Zealand until the end of the eighteenth century. The country began to be colonised by the British *then*. The Maoris resisted *them* fiercely at times. *The Maoris'* valour and physique have been much admired.
3 The Maoris are now a peaceable people. At one time *they* were divided into many tribes. *These* were often at war with each other. The tribal system scarcely exists among *them*.
4 The Maoris have a tradition. *Their* name means 'indigenous'. According to *this tradition* they originally came from an island called Hawaiki. Some people have identified *it* with Hawaii.

5 I fly to India on the twelfth and leave on the twenty-second. *This* will give me ten days there. I fly to Singapore after *that*. I plan to spend four days *there* before going on to Japan. I should reach *Japan* on the twenty-seventh.
6 In India I shall be spending most of my time in New Delhi. The shade temperature *there* can reach 45°C in June. It drops a bit after *that* because of the monsoon.
7 India has many wonderful buildings. The most famous of *them* is undoubtedly the Taj Mahal. The Emperor Shah Jehan built *it* for his favourite wife Mumtaz Mahal. *Her* body lies there beside her husband's.

8   The Taj Mahal is one of the greatest buildings in the world. *It* took twenty-two years to complete. And *it* is built of white marble, exquisitely carved and inlaid in places with semi-precious stones. (Many of *these*, incidentally, have been stolen.)

9   India has over half a billion people. After China *it* is the most populated country in the world. *This* fact weighs heavily on its rulers. *Their* birth-control policies have met with varying success.

10   Singapore has grown from practically nothing in the early nineteenth century into an independent Republic. *Singapore* is an island off the coast of Malaysia. It is linked by a road and rail bridge to *Malaysia* but seceded from *Malaysia* politically in 1965. *In the early nineteenth century* it was leased from the then owners by a British trading company. The present prosperity *of the Republic* is proverbial.

11   Japan deliberately cut herself off from the outside world from the early 1600s until 1853. So many of our consumer goods are now made *in Japan*. *In 1853* Commander Perry of the United States re-established communication. As a result of *this* Japan has not only caught up industrially with the West but has overtaken it in some respects.

12   George Bernard Shaw was an Irish playwright. A photo of *him* smiles impishly at me from the wall of my study. *He* audaciously set himself above Shakespeare. In one outrageous statement he said he despised *Shakespeare* as much as he despised Homer.

13   Shaw was, in fact, something of an intellectual clown. *This* did not prevent him from having a brilliant mind, a flashing wit and a power over the English language. *This power* is fully seen in the prefaces. He wrote *prefaces* to most of his plays.

14   GBS, as he has come to be known, did not go to university but emigrated in his youth to London. He spent a lot of time *there* educating himself in literature, music and politics. *This* led to his becoming a critic and socialist orator before becoming a playwright. He did not fully establish himself in *this* role until his forties.

15   In 1860 Abraham Lincoln and his supporters renounced slavery in the United States. A war soon broke out between the North and South as a result of *this*. *It* cost half a million lives. And *it* ruined the South. *Its* slaves had been the basis of much of the economy. *They* were set free.

16   The two best known generals on the Northern side were Grant and Sherman, while on the Southern side the most famous military leaders were Lee and Jackson. *Grant and Sherman* have both had American army tanks named after them. To the best of my belief, no military equipment has been named after *Lee and Jackson*. Since Lee is usually held to be the greatest of the four, *this* is rather ironic.

17   The turning point of the American Civil War came in 1863 at Gettysburg. *It* went quite well for the South at first. General Lee's troops were defeated

in *this* battle. And after *it* Abraham Lincoln made a speech. *It* is perhaps the most famous speech in American history.

18 The best known book to come out of the American Civil War is, of course, 'Gone with the Wind'. *Its* authoress, Margaret Mitchell, was herself brought up in the South. *There* she heard first-hand accounts of the struggle. Many of *these* she incorporated into her book.

19 Powered flight began with the two Wright brothers. *It* is perhaps the most important development of the twentieth century. *They* first achieved it on 17th December 1903. *Then* each of them made two short flights in North Carolina, USA, in the aeroplane 'Kitty Hawk'. *This* is now in the National Air Museum, Washington.

20 Their achievement would not have been possible without the work of Otto Lilienthal. *He*, a German, designed and flew a series of gliders. He unfortunately met his death in one of *them* in 1896 while experimenting with a new form of elevator control.

21 The next stage in the development of the aeroplane took place largely in France. *It* was greatly stimulated by the Wrights' achievements. *In France* Bleriot made his epoch-making cross-Channel flight in 1909. Governments were forced after *that* to take the flying machine seriously.

22 Unlike most of the aeroplanes of the time Bleriot's machine was a monoplane. *Most of the aeroplanes* were biplanes. He was the pioneer of *the monoplane* type. And *this type* has since proved itself by driving the biplane from the skies.

23 The problem of how to support a single wing was not fully solved until the 1930s. Bleriot had overcome *it* with wires from a central post. *In the 1930s* the use of thin metal or plywood allowed the construction of stronger wings. *These* needed no external support. *This* soon led to the building of such famous aeroplanes as the Spitfire and the Messerschmidt.

24 Another epoch-making flight took place in 1919. *Then* two Britons, Alcock and Whitten-Brown, flew non-stop across the Atlantic from Newfoundland to Ireland. They landed in a bog *there* after flying for over sixteen hours in an open plane of military type. *It* had been only slightly modified for the occasion.

8C Shortened constructions

Introductory note: You will already know (**8Ac**) that in defining clauses the object relatives *whom*, *which* or *that* can be left out, making the clause a little shorter. In this section we see how in most defining clauses not only the subject relatives *who*, *which* or *that* but also the verb can be left out or replaced, giving a shorter construction. This can also be done in some non-defining clauses, but, as shown below, only when there is a special relationship between the clause and the rest of the sentence. These shortened constructions follow the same rules regarding commas and tone change as their parent clauses (**8Aa, b**).

Examples

DEFINING CLAUSES **a**	NON-DEFINING CLAUSES **b**
Shortened constructions possible	**Shortened constructions impossible**
1 The McArthurs live in a house (which has)/*with* green shutters.	They live in number twenty-two, *which has* green shutters.
2 They have a large garden (that runs)/*running* right down to a river.	They spend a lot of time in their garden, *which runs* right down to a river.
3 This is an advantage for any member of the family (who is) fond of fishing.	This is an advantage for Harry McArthur, *who is* fond of fishing.
4 The boy (who is) in the garden is Harry's son Charles.	Charles, *who is* in the garden, is Harry's son.
5 The boy (who is) going fishing with Harry is his nephew David.	David, *who is* going fishing with Harry, is his nephew.
Shortened constructions impossible	**Shortened constructions possible**
6 —	David, (who had)/*with* a look of expectancy on his face, stood fishing on the river bank.
7 People *who fish* have little time for other hobbies.	David, (who was) *fishing* a little way upstream from Harry, caught nothing at first.
8 Those *who know* Harry soon find out how keen he is on fishing.	Then Harry, (who knew)/ *knowing* how disappointed David was, gave him some special bait.
9 Anyone *who is* a keen fisherman (= Any keen fisherman) likes to encourage others in the sport.	Harry, (who is) a keen fisherman, likes to encourage others in the sport.
10 The boy *who went* fishing with Harry caught a sizeable fish.	

Explanation

a DEFINING CLAUSES beginning with the subject relatives *who, which* or *that* can be shortened by the use of (1) *with* or (2) *-ing* (present participle), or

(3–5) by omitting the relative + verb *to be*, **except** when:
  i they refer to a repeated action, a habit, or a hobby (7);
 ii they contain verbs that describe mental states, and which are therefore
     without progressive forms (**1Bs**), such as *know* (8), *believe* or *like*
     (compare 'Anyone thinking of calling on Harry had better not choose a
     weekend');*
iii they contain (9) the verb *to be* + noun (*a keen fisherman*), although such
     clauses can often be shortened by rewording as shown;
 iv they refer (10) to an event completed **before** what is described in the
     rest of the sentence (compare 'The boy who fished alongside Harry
     caught a sizeable fish ⟶ The boy fishing alongside Harry . . .').

b NON-DEFINING CLAUSES can **not** be shortened (1–5) **except** when:
  i they refer to SOMETHING HAPPENING AT THE SAME TIME as what happens
     in the rest of the sentence (6, 7);
 ii they refer to the CAUSE (**3Ab**) of what happens in the rest of the sentence
     (8);
iii they provide INFORMATION THAT RELATES CLOSELY to the rest of the
     sentence (9). The shortened construction is commonly in the form of a
     noun phrase (*a keen fisherman*) placed in apposition (**8Bd**) to the subject
     (*Harry*), but may begin with an adjective or verb participle: 'Harry,
     married and with three children, is a keen family man despite his
     passion for fishing.'
The test for (**i**) and (**ii**) is to see whether the shortened construction can be
put elsewhere in the sentence, usually at the beginning but sometimes at
the end: 'David stood fishing on the river bank, (with) a look of expectancy
on his face/Fishing a little way upstream from Harry, David caught nothing
at first/Then, knowing how disappointed David was, Harry gave him some
special bait.' (Compare the clauses in 1–5, none of which could be moved if
they were shortened.) The same test can be applied to (**iii**) when the phrase
refers to the subject (*Harry*): 'A keen fisherman, Harry likes . . ./Married and
with three children, Harry is . . . .' Such phrases can, however, refer to the
object (*three children*) in a sentence, and then they cannot be moved:
     Harry has three children, Christine being (= of whom Christine is)
     the eldest, Charles the youngest.

Exercise 1

In some of the following sentences shortened constructions of the type shown
in the Examples can be used, while in others they cannot. Read out or rewrite
the sentences accordingly.

---

* Verbs expressing desire such as *want* or *wish*, although not often occurring in the progressive form, may
be used in a shortened construction after words of indefinite reference: 'People/Those/Anyone wishing to
call on Harry . . . .'

1 Marilyn has lost a purse that contained fifty pounds and a return air ticket.
2 Anyone who finds it should ring this number.
3 The loss was rather a shock to Marilyn, who was planning to fly to Chicago next week.
4 Marilyn, who is smiling all over her face, has just walked into the room waving her purse.

5 Is there anyone here who understands Japanese?
6 Willie, who is a young architect, has just got his first client.
7 His client, who is a Japanese, cannot speak much English.
8 Willie, who is anxious not to lose his client, is looking for an interpreter.

9 Lady Blenkinsop, who is a woman of considerable enterprise, is taking up farming.
10 She is taking over from one of the tenants on the estate, who farms about forty hectares.
11 Now Lady Blenkinsop, who is full of enthusiasm for her new life, gets up at five every morning to milk the cows.

12 I tell those friends of mine who have sedentary jobs that they should take regular exercise.
13 After all, bank employees, who have sedentary jobs, are often first-rate athletes.

14 Anyone who buys a second-hand car should be on his or her guard.
15 A friend of mine who knows a lot about the used car trade has opened my eyes to some of its tricks.

16 Several young mothers, who all had babies in their arms, waited patiently at the clinic.
17 There are many people who are just not patient enough to wait like that to see a doctor.

18 Anyone who is thinking of taking the exam should give his name to me.
19 But I hope there's no one who thinks it'll be an easy exam.

20 Isn't that the girl who's always saying she wants to be an actress?
21 No, that's Zena, who is a fashion model and has a pet alligator.

22 I live in the old rectory, which has a beautiful walled garden.
23 It is one of the few houses which is not up for sale.

24 You're talking about the Red Lion Hotel, which is on the right of the road, not the left.
25 On the left there is an oak tree that has branches which stretch right across the road.

26 Sir James, who has realised that his son Toby is a layabout, has told him he should get a proper job.

27 Toby, who had a note of sarcasm in his voice, asked his father if he thought his own job was a proper one.

28 I envy people who have no family ties and responsibilities.

29 You mean you envy spinsters and bachelors, who very often have no such ties and responsibilities.

30 My cousin Georgina, who has four young children, goes out to work.

31 A working mother who has four young children has her hands full.

32 Has the person who came to see us yesterday about the vacant post left her name and address?

33 I notice that some of those who have applied for the post have no qualifications at all.

34 Any motorist who wishes to take advantage of our special offer should fill in the form below.

35 A handy map-case is an ideal present for someone who drives a lot.

Exercise 2

Here we repeat some of the sentences in **8A, B,** since in each of them one or more of the relative clauses can be shortened. Rewrite the sentences accordingly.

1 Our neighbours include Sir James and Lady Blenkinsop _____ live at Blenkinsop Hall _____ stands in grounds _____ are open to the public in summer.

2 Sir James _____ is a Radical Member of Parliament is sometimes advised by those of his fellow MPs _____ are socialists to give up Blenkinsop Hall _____ was left him by his father and live in something _____ would have a less aristocratic image.

3 Sheila is one of the few teachers _____ is able to control their classes without ever raising their voices _____ is an ability _____ children appreciate highly.

4 New Zealand _____ is situated between latitudes 34°S and 47°S consists principally of two islands of _____ the southern is the larger but the northern the more highly populated.

5 The Maoris _____ at one time were divided into many tribes _____ were often at war with each other are now a peaceable people among _____ the tribal system scarcely exists.

6 The atomic bombs _____ were dropped on Hiroshima and Nagasaki had a power of twenty kilotons _____ is equal to that of 20,000 tons of TNT, whereas some of the bombs _____ have been developed since then are said to have a power as great as forty-five megatons _____ is equal to that of 45,000,000 tons of TNT.

7 These more powerful bombs _____ are now included in the arsenals of all

countries _____ call themselves nuclear powers are known as hydrogen or thermonuclear bombs.

8 A hydrogen bomb depends for its operation not only on the process of nuclear fission or splitting _____ is the basis of the atomic bomb but on nuclear fusion _____ two nuclei _____ in this case are nuclei of 'heavy' hydrogen come together to form a larger nucleus.

9 Nuclear fission _____ is the source of energy of atomic power stations results in the accumulation of harmful residues _____ are difficult to dispose of, whereas nuclear fusion _____ is the source of energy of the sun has no such residues.

10 The problem _____ scientists are faced with in trying to harness nuclear fusion as a peaceful source of energy is that it requires for its operation the high temperatures _____ are found in the sun but _____ so far have been produced artificially only by the nuclear fission _____ provides the 'trigger' mechanism of the hydrogen bomb.

9 Linking: similarity and comparison: review of *as*, *like*, *than* etc.

Introductory note: This is a section of English grammar where there is more argument among English speakers about correct usage than anywhere else, and in the Explanation below you will accordingly find a good deal of advice about what to use and what not to use. The object of this is not that you should be a conservative speaker or writer of old-fashioned English, but that your English should avoid criticism which, particularly in examinations, might be to your disadvantage.

Examples

'When I worked (1) *as* a waitress, I worked (2) *like* a slave. It was (3) *like* working in a shop, (4) *as/(like)* you said it would be. In a restaurant,	*as* AGAINST *like*	a
(5) *as/(like)* in a shop, you're at the mercy of both boss and customers. Although I worked	*as* AGAINST *like*	b
(6) *as* hard *as* the other waitresses (did), I did	*as* . . . *as*	c, d
(7) *not* get *as/so* many tips (*as* they did/them).'	*not as/so* . . . *as*	c, d
	UNCOMPLETED COMPARISONS	j
'If you did (8) *the same* job *as* they did/them but got (9) *less*	*the same* . . . *as*	c, d
	than AFTER COMPARATIVES	e
money (*than* they did/them),	UNCOMPLETED COMPARISONS	j
why didn't you leave (10) *sooner*	*than* AFTER COMPARATIVES	e
(*than* you did)? After all,	UNCOMPLETED COMPARISONS	j
(11) *the harder* you work, *the more* you should earn.'	*the* WITH PAIRED COMPARATIVES	f
'I (12) *prefer* working *to* doing nothing, and (13) I'*d rather* be a	*prefer* AGAINST *would rather*	g
waitress *than* (be) a shop assistant. It may be (14) *as* tiring	*as* . . . *as*	c
a job but it's (15) *not such a* (great) strain on one's patience	*not such (a)* . . . *as*	h
(*as* working in a shop).'	UNCOMPLETED COMPARISONS	j
'There are (16) *other* things you could do *besides/apart from*	USES OF *than*	k

working in a restaurant or
shop.'
'What could I do (17) *other*   USES OF *than*   **k**
than/except cook? And (18) I'd   *would as soon . . . as*   **c**
(just) *as soon* be a waitress *as*
(be) a cook. There's little
difference between them
(19) *except* in their wages.'   USES OF *than*   **k**

'Nonsense! A cook is quite
(20) *different in* status *from/(to)* a   USES OF *than*   **k**
mere waitress. She can keep the
customers at a distance,
(21) *whereas/while/but* a waitress   COMPARISON BY CONTRAST   **l**
is at their beck and call.'

Explanation

a *As* AGAINST *like* WITH NOUNS OR PRONOUNS: *as* indicates someone's or
something's ROLE or FUNCTION (1); *like* is for similarity only (2). Compare
also 'He waved the stick about *like* a sword' with 'He used the stick *as* a
lever to open the door.' With *-ing* (verb-noun or gerund), only *like* is used
(3).

b *As* AGAINST *like* WITH CLAUSES AND PHRASES: except with nouns, pronouns
and *-ing* (see **a** above), the standard link for similarity is *as* (4, 5), and you
are advised to use it, at least in written English. Write 'You should do as I
do' **not** 'You should do like I do.' Although the use of *like*, shown in the
Examples in brackets, is quite common for clauses and phrases, it is
considered wrong by many people.

c *As . . . as, the same . . . as* are links for equality, used with adjectives or
adverbs (6) and nouns (8) respectively; for inequality we use *not as/so . . . as*
(7). Note the use of *as . . . as* with adjective + singular countable noun in
Example 14 (compare **3Ad**) and of *would as soon . . . as* with a verb in
Example 18. Here is an example involving two different verbs: 'I'd as soon
stay in this evening as *go* to the cinema.'

d '*As . . . as*' + CLAUSE OR (PRO)NOUN: after final *as* (6, 7, 8) we can use a clause
(*the other waitresses did/they did*) or a noun or object pronoun (*the other
waitresses/them*). **But** we must avoid ambiguity or double meaning: instead
of writing 'He's as fond of the dog as Georgina/her' we should make our
meaning clear by writing either (i) 'He's as fond of the dog as Georgina/she
is' or (ii) 'He's as fond of the dog as (he is) of Georgina/her.' In spoken
English, a difference in stress can make the distinction clear: (i) '**He's** as
fond of the dog as Georgina' or (ii) 'He's as fond of the **dog** as Georgina'
(compare **2Bk, l**).

e *Than* AFTER COMPARATIVES like *less* (9) or *sooner* (10) can also (see **d** above) be followed either by a clause (*they did/you did*) or a noun or object pronoun (*them*). Again, we must avoid ambiguity by writing either 'He likes the dog more than Georgina does' or 'He likes the dog more than he likes/does Georgina.'

f *The* WITH PAIRED COMPARATIVES (11): this is not the common, everday *the* (definite article), but a link word. Note also a similar use of *the* in contexts like the following: 'What big teeth you have, grandmother!' said Little Red Riding Hood. 'All *the* better to eat you with!' said the Wolf, jumping out of bed.

g *Prefer* AGAINST *would rather*: when comparing what we *like doing* we generally use (12) *prefer* + *-ing* + *to* (preposition); when comparing what we *would like to do* we generally use (13) *would rather* (sometimes *would sooner*) + plain infinitive + *than* (**17Bg**). This is because *would prefer*, like *would like*, is followed by the full infinitive with *to* (**10Cb**), which means that, although we can say 'I'd prefer to be a waitress', we cannot complete a comparison with *would prefer* in good English: **not** 'I'd prefer to be a waitress *to/(rather) than* a shop assistant.' (See **k** below.)

h *Not such . . . as* is used instead of *not as/so . . . as* with uncountable or plural nouns ('It's not such hard *work*/They're not such hard *exercises* as I thought'). It is also used with a singular countable noun (15), but *not as/so great a strain* or *not as/so much of a strain* is a possible alternative here. *Not such a . . . (as)* can be transformed as follows: 'It's *not such a* strain (*as* working in a shop) ——→ It's *less of a* strain (*than* working in a shop) ——→ Working in a shop is *more of a* strain (*than* being a waitress).' (Compare **3Ad, 3Bb**.)

j UNCOMPLETED COMPARISONS after *as* (7, 14), comparatives (9, 10) or *such* (15) are common where the context is established, that is to say, when we know what we are talking about.

k THE USES OF *than* are as follows:

   i after comparative adjectives or adverbs (see **e**);
   ii after *rather* (see **g**);
   iii after *other* (17), although, when words come in between, *than* is much less common than *besides* or *apart from* (16). The phrase *other than* is itself less frequent than *except* (17, 19).

You are advised **not** to use *than* for **any other words** besides the above, whatever you may see or hear. Its use, for example, after *prefer* (see **g** above) or after *different* (20) in place of *from* or the less accepted *to* is quite common, but there are people on both sides of the Atlantic who regard such use as an 'abominable pestilence' (to quote from H. L. Mencken's classic book *The American Language*). So beware!

l COMPARISON BY CONTRAST (21) is linked with *whereas* or *while*; or, less

mally and more emphatically, with *but*. Only *whereas* can introduce the
itrast: 'Whereas a waitress is at the customers' beck and call, a cook . . . .'

m See also *as if (*1Fc) as a link for similarity.

Exercise 1

Replace each number by the appropriate link.

This year has not been a bit (1) last year. The summer has not been nearly
(2) warm, and our harvest is likely to be smaller (3) it has ever been. (4) this
time last year we were cutting the corn, this year it is still green. However,
other (5) give up farming altogether there is nothing we can do about it.

One of the difficulties of English is that it is not spelt (6) it is pronounced.
Some letters, (7) in *though* or *know*, might just (8) well not be there. Another
difficulty is that American spelling is different (9) some respects (10) British.
Since it is nearer to English pronunciation, I prefer it (11) British spelling.

Usually Marilyn regards me (12) an equal, and talks to me (13) she does to her
other friends. Sometimes, though, she treats me (14) a child, although I have
the same degree (15) she has and am (16) good a typist. Perhaps she treats me
(17) that because she thinks I'm not (18) a good business woman (19) she is.
Give me time and I'll show her I'm just (20) good.

'Why is Ken dressed (21) a woman?'
'Because he's going to the Blenkinsops' fancy-dress party. What are you going
(22)?'
'I'm going (23) I am. I've got nothing else to wear (24) a dinner-jacket, and I
don't want to go looking (25) a waiter.'
'Why not? If I went (26) a waitress we'd make a fine pair.'
'The Blenkinsops would probably put us both to work for the evening
(27) unpaid servants. (28) less attention you draw to yourself at a fancy-dress
party (29) better.'
'But you'll draw all (30) more attention to yourself by not going in fancy
dress!'

Sheila and Helen are very different (31) appearance. Helen's tall and willowy
(32) Sheila's on the plump side and hasn't (33) a good figure. Helen's dark and
green-eyed (34) Sheila's fair and blue-eyed. Sheila looks pleasant rather
(35) pretty, (36) Helen looks (37) a film star. In short, Sheila's no beauty, but
I'd prefer her (38) a friend (39) Helen. (40) my mother says, there's more to life
(41) appearances, and in character Sheila stands head and shoulders above
Helen.

Crossing the rope bridge over the ravine was more (42) climbing (43) walking.
There were other people on it (44) myself, and they made it bob about (45) a
clothesline. The leader went over (46) a man crossing the street, (47) all I could

do (48) last in the queue was to hold on (49) grim death and inch my way across (50) a spider.

'Why don't you and your husband emigrate to the States (51) us? Wouldn't you rather live there (52) in Britain?'
'No, I don't think so. I prefer smaller countries (53) larger ones. For one thing, I wouldn't want to be any further from the sea (54) I am.'
'I'd (55) soon live near mountains (56) the sea. California's got both, (57) the whole of the West Coast. That's where we hope to be in three months' time. (58) sooner (59) better (60) far (61) I'm concerned.'
'Really? Well, I can see there's no more point in my trying to persuade you to stay (62) in your trying to persuade me to go. We might (63) well save our breaths. I'd only add that I don't think it's (64) important where you live (65) how you live.'

Exercise 2

Re-form the following using a comparative and *than*, in the way shown in the examples below. If you can, do the Exercise **orally**, without the book and with someone saying the sentences to you.

He's not so tall as *she is*. ⟶ *She's* taller than he is.
Her car's not nearly so economical ⟶ *My car's* much more economical as *mine*. than hers.
The play isn't such a flop as *I* ⟶ *I thought the play would be* more of *thought it would be*. a flop than it is.

 1 The dining room hasn't as many chairs in it as the sitting room.
 2 Upstairs the ceilings aren't as high as they are downstairs.
 3 The house next door isn't so well built as this one.
 4 We didn't arrive as early as we expected to.
 5 It isn't nearly as noisy here as it was at the airport.
 6 We don't live as near the town as we'd like to.
 7 We haven't done as much homework as we should have.
 8 London isn't such a big city as Tokyo.
 9 The Atlantic isn't as salty as the Mediterranean.
10 Russia's not so densely populated as India.
11 Arabic isn't such a hard language as Chinese.
12 We're not so good at judo as the Japanese are.
13 Jupiter's not so far from the sun as Saturn.
14 Southerners are not so fair as northerners on the whole.
15 People aren't so friendly here as they are in the north of England.
16 There isn't as little petrol in the tank as you thought there was.
17 Flies are not such a nuisance as mosquitoes.
18 Salmon weren't nearly so scarce twenty years ago as they are now.
19 Inflation's not so bad this year as last.

"GRAMMAR IN CONTEXT" GETHIN (COLLINS) 1983

20 Being rich isn't such an advantage as people think.

Exercise 3

Re-form the following using a negative followed by *as/so . . . as* or *such . . . as*,
in the way shown in the examples below. If you can, do the Exercise **orally**,
without the book and with someone saying the sentences to you.

My car's much more economical   ⟶   *Her car*'s not nearly as/so
than *hers*.   economical as mine.
I thought the play would be more   ⟶   *The play isn*'t such a flop as I
of a flop than *it is*.   thought it would be.

 1 Our grandparents worked harder than we do.
 2 We have a higher standard of living than they have.
 3 They live further from the town than we do.
 4 They have less money than we have.
 5 We have more confidence in the future than they have.
 6 Young people are a lot more active than old people.
 7 We have fewer responsibilities than they have.
 8 Children are more of a responsibility than pets.
 9 Dogs are more of a nuisance than cats.
10 They used to greet us in a more friendly way than they do.
11 We see them more often than we used to.*
12 They speak the language better than we do.
13 German has a more complicated grammar than English.
14 She has less self-confidence than I expected.
15 He smokes more than he used to.*
16 We eat more than we should.
17 We behaved worse in our youth than the present generation does.
18 The house is better furnished than I thought it would be.
19 This is a better table than ours.
20 Inflation was a lot worse last year than this.

* See 11Ba for negative forms of *used* [juːst].

10 The infinitive and -*ing*

Introductory note: This section is supported by study lists **17B, C, D** and their accompanying notes, which are placed towards the end of the book so that you can more easily avoid looking at them while doing the section Exercises. The lists are as follows:

17B Verbs and phrases followed by the plain infinitive (= without *to*)
17C Verbs followed by an object + full infinitive (= with *to*)
17D Verbs and phrases followed by -*ing* (gerund)

Common verbs not on these lists may:

 i be **directly** followed by a full infinitive (as mentioned in **10B**, Exercise 2) or
 ii be followed by an infinitive or -*ing* (gerund or present participle) according to use or meaning, in which case they are dealt with in **10C** and **10D**.

10A The infinitive

Examples

INFINITIVE (in *italics*)   FORM OF INFINITIVE

1 You may *take* a horse to the   PLAIN
  water but you can't *make* him   PLAIN   a
  drink.   (Proverb)   PLAIN
2 In other words, it's
  impossible *to force* people   FULL
  to do what their basic nature   FULL   b, c
  tells them not *to* (*do*).   FULL (SHORTENED)
3 'What do you think you'll *be
  doing* this time next week?'   PROGRESSIVE (PLAIN)
  'I hope *to be eating* pineapples   PROGRESSIVE (FULL)   d
  on a beach in Acapulco and
  (*to be*) thoroughly *enjoying*   PROGRESSIVE (SHORTENED)   e
  myself.'
4 'Must the flight *be booked*   PASSIVE (PLAIN)
  now?/Does the flight have
  to be booked now?'   PASSIVE (FULL)   f
  'Yes, she wants it (*to be*)
  booked straight away.'   PASSIVE (SHORTENED)

5 'She clearly expected you
   to have booked it/it   PERFECT (FULL)
   to have been booked already.'   PASSIVE PERFECT (FULL)   **g**

Explanation

a PLAIN INFINITIVES (1) like *take*, *make* and *drink* are used after the verbs and phrases listed in **17B**. The list and accompanying notes will show you that some of these verbs, including *make*, are used with an object (*him*).

b The FULL INFINITIVE (2) may follow any part of speech except prepositions. Thus it may follow adjectives (*impossible*) or the object of verbs such as *force* or *tell* (listed in **17C**) to give an object + infinitive construction. When it is unnecessary to use the full infinitive because it is understood from the context, it is often shortened to *to* as shown.

c The full infinitive can also stand as grammatical subject at the beginning of a clause or sentence, as it does in the well known quotation* 'To err is human, to forgive, divine'; but in modern English the infinitive as subject is nearly always introduced by *it* (**8Ap**), so that instead of 'To force . . . is impossible' we have the construction as shown (2). For special emphasis (on *impossible*) the full infinitive may be introduced by *what* (**8Am**):
     What's impossible is to force people to do something their basic nature tells them not to.
See also an example of introductory *it* used with *for* and the infinitive in **10Be**.

d The PROGRESSIVE INFINITIVE (3) is used to form the future progressive tense (*will be doing*) and other verb combinations (*hope to be eating*) that refer to something in progress, and therefore uncompleted, at a time-point such as *this time next week* (**1Bn**).

e A second (or third etc.) infinitive in series may be shortened down to the last element (*enjoying*) as shown (3). Other forms of infinitive (2, 4, 5) may be similarly shortened:
     I want *to eat* pineapples, *lie* in the sun and *get* brown.
     The flight must *be booked* today and *paid* for tomorrow.
     She expected it *to have been booked* and *paid* for already.

f The PASSIVE INFINITIVE (4) may be shortened without being in series when it occurs after *wish*, *want* etc. (see **10Cb**) in an object (*it*) + infinitive (*to be booked*) construction. The use of the infinitive (active or passive) in passive constructions is dealt with in **13B**.

g The PERFECT INFINITIVE (5) relates to time **before** that of the introductory

---

*From *Essay on Man* by Alexander Pope.

verb (*expected*). The relationship can be shown as follows (and see also **13Bb**):

> She clearly expected you *to book* it (= she
> clearly thought (that) you *would book* it).   INFINITIVE
> She clearly expected you *to have booked* it
> (= she clearly thought (that) you *had booked* it).   PERFECT INFINITIVE

The perfect infinitive may also be in plain or in progressive form:

> You should *have booked* it already.
> You seem *to have been making* a lot of mistakes lately.

h A PASSIVE PROGRESSIVE INFINITIVE exists but has not been included in the Examples or Exercise because it is phonetically awkward and rarely used: 'The Government's counter-inflation strategy may *be being blown* off course.'* A possible rewording would be 'is perhaps being blown off course.'

Exercise

Use the correct form of infinitive for the verbs in brackets. In preparation you should look not only at the Examples and Explanation above but also at study lists **17B, C** (see Introductory note to this section).

Before she went to Paris, Zena said she needed (**1** brush up) her French, so I gave her a few lessons. 'Why not (**2** stay) for a few days after your work is over and (**3** practise) the language?' I suggested.
On her return Zena was made (**4** open) all her bags at the customs. They must have been very suspicious of her, for they finally made her (**5** turn) out all her pockets. It hardly helped matters when she said in a loud voice: 'How dare you (**6** suspect) me of smuggling?'
She then turned to me, who happened (**7** travel) with her, and said: 'How can you stand there and let me (**8** accuse) of something you know I haven't done?' Although I knew Zena was innocent of smuggling, I dared not (**9** interfere), as I didn't want my bags (**10** search) like hers.

Things appear (**11** go) from bad to worse on the stock market at the moment, but I think I'd still rather (**12** be) a stockbroker than anything else. As the firm's senior partner, though, I do expect (**13** tell) about things as soon as they happen. It would have been easy for my colleague (**14** pick) up the phone and (**15** give) me the necessary information, but he just couldn't be bothered.

'I don't want there (**16** be) any secrets between us when we're married,' said Denis to Helen. 'We'd better not (**17** have) any before we're married either,' replied Helen ominously. Later Helen let (**18** fall) a remark that suggested her engagement to Denis might soon be off. 'Why (**19** get) married at all?' I heard her say, before her voice was drowned in the general conversation.

*From *The Guardian* newspaper for 29th September 1981.

Ken's a versatile athlete; I've known him (**20** compete) in four events at a sports meeting and (**21** win) two of them. It's a pity Willie can't find more time for sport; he seems always (**22** work).

When I called on the McArthurs, Harry chanced (**23** garden) for once, not (**24** fish), and so I·was able to have a chat with him. He and Mary seem (**25** have) a very happy marriage so far, don't they? But their son Charles played rather a nasty trick on them the other day, when he pretended (**26** injure) in a cycle accident that had never taken place. When he told them the truth he made matters worse by saying they'd been stupid (**27** believe) his story. His mother was so upset by his behaviour that she wants his pocket-money (**28** stop) for six months.

Can you help me (**29** find) better accommodation and a more understanding boss? When he came back from a business meeting this afternoon he expected me (**30** type) all the letters he had given me and (**31** have) them ready for him to sign. I was quick (**32** let) him (**33** know) I'd had other things (**34** do) besides typing his letters. I hope soon (**35** work) in a new job and (**36** live) in a flat of my own.

10B   The -*ing* form as gerund

Examples

THE GERUND:

1 '*Winning* is important,' says Ken, 'but *breaking* the local club records is what really matters to me.'	AS SUBJECT	**a**
2 When the athletic season approaches, Ken works hard at *keeping* fit. His training programme includes *running* up and down stairs twenty times before breakfast.	AS OBJECT	**b**
3 I dislike *him/his doing* it, but it's no use *(me/my) trying* to stop him.	AFTER PRONOUN/ POSSESSIVE	**c, d**
4 It was the duty of the police to prevent the *President* (from) *being shot*.	AFTER NOUN PASSIVE	**e, f** **g**
5 A woman reported *seeing/(having seen)* an armed man in the crowd before the	(PERFECT)	**h**

shooting, but no one reported
*being searched/(having been
searched*) for weapons by the   (PERFECT PASSIVE)   **h**
police.   **j**

Explanation

a   The gerund or verb-noun can be a grammatical subject in a sentence (1),
either by standing alone (*Winning*) or heading a phrase (*breaking the local
club records*). For emphasis, the gerund may be introduced by *it* or by *what*:
> It's breaking the local club records that really matters to me.
> What really matters to me is breaking the local club records.

(Compare the infinitive as subject, **10Ac**.)

b   The gerund may be a grammatical object (2) like *keeping* or *running*, after:
  i   any preposition (*at*), including those of prepositional phrasal verbs like
  set about, *get out of* (**17Gii**)
  ii   verbs such as *include* (2), which are listed in **17D**.

c   The gerund also occurs after a few phrases like *it's no use* (3), also listed in
17D.

d   The gerund, instead of *directly* following a preposition, a verb or a phrase,
may (3) have before it an object pronoun (*him*) or possessive (*his*) to indicate
a change of reference from the subject (*I*) to someone else (*him*). This
construction is the equivalent of an object + infinitive (**10Ab**), as the
following may help to show:
> I dislike *doing* it and so   GERUND
> I don't want *to do* it.   INFINITIVE
> I dislike *him/his doing* it and so PRONOUN/POSSESSIVE + GERUND
> I don't want *him to do* it.   OBJECT + INFINITIVE

Where (3) the reference to the subject of the sentence (*I*) is clear, there is no
point in using the pronoun/possessive (*me/my*) before the gerund except for
emphasis: 'I dislike him doing it but it's no use *my* trying to stop him.
Perhaps *you* could have a go.'

e   The gerund may (4) be preceded by a noun instead of a pronoun. The
possessive of nouns, corresponding with *his*, *my* (3), is rarely used: **not** in 4
'the President's being shot.' It is only at the beginning of sentences that it
may be preferred to the corresponding noun, but both are usually avoided:
> The President's/(President) mixing with the crowd was obviously
> dangerous ⟶ *It* was obviously dangerous *for the President to mix*
> with the crowd *as he did*.

(Without the last three words it would not be absolutely clear that the
President *did* mix with the crowd: 'It was obviously dangerous for the
President to mix with the crowd, and so he didn't.')

f   With one or two verbs such as *prevent* (4), the use of a preposition (*from*) before the gerund is optional (see **17D**).

g Note (4) the passive gerund (*being shot*).

h The use of the perfect gerund (5), either active (*having seen*) or passive (*having been searched*), is seldom necessary, since the time relationship of gerunds such as *seeing* and *being searched* is normally clear:

reported *seeing* = reported that they *had seen*
reported *being searched* = reported that they *had been searched*

Only in contexts such as the following is a perfect gerund necessary:

He admitted *having had* the intention of shooting the President
(= admitted he had (once) had the intention).
He admitted *having* the intention of shooting the President
(= admitted he (still) had the intention).

j It is worth pointing out here that words ending in *-ing* are **not** all gerunds. Some (see *ending* in the previous sentence) are verb-adjectives or present participles (**10D**). Others (*the shooting* in Example 5) are true nouns. Unlike gerunds or verb-nouns, true nouns cannot of course take an object and require a preposition to relate them to another noun. Compare:

It is the duty of the police to stop *the shooting of* Presidents.   NOUN
It is the duty of the police to stop *shooting* Presidents.   GERUND

Note the difference in meaning! (See also **3Bd, m.**)

Exercise 1

For the verbs in brackets, use the *-ing* form (gerund), either active or passive, as shown in the Examples. An object pronoun/possessive may be required (see Example 3).

1 Are you against children (watch) television?
2 Of course not. I've got used to (do) all sorts of things we never did as children.
3 But I'm against television (watch) too often, either by children or adults.
4 Please forgive (be) so late; I was unavoidably detained.
5 Most people detest (keep) waiting, and I'm sure you're no exception.
6 Although Sheila looks quite like her younger sister, she is very different from her in character and dislikes (mistake) for her by strangers.
7 Sheila's kind but firm with the children in her classes, and doesn't tolerate anyone (fool about).
8 'I haven't finished (talk) to your father yet,' said Mary McArthur to her son Charles, 'so don't interrupt.'
9 'Then I'd appreciate (tell) me when you've finished so that I can get a word in,' replied Charles cheekily.

10 Pardon (mention) it, but could I have the ten pounds back that I lent you last month?
11 I grudge (lend) money to people who are less than meticulous about (pay) it back.

12 (Be) my boss doesn't excuse (treat) me the way you do.
13 In fact I'm not going to stand (treat) like a slave any longer.

14 Pressure of work prevented (take) my usual summer holiday this year.
15 Now I'm very much looking forward to (go) to Italy in the autumn.
16 I can't foresee anything (happen) to stop (go) there.

17 Willie's contemplating (learn) Russian with a view to (read) Tolstoy in the original.
18 (Learn) Russian does, of course, entail (learn) a new alphabet, but that's the least of one's difficulties.

19 I escaped (have) to go into the army when I was young because the Government abolished conscription.
20 As I'm nearly forty I don't anticipate ever (call up) now.

21 Robert admits (have) too much to eat when he broke the chair he sat on.
22 I don't recollect (apologise), which he certainly should have done.

23 Charles's sister's in the garden practising (stand) on one leg, as she's got the part of a stork in her college pageant.
24 I can't bear (stand) there all by herself looking so sad and lonely.

Exercise 2

Before doing this Exercise you are advised again to study lists **17C** and **17D**, as well as the following examples. Any italicised verb in the Exercise that is not on those lists will be **directly** followed by the full infinitive, like *seem* below; and any adjective or phrase that is not listed will be followed by the full infinitive, like *it's wrong* below. This and the previous Exercise cover between them nearly all the verbs and phrases listed in **17D**.

it's wrong	I don't think we should eat songbirds like thrushes or blackbirds.	→ I think it's wrong (for us) *to eat* songbirds like thrushes or blackbirds.
justifies	Surely hunger gives one the right to eat anything.	→ Surely hunger justifies *eating* anything.
seem	It looks as if most people around here have given up the habit.	→ Most people around here seem *to have given up* the habit.
continue	I'm sure they won't stop doing it unless there's a law against it.	→ I'm sure they'll continue *doing/to do* it unless there's a law against it.

order	You're not going to demand that I shouldn't do it, are you?	$\longrightarrow$	You're not going to order *me* not *to do* it, are you?

Without altering the meaning, reword the following sentences by using the words in *italics* either with the *-ing* form (gerund) or with the full infinitive/object + full infinitive, as shown in the examples above. Do not change the italicised words in any way.

1 *suggests*   Helen proposes that we go to the Upper Crust disco.

2 *necessary*   Do you have to be a member to get in?

3 *managed*   The last time I went I succeeded in getting in all right.

4 *we're unlikely*   Ken's a member, and so I don't expect we'll have any difficulty.

5 *fancy*   Do you want to go to the disco, Sheila?

6 *put her off*   Don't say anything that will make her not want to go.

7 *mind*   Will your mother object to your taking her car?

8 *she allows*   She has said I can use it whenever I like.

9 *worth*   There's no point in going all the way home to fetch mine.

10 *risk*   You may be stopped by the police if you drive without seat belts.

11 *caused*   Ken lost control of his car because there was a blowout in one of the front tyres.

12 *avoid*   I never drive that way into town.

13 *given up*   I no longer count the times Denis has damaged the company car.

14 *forbid*   Why don't you say he mustn't use it under any circumstances?

15 *no use*   He can't possibly plead ignorance of the company rules, because he was given a copy of them.

16 *deserve*   It's not right that he should get away with things the way he does.

17 *denies*   Denis says he didn't break the calculator.

18 *can you imagine*   You don't think he'd ever admit it, do you?

19 *impossible*   My secretaries can't possibly cope with the work in this office without the calculator.

20 *enables*   With it they can do the work in a fraction of the time.

21 *miss*   I find it a great disadvantage not to be able to use one whenever I want.

22	*the last . . . the first*	Denis usually arrives last in the office in the morning, but seldom leaves first in the evening.
23	*surprised*	I hear the boss thinks quite highly of him, which surprises me.
24	*I dare*	I bet you'd never tell Denis to his face what you really think of him!
25	*he's certain*	I'm sure he'll ask you your opinion of Helen.
26	*rely on*	Yes, you can always be sure Denis will ask awkward questions!
27	*can't afford*	It would be a bad thing if I made an enemy of Helen.
28	*put off*	I've decided not to go to Tokyo till Monday.
29	*involve*	Leaving tomorrow would mean that I missed the finals of the Wimbledon tennis tournament.
30	*arranged*	Ken and I are going to meet in London when I return from Tokyo.
31	*considering*	We think we might hire a boat for a week's cruise on the Thames.
32	*I enjoy*	Messing about in boats is fun.
33	*intend*	My aim is to get a boat of my own one day.
34	*resent*	I strongly object to paying excessive rents to profiteering boat-hirers.
35	*persuade*	I'm trying to convince Willie he should come with us.
36	*keep*	I tell him repeatedly that he needs a holiday.
37	*advised*	His own doctor has told him he should have one.
38	*warned*	He has told him he should not overwork.
39	*recommends*	My doctor says one should take shorter, more frequent holidays.
40	*be made*	Someone must make Willie see sense.
41	*expect*	How much longer do you think Marilyn will stay in the States?
42	*plans*	Her idea is to return next month,.
43	*encouraging*	Her American friends are probably trying to make her stay longer.
44	*resist*	They're so hospitable that she may find it hard not to stay a little longer.
45	*foresee*	But I don't think she'll stay there over Christmas.
46	*difficulty*	Some Americans find her Midlands English accent difficult to understand.
47	*mentioned*	By the way, she said she'd met Toby the other day.
48	*she happened*	It so happened she was staying at the same hotel as he was.

103

| 49 *necessitate* | To get to know Toby well, one would have to share his leisure pursuits.* |
| 50 *propose* | That's not something I'm thinking of doing. |

10C   Verbs taking a full infinitive or -*ing* (gerund) according to meaning

begin	d	*go on*	e	*mean*	e	*remember*	a
cease	d	*hate*	b	*need*	e	*start*	d
dread	c	*like*	b	*prefer*	b	*try*	e
forget	a	*love*	b	*regret*	c	*understand*	e
						want	e

These verbs fall into five groups, which are dealt with in turn below (a–e).

Examples and Explanation

a   *Remember, forget.* If *remember* means not to forget **beforehand** to do something, it takes the infinitive, but if it means to recall or recollect something **afterwards** it is followed by -*ing*:

I must remember *to ask* Zena if she remembers *going* to Paris as a child.

Similarly, *forget* takes the infinitive if it means not to remember **beforehand** and -*ing* if it means not to remember **afterwards**:

I forgot *to ask* her whether she has completely forgotten ever *going* there.

b   *Like, love, prefer, hate* take the infinitive when we have feelings **beforehand** about what may happen,† so that the meaning of these verbs is then *(not) wish, (not) want* or *hope*:

I didn't like *to disturb* her (= I didn't want to . . .).
I don't like *to disturb* her (= I don't want to . . .).
I wouldn't like *to disturb* her (= I hope I won't . . .).
I'd love *to come* skiing with you (= I very much want to . . .).
I'd prefer not *to go out* this evening (= I hope I won't have to . . .).
I'd hate him *to suffer* a lot of pain (= I very much hope he won't . . .).

When our feelings **accompany** or **follow** what happens (or what we know will happen) so that the meaning is *(not) enjoy* or *(not) take pleasure in*, these verbs take -*ing* or (when affirmative) the infinitive:

I didn't like *disturbing* her (which I did).
I don't like *disturbing* her (which I've done/I do).
I shan't like *disturbing* her (which I shall do).

---

* Note that the infinitive *To get* is not acting here as subject (**10Ac**) but is an infinitive of purpose (= 'In order to get to know . . .'). Avoid using it as the subject of *necessitate* (see **10Ba**).

† What **does** happen depends on circumstances: 'I don't like to disturb her, and so I'll call again later/but I'm afraid I must.'

I love *skiing/to ski* in the early spring (which I've done/I do).

I prefer *staying/to stay* in on cold winter evenings (which I do when I can).

I hate him *suffering/to suffer* so much pain (which he has done/does).

Note that for comparisons (**9g**) *prefer* should be used with *-ing*, not the infinitive:

I prefer staying in to going out on cold winter evenings.

Note also that, like *hate* above, all these verbs may be used with an object + infinitive. In this construction the infinitive *to be* is often omitted before a past participle, an adjective or an adverbial, as it is with *wish* or *want* (**10Af**):

I'd like my steak (to be) well done, please.

I know you prefer yours (to be) nearly raw.

She'd like us (to be) there by nine o'clock.

I'd hate my hair (to be) as long as that.

c *Dread, regret* are used respectively with the infinitives *to think* and *to say* (also *to tell, to inform* etc.), but with the *-ing* of verbs that describe what almost certainly will happen (*dread*) or what has happened (*regret*):

I dread *to think* what may happen (and so I'll try not to think about it).

I dread *going* to the hospital (but I'm going).

I regret *to say* your husband is seriously ill (= I don't like to say what I'm going to say, but . . .).

Do you regret *telling* her what you did?

d *Begin, start, cease.* Usage with *begin* and *start* can be shown in the following example:

It *begins to get/getting* cold in early October, when the leaves *are starting to turn*. It's then that we *begin to realise* that the year is dying and that we *start getting/to get* ready for winter.

As the example shows, *begin* and *start* may be used with either the infinitive or *-ing*, but there is a tendency to use the infinitive for events that are impersonal (*It begins to get cold*) or involuntary (*I began to get cold*) and *-ing* for voluntary actions (*we start getting ready*). However, both *begin* and *start* are used with the infinitive when:

i they are in the progressive form (*are starting*) and

ii the verb that follows (*to realise*) has no progressive form (**1Bs**).

Cease, which is generally a formal or literary alternative to *stop* (**17Df**), is like *begin* and *start* in points i and ii but otherwise:

iii usually takes *-ing*:

i Our firm *will* shortly *be ceasing to produce* this particular model.

ii Many people *have ceased to believe* in the efficacy of the nuclear deterrent.

iii When *shall* we *cease squabbling* and *fighting* among ourselves?

e *Go on, mean, need, try, understand, want* are used either with the infinitive or the gerund according to their meaning, as follows:

go on	= proceed	+ INFINITIVE
	= continue	+ -*ing*
mean	= intend	+ INFINITIVE
	= entail	+ -*ing*
need	= have a need (people)	+ INFINITIVE
	= be in need of (things)	+ -*ing* OR PASSIVE INFINITIVE
try	= attempt, endeavour	+ INFINITIVE
	= experiment with	+ -*ing*
understand	= have the impression	+ INFINITIVE
	= understand why	+ -*ing*
want	= wish	+ INFINITIVE
	= be in need of	+ -*ing*

The following examples should help to make these distinctions clear:

After eating two dozen oysters, Charles *went on to consume* a kilo and a half of strawberries.
He *went on eating* long after the others had finished.
He *meant to get up* early but overslept.
Tell him that getting up earlier *will mean going* to bed earlier.
We *need to be* sure we can afford the alterations.
Most of the house *will need rebuilding/will need to be rebuilt*.
Christine *has tried to stop* hiccuping for over an hour.
Has she *tried drinking* salted water?
I *understood* her *to say* she didn't like strawberries.
I can't *understand* anyone not *liking* them.
Except for the money, who'd *want to be* a lawyer?
The whole matter of the inheritance *wants looking into*.

Exercise

Choose the correct form, full infinitive or -*ing*, for each number. As well as the verbs dealt with in this section there are the words *good*, *help* and *stop*, for which adequate preparation is given in study lists **17C, D**.

Helen should stop (**1** criticise) people behind their backs. Has she, I wonder, ever stopped (**2** think) what people must be saying about her in return?

'If you say I sent Sheila and Ken an invitation to our party I suppose I must have, but I completely forget (**3** do) so.'
'You certainly did, because here it is; you gave it to me to hand on to them, but I forgot (**4** do) so.'

I regret (**5** say) that Sheila didn't get the headmistress's post she applied for. She now regrets (**6** apply) for it, because the application took up a lot of her time.

Although I don't like (**7** look after) Zena's alligator while she's away I do ¦ because I wouldn't like Zena (**8** think) I was afraid of it.

The McArthurs' elder daughter simply loves (**9** ski), and would clearly love nothing so much as (**10** turn) professional and (**11** become) an instructor.

The world's political and social problems have, quite honestly, ceased (**12** interest) me. I ceased (**13** try) to put the world in order soon after leaving university.

'Do you mean (**14** tell) me that Willie's firm of architects didn't accept that wonderful contract with the Town Hall?'
'Yes, I do, because if they had it would have meant (**15** give up) an even better contract in New York.'

It was getting dark and storm clouds were beginning (**16** form) when we eventually arrived at the mountain hut. We'd begun (**17** think) we might have lost our way.

Robert is putting on weight. He says he can't help (**18** eat) large meals however hard he tries. He hopes that the new football season may help him (**19** take) off a few pounds.

You say you've tried (**20** stop) (**21** snore) but have failed. Have you tried (**22** sleep) on your stomach?

Although I generally prefer (**23** be) frank to (**24** be) secretive, on this particular occasion I prefer (**25** keep) my opinion of Denis to myself, if you don't mind.

My uncle started (**26** smoke) heavily a couple of years ago and now his health is starting (**27** deteriorate).

Lady Blenkinsop says she got my cheque. Well, I remember (**28** write) it, but I don't remember (**29** post) it to her.

However good one may think it is (**30** get) out into the fresh air at weekends, it's no good (**31** try) (**32** convince) Toby of that; he prefers indoor pursuits like billiards.

'I see that Ken has arrived to play tennis with us. I understood him (**33** say) yesterday that he wouldn't have time for a game today, didn't you?'
'Yes, I did, but I can understand him (**34** change) his mind when he heard Sheila was here.'

I dread (**35** think) what my father's reaction will be when I tell him the news. That's why I'm dreading (**36** go) home tomorrow for the weekend.

I hate him (**37** criticise) me the way he does. But I'd hate him (**38** think) his criticism had any effect upon me, and so I keep quiet.

My mother wants me (**39** cut) the lawn. I know it wants (**40** cut), but I really haven't time this weekend.

You can't say Harry McArthur hasn't tried (**41** interest) his son Charles in fishing. He has even tried (**42** give) him a prize for every fish he catches, but all in vain.

You need (**43** be) a little more careful in what you say to Sheila's mother. I know her ideas need (**44** modernise), but there it is; she strongly objects to risqué stories.

If I've forgotten (**45** lock) the car it's the last time I'll forget (**46** do) so because it's sure to have been stolen!

After he'd talked about politics for a bit, Sir James went on (**47** tell) us about his experiences in Brazil. I must say this was a relief, because if he'd gone on (**48** talk) about politics most of us would have got a bit bored.

I'd have very much liked (**49** have) your advice yesterday on a financial matter, but I didn't like (**50** ring) you in case you were busy.

10D   Verbs taking the infinitive or -*ing* (participle) according to meaning

be	d	*get*	c	*leave*	c	*see*	a
come	b	*go*	b	*notice*	a	*send*	b
feel	a	*have*	c	*observe*	a	*take*	b
find	c	*hear*	a	*overhear*	a	*watch*	a

These verbs fall into four groups which are dealt with below (**a–d**), after the Introductory note.

Introductory note: The present participle or verb-adjective in -*ing* has already occurred in this book as a causal link (**3A**), a time link (**7**) and in shortened relative constructions (**8C**). It is important that you should be familiar with its use in these contexts and in those given below rather than worry about the grammatical difference between it and the gerund or verb-noun (**10B**), a difference that sometimes disappears. However, there is an important practical difference, which is that the present participle, unlike the gerund (**10Bd, e**), can **not** be preceded by a possessive:

We saw him (**not** his) leaving by the back stairs.
The object of *saw* is *him*, which can become the subject in a corresponding passive:

He was seen leaving by the back stairs.
Compare with these sentences the following, in which the respective object and subject is *his leaving* (gerund) *secretly like this*:

We saw (= regarded) his leaving secretly like this as something very suspicious.

His leaving secretly like this was seen as something very suspicious. Besides *see*, there are a number of verbs that can be followed by an object + -*ing* (participle), such as *catch* (*a candidate cheating*), *keep* (*an applicant waiting*), *set* (*a clock going*), *smell* (*something burning*). But most verbs, including *see*, that take -*ing* like this can also take an object + infinitive (plain or full), depending on meaning, and it is these verbs, together with a few others that are used without an object, that are dealt with here.

Examples and Explanation

a *Feel*, *hear*, *notice*, *observe*, *overhear*, *see*, *watch* (verbs of three senses) are followed by an object + infinitive to refer to a complete event and by an object + -*ing* to refer to part only of an event:

> Yesterday I *saw Robert eat* a whole cake in twenty minutes. You often *see him eating* huge platefuls of food after a football game.

We see the complete action of eating the cake, because it is a short event in one place, but we do not see the whole of the 'eating huge platefuls . . . .' When these verbs are in the passive the principle is the same, but the full, not plain, infinitive is then used (see **17Be**).

> I *was overheard criticising* my boss yesterday. But luckily I *wasn't heard to say* I didn't like him.

b *Come*, *go*, *send*, *take* are verbs of movement which may be used with an infinitive of purpose (**4Aa**) or in a phrase with -*ing* to describe an activity (*go fruit-picking* etc.):

> In the old days, when people were poorer than they are now, tramps used to *come knocking* on our door (in order) *to beg* a crust of bread.

Send and *take* are followed first by an object:

> Although Mary McArthur sometimes *sends her son Charles shopping*, she has learnt not to *send him to buy* strawberries.

Take, as well as being a verb of movement ('I took Christine skiing/to see the ski-jumping'), may also mean *interpret* when used with the infinitive:

> I *take you to mean* that Charles eats most of the strawberries himself.

c *Find*, *get*, *have*, *leave* are used with an object + infinitive (full except after *have*) or -*ing* according to meaning as follows:

find (by investigation = find that . . .)	+ INFINITIVE*
(by chance)	+ -*ing*
get/*have* (causal)	+ INFINITIVE
(expressing result)	+ -*ing*
leave (with a commitment)	+ INFINITIVE
(in a condition, position etc.)	+ -*ing*

* Usually *to be* or *to have*.

The following examples should help to make these distinctions clear:

> The police, searching for the murderer, *found a man hiding* in a ditch (**not** The police found that a man was hiding . . .).
> They later *found him to be* unconnected with the crime (= They later found that he was unconnected . . .).
> I'll *get him to repaint/(have him repaint)* the whole room.
> I'll soon *get/have the house looking* nice and smart.
> Georgina often *leaves her older children to look after* the younger ones.
> One day they *left the tap running* and flooded the house.

Get is much more common than *have* when used causally with the infinitive (*to repaint*), but when these verbs are used causally with the past participle *have* is probably more common than *get*:

> I'll have/get the whole room repainted.

Get expressing result cannot be used for present time except as a supplement (*got*) to *have*:

> I've got/I have the house looking nice and smart now.

For *have* expressing obligation, see **11D**; for its use in the auxiliary passive, see **13Al**.

d The verb *be* is of course used with -*ing* to form the progressive infinitive (**10Ad**) and progressive tenses (**1B**). It is also used with the full infinitive to mean *can* and *must*, and to express an arrangement (**11E**), including the 'arrangements' of fate. Some of these uses, like the first two below, are in questions that are rhetorical, that is to say, that do not really expect an answer.

> What*'s to become* of us? (= What will be our fate?)
> What *am* I *to do*? (= What can I possibly do?)
> You*'re to calm down* and not *get* so excited. (= You must . . . .)
> I*'m to phone* Sir James at six, as he said he might be able to help us.
> (= The arrangement is that I should phone . . . .)*

Exercise

Choose the correct form, infinitive or -*ing*, for each number.

I'm glad Zena's learning to relax. I saw her yesterday evening quietly (**1** read) a book. All I'd ever seen her (**2** do) before was (**3** open) one to flip through the pages.

Marilyn called on her mother the other day and found her (**4** lie) on the sofa scarcely able to move. When they got her to hospital she was found (**5** suffer) from pernicious anaemia.

When there is a bit of home decorating to be done the rest of the family are enthusiastic to begin with, but usually leave me (**6** finish) the job. Once, when their favourite television programme came on, I was left (**7** stand) on the

---

*For the use here of *should*, see 11Fa.

stepladder (**8** hold) the end of a piece of wallpaper.

'How are you (**9** get) to Amsterdam on Thursday, by rail or by air?'
'I haven't decided. Whichever way I go, the problem is to know how I'm (**10** get) there in time for the committee meeting at two.'

Marilyn got her father (**11** lend) her some money to start her business with. I hear she's got her office (**12** run) very smoothly now.

'You want to see Harry McArthur? I'm afraid he's gone (**13** fish) and won't be back for some time.'
'Really? I thought he'd gone (**14** meet) Christine at the station and would be back quite soon.'

'The Managing Director says Denis isn't (**15** use) the company cars without his personal permission. Apparently he damaged one the other day.'
'He damaged mine once. I can assure you he's not (**16** borrow) it again under any circumstances.'

The sound of gunfire sent us all (**17** run) for cover. When silence reigned once more we sent two of the platoon (**18** find) out what had happened.

'Sir James is very persuasive; I can see he'll soon have you (**19** vote) for him if you listen to him any longer.'
'What would you have me (**20** do), then – not (**21** go) to any more of his political meetings?'

Do you know what I've just heard Sheila (**22** say)? She said she'd never speak to Helen again. Apparently Helen's been overheard (**23** say) uncomplimentary things about Sheila's mother. Among other things, she was heard (**24** say) she was practically illiterate.

Mary McArthur's taking Charles and Christine up to London tomorrow (**25** see) the sights. While his wife takes his son and daughter (**26** sightsee), Harry's taking his nephew David (**27** fish). I take this (**28** mean) that he wants David to catch the fishing bug too.

I was watching Willie in his architect's office the other day (**29** work) on the plan of a new building when I saw him absent-mindedly (**30** write) 'Sheila' in one of the rooms. He noticed me (**31** watch) him and blushed.

First I heard the door (**32** click). Then, as I lay there in the dark, I heard footsteps slowly (**33** approach). Then I heard them (**34** stop). I could feel my heart (**35** beat). The police had observed a man (**36** loiter) outside the block of flats several days before, and had come (**37** tell) me about it. He had been seen (**38** be) particularly interested in the first-floor flats. Could this be the person that had come (**39** creep) into my flat in the middle of the night? I was never (**40** know), because at that moment my corgi gave a sleepy growl – enough, apparently, to scare the intruder away.

11 Auxiliary verbs: particular uses

Introductory note: Auxiliary verbs like *will, have, may, should* are so called because they cannot be used alone* but only as an aid or auxiliary to another verb. A few of them, such as *will* and *have*, are auxiliaries for tense (**1B**), but all except *do* are MODAL auxiliaries in that they are used with other verbs to convey a particular sense or 'mood' like the following:

She*'ll* be there by now.	ASSUMPTION
She *has* to be in the office by eight.	OBLIGATION
She *may* have missed the bus.	POSSIBILITY
She *should* have got up earlier.	ADVISABILITY

Auxiliary verbs can form the interrogative or negative without *do*; and the negative *not*, except after *may*, can be contracted to *n't*:

> *Will* she be there yet?
> *Has* she (got)/*Does* she *have* to be in the office by eight?
> She *may not* have caught the bus.
> She *shouldn't* have overslept.

Most auxiliary verbs combine with the plain infinitive (see **17B**), but *be, have, ought* and *used* [ju:st] take a full infinitive. The following is a list of modal auxiliaries together with the 'moods' they express and the sections in which they appear:

is to, was to etc.	ARRANGEMENTS ETC.	**10Dd, 11E**
can, could	ABILITY, PERMISSION, POSSIBILITY	**11A**
could ...!	DUTY (WITH REPROACH!)	**11E**
cannot, could not	INABILITY, PROHIBITION, IMPOSSIBILITY	**11A**
cannot (have), could not have	CONCLUSION	**11C**
dare	**17Ba**	
have to	OBLIGATION (NECESSITY ETC.)	**11D**
may, might	PERMISSION, POSSIBILITY	**11A**
may (... but)	CONCESSION	**11B**
might ...!	DUTY (WITH REPROACH!)	**11E**
must (not)	OBLIGATION (COMMAND ETC.)	**11D**
must (have)	CONCLUSION	**11C**
need ...?†	OBLIGATION (WEAK)	**11D**
need not	ABSENCE OF OBLIGATION	**11D**

---

* Except where the context is understood: 'Do you think she'll be there by now?' 'Yes, I think she will.'
† *Need* used affirmatively ('I *need* to .../I *need* a ...') is a non-auxiliary or main verb (see **10Ce, 17Bf**).

ought to, should	EXPECTATION 11C;
	ADVISABILITY, DUTY 11E
should	SUGGESTIONS, OPINIONS, FEELINGS
	ETC. 11F
used [juːst] *to*	PAST ACTIVITY OR STATE 11B
will, would	HABIT 11B
will (have)	ASSUMPTION 11C
will not, would not	REFUSAL 11B
would	TYPICAL BEHAVIOUR 11B

11A   Ability, permission, possibility

ABILITY/INABILITY	*can/cannot, could/could not*
PERMISSION	*can, could, may, might*
PROHIBITION	*cannot, could not, may not*
POSSIBILITY	*may (not), might (not), could*
POSSIBILITY/IMPOSSIBILITY	*can/cannot, could/could not*

Examples

USES

1 I hear you're organising another
   walking tour in the Highlands.
   Can/May I join it?   PERMISSION   a
2 Certainly you *can/may*. Only   PERMISSION   b
   nonagenarians and toddlers
   can't join my walking tours.   PROHIBITION   c
3 I *can* (= I'm able to) carry a   ABILITY   d
   loaded rucksack thirty
   kilometres without getting
   terribly tired. And I'm sure I
   can (= I'll be able to) get the   ABILITY   d
   necessary time off from work.
4 Good. Bring warm clothing. It
   may/might/could snow while   POSSIBILITY   e
   we're up there. It *can* snow   POSSIBILITY   f
   there even in summer. You *can't*   IMPOSSIBILITY   g
   rely on Scottish weather.
5 I*'ve been able to/was able to*   ABILITY (REALISED)   h
   borrow Ken's large rucksack for
   this trip. Last year I *wasn't (able*   INABILITY   j
   to)/was unable to/couldn't.

Explanation

a In **asking for** PERMISSION (1), *may* is more polite than *can*. They are replaced by *might* or *could* when the speaker is being cautious, tactful, timid or extra polite:
> Might I perhaps/Could I possibly join it?

(*Might* can also be used ironically: 'Might I be so bold as to ask why you never offer to do the washing-up?') Note that in asking about permission *can*, not *may*, is used:
> Can you (= Are you allowed to) take your pet mice to school?

b In **granting** PERMISSION (2), we use *can* or *may*, not *might* (but see **k** below). *Could* is used for permission granted in the past:
> At my school we could (= were allowed to) keep pet rabbits.

c For PROHIBITION, the use of *may not* instead of *cannot* (2) is chiefly limited to quick responses to *may*: 'May I . . . ?' 'No, you may not!' *Could not* expresses past prohibition:
> We couldn't (= weren't allowed to) keep pets at my school.

d *Can* expressing ABILITY (3) is replaced by *could* as follows:
  i for past ability or potential, when no reference is made to an actual achievement or success:
> 'In my younger days I could (= was able to) walk for miles and miles without getting tired.'

  Note there is no reference to an actual achievement (compare **h** below).
  ii in a context of NON-FACT (see **1Df, Eb**):
> 'I could (= would be able to) get time off if I wanted.'
> 'I wish I could (= was/were able to) get time off.'

e *May* is replaced by *might* or *could* to express less POSSIBILITY (4). All three cover **present** possibility with reference to the future, present or past as follows:
  i It may/might/could *snow* (= It *is* possible that it *will* snow).
  ii It may/might/could *be snowing* (= It *is* possible that it *is snowing*).
  iii It may/might/could *have snowed* (= It *is* possible that it *(has) snowed*).
  May not and *might not* express possibility negatively: 'Bring warm clothing; it may not be as cold as it was last year, but you never know.' *Could not*, however, expresses impossibility (see **g** below).

f *Can* covers **general** POSSIBILITY without reference to past, present or future (4), and *could* covers **past** possibility and possibility in a context of NON-FACT (see **d** above), as follows:
  i It *can* snow there even in summer (= It *is* possible for it *to snow* . . .*).
  ii I remember how it *could* snow there even in summer (= I remember how it *was* possible for it *to snow* . . .*).

---

* These constructions in Examples and Exercises are for explanation only; although they are grammatically correct, they are non-idiomatic.

iii One *could* perhaps ski there even in summer (= It *would* perhaps *be*
   possible *to ski* . . .).
As an extension of **iii**, *could* is often used in polite REQUESTS:
   Could you (= Would it be possible for you to) give me her address?

g *Cannot* expresses **general** IMPOSSIBILITY (4) and *could not* expresses **past**
   impossibility and impossibility in a context of NON-FACT (see **d** above) as
   follows:
   i You *can't* rely on Scottish weather (= It *is* impossible *to rely* . . .).
   ii I remember how you *couldn't* rely on Scottish weather (= I remember
       how it *was* impossible *to rely* . . .).
   iii You *couldn't* grow maize up there however much you tried (= It *would
       be* impossible *to grow* . . .).
As an extension of **iii**, *couldn't* can be used in **not**-so-polite requests
   (compare **f** above):
   Couldn't you (= Wouldn't it be possible for you to) give me her
   address?

h For past ABILITY which is **realised** in some actual **achievement** or **success**
   (compare **d** above), *could* is replaced by the past or present perfect tense of
   be able (5). Note, therefore, that 'I could borrow Ken's large rucksack for
   this trip' can **only** be supposition about the future as in **dii** above; it can
   not be past fact.

j Past INABILITY, whether or not reference is made to an actual occasion, can
   be expressed by *couldn't* as well as by the past tense of *not be able* or *be
   unable* (5). However, like *could*, *couldn't* cannot replace the present perfect ·
   tense: 'I haven't been able to (**not** couldn't) do much walking since I broke
   my leg.'

k See **12Aa** for the use of *could* and *might* in reported speech.

Exercise

Replace the words in italics with a construction using one of the auxiliary
verbs dealt with above, **except** where the use of *be able* is required (see
Explanation **h**, **j**). For impersonal constructions, use *one* or *you*.

It's possible that Robert *will* be   ⟶   Robert *may* be kicked out of his
kicked out of his football team.   football team.
Is it possible to be kicked out for   ⟶   *Can you* be kicked out for putting
putting on a bit of weight?   on a bit of weight?
I *was able to* speak Mercian quite   ⟶   I *could* speak Mercian quite well as
well as a child.   a child.
Now I've forgotten a lot, but I *was*   (No change)
able to ask my way to Peter's house
this morning.

1 I remember that *it was possible for** our parents *to* be very strict with us at times, but that on the whole they *were able to* control us through kindness and laughter.

2 We certainly *weren't allowed to* do exactly what we wanted like Georgina's children. *Are* your children *allowed to* do exactly what they want?

3 *It's possible that* mankind *will* have no future if it*'s unable to* mend its ways.

4 *It's possible that* what they said *wasn't* true, but *it wasn't possible for us to* ignore it.

5 *Would you allow me to* use your phone for a moment? *It's possible that* I left my keys at home, and I'd like to ring and ask my wife about them.

6 *It would be quite impossible for me to* pay back what I owe you by Saturday. *Wouldn't it be possible for* you *to* let me have a little more time?

7 Did you hear that noise? I think *it's possible that* the clock *has* fallen off the wall in the room next door. *Would it be possible for* you *to* go and see?

8 I*'m unable to* go myself because I*'m unable to* leave the baby.

9 Mary and Harry McArthur *have* at last *been able to* do what they have always wanted to do: visit Australia. Unfortunately it *wasn't possible for* Christine *to* go with them.

10 I*'m* usually *unable to* get a seat on the bus in the morning and have to stand, but I *was able to* get one this morning.

11 When my grandfather was a young man *it was possible to* park your car almost anywhere you liked without difficulty. But *it's impossible to* do that now.

12 *It's possible to* spend hours looking for a parking place. The other day, when I *was able to* find one after only twenty minutes, I was amazed.

13 'Under no circumstances,' shouted Helen's father, '*will I allow* my daughter *to* marry Denis Chambers! *I'll not let him* go around calling himself her fiancé any longer!'

14 '*It's impossible to* adopt that sort of attitude,' said Helen's mother. 'You should know you*'re unable to* stop Denis calling himself whatever he wants.'

15 '*Would you allow me to* make one small suggestion?' she went on. '*Wouldn't it* at least *be possible for us to* show some regard for Helen's feelings by asking him to supper?'

16 '*It's possible* after all *that* he *isn't* so bad as you think. When you*'ve been able to* form a considered opinion of him, we*'ll be able to* think again.'

17 Later, with her mother's help, Helen *was able to* convince her father that *it would be possible for them to* ask Denis to supper without precipitating a marriage.

18 'All right,' he said, '*I'll allow* you *to* ask him to supper just so that I*'ll be able to* confirm my low opinion of him.'

19 *It would be impossible to* criticise Denis's behaviour on that first evening with Helen's father. Denis turned on the charm — and he*'s* certainly *able to*

* See footnote, p. 114.

turn it on when he wants to – and by the end of the evening he *was able to* say to himself: 'I've made a hit!'

20 *It's possible to* fool all the people some of the time and some of the people all the time, but *it's impossible to* fool all the people all of the time. (Abraham Lincoln in this, his famous saying, used *you*, not *one*.)

11B   Past activity, habit, refusal, etc.

PAST ACTIVITY OR STATE	*used* [juːst]
HABIT	*will, would*
TYPICAL BEHAVIOUR	*would*
REFUSAL	*will not, would not*
CONCESSION	*may (. . . but)*

Examples

	USES	
1 Harry McArthur *used* to be a cigarette smoker.	PAST STATE	a
2 He *didn't use* [juːs]/*usedn't* [juːsnt] to worry about his health or his pocket.	PAST ACTIVITY	a, c
3 He*'d* sometimes get through a couple of packets a day.	HABIT (PAST)	b, c
4 Now he smokes a pipe, and *'ll* sit smoking it even when it's out – which is a cheap way of smoking.	HABIT (PRESENT)	b
5 The trouble is that he *will* empty the ashes into the nearest flower vase.	PERSISTENT HABIT	d
6 'Harry *would* do a thing like that,' says his wife Mary, 'he's so lazy.'	TYPICAL BEHAVIOUR	e
7 'He just *won't* be clean and tidy.'	REFUSAL	f
8 'I haven't thrown him out of the house yet, though. He *may* have dirty habits, *but* I still love him.'	CONCESSION	g

Explanation

a The auxiliary verb *used* occurs in the affirmative (1), in the negative as *used*

117

not or *usedn't* (2) and in questions ('Used Harry to smoke cigarettes?').
However, it is the non-auxiliary form with *did* that is probably the more
common both in the negative (2) and in questions:

Did Harry use to smoke cigarettes?

But there is no such verb as *use* [juːs] referring to present time (**not** 'He uses
to smoke a pipe now/Does he use to smoke a pipe now?/He doesn't use to
smoke cigarettes now'). Do **not** confuse the auxiliary with:

 i the past tense *used* [juːzd] of the verb *use* [juːz];
 ii the adjective *used* [juːst], meaning *accustomed*, that occurs in phrases
    with *be* or *get* and the preposition *to*: 'Harry is used/has got used to
    (smoking) a pipe now.'

And do **not** confuse the non-auxiliary *use* [juːs] (2) with the noun *use* [juːs]
that occurs, for example, in the phrase *it's no use* (**17D**).

b *Would* (past) and *will* (present) refer to activities or events that are repeated
and which we notice, such as people's habits (3, 4) or characteristics of
things such as weather:

In the Western Isles it'll rain (= it's liable to rain) for days on end.

They are also used for characteristics such as standard capacity or
performance:

Don't worry, the lift'll hold ten people.

Ken's new car isn't as fast as his old one, which would do 175 kph.

Compare the use of *can* and *could* (**11Af**), which in the above two sentences
would convey the idea of **possible** rather than **standard** capacity or
performance.

c *Would* and *used* may occur in similar sentences (see Examples 2 and 3):

He wouldn't worry about his health or his pocket.

He used sometimes to get through a couple of packets a day.

There is usually a difference of emphasis, however. With *would(n't)* we
tend to be more interested in what actually happened (3) than in the fact
that it happened in the past; while with *used(n't)* it is the past itself that can
interest us (2), because it is different from the present (Harry, it seems, now
does worry about his health or his pocket). Note that *would*, since it can be
used only for activity, cannot occur in sentences similar to Example 1.

d For persistent activity or habit, that is to say for something repeated in spite
of our dislike or opposition, *will* and *would*, instead of being unstressed and
often contracted (3, 4), are stressed and uncontracted (5).

e If behaviour, repeated or unrepeated, past or present, strikes us as typical
of the person in question, we may refer to it (6) with stressed, uncontracted
would (= 'It's typical of Harry/How like Harry/I might have expected
Harry to do a thing like that'). Unlike *will* and *would* above (**b, c, d**), it may
stand on its own:

Denis denies breaking the calculator.

Well, he *would*, wouldn't he?

'Behaviour' can be extended to inanimate things like the weather:

   It *would* rain on our wedding day!

Note that the typicality of behaviour strikes us when it annoys rather than when it pleases!

f   *Will*, when used as an auxiliary for the future tense (**1Bf**), carries little idea or 'mood' (see Introductory note, p. 112) of will or willingness except when stressed:

   'I *will* be clean and tidy,' said Harry to himself.

But *will not* or *won't* (not *'ll not*) fully carries the idea of unwillingness or refusal in certain contexts (**7**) whether it is stressed or not. Compare the following, in which the stress can be the same:

He won't be there tomorrow.	*Won't* AS TENSE AUXILIARY
He won't come with me.	*Won't* = *refuses to*: MODAL AUXILIARY

Would not may express refusal in the past. Compare:

I knew he wouldn't be there.	TENSE AUXILIARY EXPRESSING FUTURE IN THE PAST
I knew he wouldn't come with me.	MODAL AUXILIARY EXPRESSING REFUSAL IN THE PAST

Will/would not may also express 'refusal' in inanimate objects:

   This window won't open (= is meant to be opened but can't be).

Compare 'This window doesn't open (= is not meant to be opened).'

g   *May* used with *but* (**8**) can be a substitute for *although* etc. (**5a, b**). Note that *may* is not being used here to express possibility (**11Ac**), but certainty (= 'Although he *has* dirty habits, I still love him'). It can be used with the perfect infinitive to refer to the past:

   Denis may have denied breaking the calculator, but I know he did
   (= Although Denis *(has) denied* . . .).

Exercise

Replace the words in *italics* with a construction using one of the auxiliary verbs dealt with above. Where it appears that either *used* or *would* could be used, base your choice on note **c** in the Explanation and the following two examples:

Napoleon in exile on St Helena *had the habit of standing* for hours staring out to sea in the direction of France. ⟶ Napoleon in exile on St Helena *would stand/(used to stand)* for hours staring out to sea in the direction of France.

At one time Harry McArthur *fished* more than he does now. ⟶ Harry McArthur *used to fish* more than he does now.

1 As a child, Willie *was in the habit of spending* a lot of time reading his father's books, and *didn't usually* play much with other boys.

2 He learnt to avoid their company because they *persistently teased* him about his bookish habits.

3 When people asked him what he was going to be he *always smiled* and *said* nothing.

4 *There was a time when* he *was* very shy and never went to parties, although now he *normally accepts* most of the invitations that come his way.

5 In fact he *often tells* people that he *kept* himself to himself *in the past* so as to be able to get on with his studies.

6 *Although* he kept quiet on the subject, he always knew what he wanted to be.

7 *At one time* Denis and Helen's father *weren't* on speaking terms, but now they're as thick as thieves.

8 Yes, *it's just like* Denis *to* know how to get round the boss!

9 *Although* he is the boss's future son-in-law, I'm damned if I'm going to run about for him!

10 You *won't stop criticising* Denis in this rather nasty way. Why?

11 Charles, why *do* you *insist on interrupting* while I'm speaking to your father? Why *do* you *refuse to* wait till I've finished?

12 Charles *refused to* admit he was in the wrong. *Although* he's a nice boy, he can be very stubborn.

13 I can see that your cat *usually lies* about doing nothing for most of the day like ours. *Was* it more active *at one time*?

14 Oh yes, *at one time* she *was* far more active. You should have seen her as a kitten, when she *never kept* still for an instant. But like everything else, cats *insist on growing up, do*n't they?

15 People *never stop leaving* their litter about instead of putting it in litter baskets. *There was a time when* this picnic site *looked* quite tidy, but now it's a disgrace.

16 *In the old days* there *was*n't anything here at all except a clearing in the forest where a few people *were in the habit of coming* for this wonderful view of the mountains.

17 When I told Christine that Robert had put on a lot of weight just before the start of the football season, she replied: '*That's just like* Robert! *Although* he pretends to be the healthy sporting type he's actually much more fond of his food than the rest of us.'

18 I agreed. Robert's one of those pleasant, genial people who *habitually* sits in cafés for hours and hours laughing and joking, and getting fatter and fatter.

19 *One might have expected* him *to* go and spoil his chance of getting into the team.

20 I remember when we were children Robert *had a habit of saying* with a

little smile that one day he would be famous. *Although* he said that, has he now the will to make it come true?'

11C   Expectation, assumption, conclusion

EXPECTATION	*should (have), ought to (have)*
ASSUMPTION	*will (have)*
CONCLUSION	*must (have), cannot (have), could not have*

Examples

USES

1 Ken's taking his Advanced Motorists' test tomorrow. He's a pretty good driver, so he *should/ought to* pass.   EXPECTATION   **a**

2 Christine has just taken her exams. She worked extremely hard for them, so she *should have/ought to have* done well.   EXPECTATION (PAST REFERENCE)   **a**

3 It's no use ringing Harry at home now. It's past eight o'clock and he *won't* be there. He*'ll have* left for the office.   ASSUMPTION (NEGATIVE)   **b, c**
ASSUMPTION (PAST REFERENCE)   **b, c**

4 His wife *'ll* probably be at home, though.   ASSUMPTION (QUALIFIED)   **c**

5 What a terrible draught! The front door *must* be open.   CONCLUSION   **d**

6 It *can't* be. I shut it when I came in.   CONCLUSION (NEGATIVE)   **d**

7 You obviously *can't have/couldn't have*. Look, it's wide open.   CONCLUSION (NEGATIVE, PAST REFERENCE)   **d, e**

8 I can assure you I did. The wind *must have* blown it open.   CONCLUSION (PAST REFERENCE)   **d**

Explanation

a EXPECTATION, as the word is used here (1, 2), means believing that things are or will be as we wish them to be. We would not use *should* or *ought* if, for example, we expected someone to fail a test – unless we wanted him or

121

her to fail. We would normally say 'I'm afraid he'll fail' or 'I'm afraid she may not have done very well.' Note that *should* as a modal auxiliary (see Introductory note, p. 112) is never contracted to *'d*, unlike conditional *should* (1Dh).

b   An ASSUMPTION (3) is based not upon our wishes but upon our knowledge of people and things – their daily routine, character, qualities – and is therefore more realistic than expectation. It can consequently be unfavourable: 'Christine didn't do much work for her exams and won't have done very well, I'm afraid.'

c   The assumption in Example 3, based perhaps on our knowledge of Harry's routine, could be made on any working day, ignoring the fact that Harry might be ill or taking a day off. Similarly, in **b** above, we may know Christine and that she is no exception to the general rule that people have to prepare for examinations to do well in them; but we may not know that special circumstance did not require her to work hard for these examinations. Sometimes we make allowance for this kind of ignorance by qualifying our assumptions with adverbs like *probably* (4) or with an *if* etc. (1C) clause:
   His wife*'ll* be at home, though, as long as she hasn't already gone out
      shopping.
There is little difference in realism or degree of certainty between a qualified assumption (4) and the use of *should/ought*: 'His wife should be at home, though.'

d   CONCLUSIONS (5–8) are based on particular experiences and occasions, and therefore, being more adapted to circumstances than assumptions, are generally more accurate. We would **not** normally say (see Example 3) 'It's past eight o'clock and Harry can't be there'; we would investigate further: 'I've rung, but there's no answer, so Harry can't be there; he must have left for the office.' Although our conclusions are sometimes wrong (6) we do not make allowance for this when using *must* or *can't*. On the contrary, if we qualify them at all we do so confidently with such adverbs as *obviously* (7).

e   Note that *can't* with the infinitive may express inability, prohibition, impossibility (11A) **or** a negative conclusion, but that *couldn't* with the infinitive expresses only the first three. To express a conclusion with past reference, either *can't* or *couldn't* is used with a PERFECT infinitive. Compare the following:
   She couldn't ring Harry, as the phone was out of order.

INABILITY/IMPOSSIBILITY

   She can't have/couldn't have rung Harry, as the phone was out of
   order.   CONCLUSION

f   In some contexts a choice of *should/ought*, *will* or *must/cannot* is possible, depending on the degree of confidence we feel, since the three categories of expectancy, assumption and conclusion are in ascending order of certainty.

Take, for example, a situation in which we want to contact Harry and already know that he has left home for work:

> It's nine o'clock, so ring Harry's office; he should/'ll/must be there by now.

Exercise

Use the verbs in brackets with the appropriate auxiliary to express expectation, assumption or a conclusion. Alternatives are sometimes possible. If no verb is given (_____), then only the auxiliary is needed (see Example 7).

'My daughter works in Washington. They're five hours behind us over there. Just now, while we're having our lunch, she (1 go) to work.'
'You've forgotten one thing. It's the fourth of July, Independence Day in the States. So they (2 not|go) to work over there. They (3 enjoy) a public holiday.'
'Oh, really? I suppose they taught me that at school, but I (4 forget) it. Look, there's the postman. I wonder if he has brought anything for me. He certainly (5 _____). There (6 be) at least one letter from my daughter.'

'You (7 be) very excited at the prospect of seeing your daughter again after so long.'
'Yes I am. And she (8 look forward) to seeing me again too. It's one o'clock, so her plane (9 take off) already if it's on schedule. Will we be at the airport in time to meet her?'
'We (10 be) in plenty of time. It's normally only a two-hour run from here by car.'

'I can't see my daughter among the passengers. She (11 miss) the flight.'
'Let's ask the airline. If she has missed the flight they (12 know).'
'Poor dear! She (13 be) frightfully worried if she has missed it.'
'Your daughter, madam, (14 cancel) her booking, because her name does not appear on the passenger list.'

'The light's not on in the office. Willie (15 go) home.'
'No, no. I'm sure he (16 not|go) home yet. He (17 sit) there in the dark, dreaming of his next architectural creation.'
'Really? He (18 be) crazy.'

'Look in the fridge and see if there's enough milk in there for the weekend, will you? There (19 be).'
(Holding up the bottle): 'You (20 drink) much milk if you think this is enough. Shall I get you some? It's not eight yet, and so the supermarket down the road (21 still|be) open.'

'Is that the Red Lion Hotel?'
'I don't know. It (22 be) according to the map, but I don't see any sign.'
'I think we (23 pass) it back there in the dark.'

'We (24 _____). We would have seen some lights. Let's ask that man over there.'
'He (25 not|know). He looks as lost as we are.'

'Do you think Christine (26 get) the results of her exams by now?'
'She (27 _____). They don't usually take more than a month to come through.'
'She (28 be) very disappointed if she hasn't passed.'

'Did you say that girl over there was your cousin Georgina? It (29 be)! She looks far too young. If it is, then she (30 have) some beauty treatment.'

11D   Obligation, absence of obligation

OBLIGATION (NECESSITY ETC.)	*have (got) to*
OBLIGATION (COMMAND ETC.)	*must (not)*
OBLIGATION (WEAK)	*need (to)*
ABSENCE OF OBLIGATION	*does not need to/have to, have not got to, need not (have)*

Examples

1 Harry McArthur *has (got) to* go to Hong Kong at short notice for his firm. He *has (got) to* get up very early tomorrow to catch his plane.	OBLIGATION	b, j
	OBLIGATION (NECESSITY)	b, j
2 (Mary, his wife): You *must* phone me as soon as you get there. You *mustn't* forget.	OBLIGATION (COMMAND)	· a, e
	OBLIGATION (COMMAND)	a, e
3 Now I *must/have (got) to/need to* get your clothes ready for packing.	OBLIGATION (PRESENT)	a, c, d, f, j
4 I see you've got only three decent shirts; you *must/'ll have to/'ll need to* buy some more when you get there.	OBLIGATION (FUTURE)	c, d, f
5 I remember you *had to* do that the last time you went abroad.	OBLIGATION (PAST)	d
6 (Harry): Relax! You *needn't* get my clothes ready now; I'll do it later. I *don't need to/don't have to/haven't got to* leave for another eight hours.	ABSENCE OF OBLIGATION (PRESENT)	g
	ABSENCE OF OBLIGATION (PRESENT)	g, j

7 I hope the plane leaves on time
and that I *won't need to/won't*   ABSENCE OF OBLIGATION
have to wait at the airport.   (FUTURE)   g

8 (Mary): Did you go to the bank?
(Harry): No, I *didn't need*   ABSENCE OF OBLIGATION
to/didn't have to; I got enough   (PAST)   h
money from the office to take
with me.

9 (Mary): The last time you went
you took Hong Kong dollars
with you. (Harry): Yes, but I
needn't have; it's easy to change   ABSENCE OF OBLIGATION
money when you get there.   (PAST)   h

Explanation

a *Must* or *mustn't* [mʌsnt] expresses the 'internal' OBLIGATION that has its
origin in the speaker or writer. This may be a command, that is to say,
obligation imposed by the speaker on someone else (2); or it may be
obligation imposed by the speaker on herself (3).

b *Have to* (1) expresses the 'external' obligation that has its origin in
circumstance (necessity) or in a person **other than** the speaker or writer.
The person in this case may have been Harry's boss: 'Harry *must* go to
Hong Kong.' This, in the writer's words, becomes 'Harry has to . . . .'

c Sometimes (3, 4) the context allows the use of either *must* or *have to*,
depending on whether the speaker feels that the obligation comes from
herself or from elsewhere.

d *Must* covers both present (3) and future (4) time. *Have to* has tenses for the
present (3), the future (4) and also for the past (5), for which *must* cannot be
used.

e *Must* and *mustn't* expressing a command (2) are similar in meaning to (i) the
corresponding imperative* or (ii) the use of *is/am* etc. *(not) to* (10Dd):
   i Phone me when you get there; don't forget.
   ii You're to phone me when you get there; you're not to forget.
These uses (and particularly the second) are generally more abrupt and less
polite than the use of *must* and *mustn't*.

f *Need to* expresses a weaker sense of 'external' obligation than *have to*, to
which it corresponds in the present (3) and future (4) tenses. A past tense
(*needed to*) is rarely used except in the interrogative: 'Did you need to . . .?'
It is only in the interrogative present tense that *need* can be used as an

---

* The imperative of a verb is basically similar in form to the plain infinitive (10Aa): *'Stop! Go! Don't slow
down.'*

auxiliary without *do*: 'Need you go/Do you need to go?' It may be used in this way with the perfect infinitive for past reference, but now there is a difference in meaning between the auxiliary and non-auxiliary forms:

Need you have gone (= Was your journey necessary)?

Did you need to go (or were you able to stay)?

Compare *need not have* and *did not need to* in **h** below.

g To express the ABSENCE OF OBLIGATION in the present (6) or future (7), we can use the auxiliary *needn't* or the non-auxiliary *don't need to/have to* or *won't need to/have to*. However, there is a strong tendency to use *needn't* for the absence of 'internal' obligation (that is to say, as a counterpart of *must*) and *don't need to* etc. for the absence of 'external' obligation (as a counterpart of *have to*).

h To express absence of obligation in the past, we use *didn't need to/have to* when we did **not** do anything **because** it was not necessary (8) and *needn't have* when we **did** do something **although** it was not necessary (9).

j *Got* is often used with *has to/have to* and may convey a sense of urgency. Usually there is contraction (1, 3): 'He's got to get up very early/Now I've got to get your clothes ready.' Similarly, *haven't got to* may replace *don't need to/have to* (6).

Exercise

Use the verb in brackets with the correct form of auxiliary to express obligation or absence of obligation. If no verb is given (_____), use only the correct auxiliary, as in Examples 8 and 9. The affirmative use of *need to* (see Examples 3 and 4) is possible in one or two of the sentences, but is not required.

'I (**1** lock) my front door when I go out; this is a very honest neighbourhood.'
'You're lucky! We (**2** lock) ours! Our neighbourhood is far from honest.'

'Luckily enough I (**3** wait) more than a couple of minutes for a bus yesterday.'
'Oh, I (**4** worry), then. I imagined you standing there in the freezing cold for half an hour.'

'You (**5** pay) me now if you are short of money.'
'I (**6** _____). It's a principle of mine never to owe money.'

'You're very fortunate, because in your kind of job you (**7** get up) early in the morning if you don't feel like it. In mine I (**8** get up) at six every morning whether I like it or not.'
'You (**9** get up) so early if you lived nearer your job.'
'I realise that. But I (**10** pay) more rent.'

'You (11 turn off) the radio, you know. It wasn't disturbing me.'
'Perhaps not, but it was disturbing me. I (12 finish) this work by five o'clock or I shall be in trouble.'

'Presumably when you marry Denis you (13 go on) working if you don't want to.'
'Indeed I (14 _____)! We're going to be as poor as church mice.'

'(15 you|call) the doctor for Dad last night?'
'No, we (16 _____), I'm glad to say. He's much better.'

'Georgina has just gone to the dentist. I hope she (17 have) any teeth out.'
'So do I. If she has any more out she (18 have) false ones.'

We (19 buy) any fish while we were on holiday because we caught them ourselves. But we (20 buy) a fishing licence which was more than the price the fish would have been!

'You see! What did I tell you? You (21 worry) like that, because everything has turned out all right.'
'Yes, I know, but I feel one (22 worry) sometimes so that everything **will** turn out all right!'

I (23 take) my car to the garage after all; I put it right myself. But I (24 take) it soon, because there's something else wrong with it which I can't put right.

If there is any damage to the firm's cars, we (25 report) it to the insurance company, so you (26 let) me know at once if anything happens while you are driving them.

Tell Ken he (27 drive) me to the station; I'll take a bus. I (28 be) there until six, so I've got plenty of time.

You (29 be) frightened! I'm not going to eat you! You really (30 try) to be a little less timid!

11E   Duty and arrangement, with non-fulfilment

DUTY, ADVISABILITY	*should (not), ought (not) to*
DUTY (WITH REPROACH!)	*could ...! might ...!*
ARRANGEMENT	*is to, was to* etc.
NON-FULFILMENT	(expressed with the perfect infinitive)
	should have, might have, was to have etc.

Examples

	USES	
(There is some doubt whether Denis and Helen will keep their appointment with us):		
1 People *should/ought to* let one know before failing to keep an appointment.	DUTY	**a**
2 I agree; people *shouldn't/ oughtn't to* just fail to turn up without saying anything.	DUTY (NEGATIVE)	**a**
3 I think you *should/ought to* check to see if Denis and Helen are coming.	ADVISABILITY	**a**
4 They *could/might* at least tell us if they're not coming!	DUTY (WITH REPROACH!)	**b**
5 We *were to* meet at the cinema at half-past seven.	ARRANGEMENT	**c**
(After half-past seven, when Denis and Helen fail to turn up):		
6 Denis and Helen *should have/ought to have* let us know that they weren't coming.	NON-FULFILMENT (OF DUTY)	**d**
7 Yes, I do think they *could have/might have* told us they weren't coming.	NON-FULFILMENT (OF DUTY, WITH REPROACH!)	**d**
8 We *were to have* met at the cinema at half-past seven.	NON-FULFILMENT (OF ARRANGEMENT)	**d, e**

Explanation

a *Should/ought to*, as well as being used for expectation (11Ca), is used for DUTY (1, 2) and ADVISABILITY (3). *Should* in these uses is **not** contracted to *'d*, unlike conditional *should* (1Dh).

b *Could* and *might*, as well as expressing possibility etc. (11A), may also be used to convey REPROACH if we consider that people are failing in their duty. They usually occur with phrases like *at least* (4), *I do think* (7) or with an exclamation mark (4). In spoken English this use of *could* and *might* can be distinguished from their use to express possibility etc. by the stress and intonation. Compare the following:

They **could/might tell** us if they're **not** coming!	LEVEL TONE, DUTY WITH REPROACH!
They **could/might tell** us if they're not coming.	FALLING TONE, POSSIBILITY ETC.

c We have already seen (**10Dd**) that *is/am* etc. *to*, as well as being used instead of *can* or *must*, is used to express an ARRANGEMENT. The past ten is used in Example 5 because there *was* an arrangement which we now realise may not stand. 'We *'re to* meet at the cinema at half-past seven' implies that the arrangement **does** stand. In such contexts, however, the present progressive tense (**1Bm**) is more common: 'We're meeting . . . .'

d To express the NON-FULFILMENT of a duty or arrangement we use the appropriate verb with the perfect infinitive, as shown (6–8).

e If we drop the *have* with *was/were* (8) we do not know whether the arrangement was fulfilled or not (compare Example 5) unless we add the necessary information: 'We were to meet at the cinema at half-past seven but they never turned up.' However, even with this information, it is common to use the perfect infinitive (*were to have met*) to express non-fulfilment.

f Note that *should have/ought to have*, in addition to expressing the non-fulfilment of duty or advisability, may also express, according to context, (i) EXPECTATION with past reference (**11Ca**) or (ii) the NON-FULFILMENT of expectation:
  i They should have arrived by now (= I expect they have).
  ii They should have arrived by now (but they haven't).

g Similarly, *could have*, as well as expressing the non-fulfilment of duty (with reproach!) may also express (i) POSSIBILITY with past reference (**11Ae**) or (ii) the NON-FULFILMENT of ability or possibility:
  i They could have arrived by now (= perhaps they have).
  ii They could have arrived by now (but they haven't).

Exercise

Use the verbs in the brackets with the auxiliaries given in the Examples so as to express duty, arrangement etc. or their non-fulfilment. Alternatives are sometimes possible.

'I do think Denis and Helen (**1** apologise) for not turning up yesterday! We haven't heard a word from them so far.'
'I quite agree. People (**2** not|behave) like that.'

'Sheila (**3** go) to Cambridge last Saturday to see her brother. Ken (**4** take) her in his car, but I'm told it was out of order, so they may not have gone.'
'I find that rather funny, as Ken is always telling people they (**5** keep) their cars in good running order.'

'Ouch! At least you (**6** tell) me this handle was red-hot! I nearly dropped the soup all over the floor.'

'You (**7** tell) me first you were going to pick it up, and then I would have warned you.'

'I hear Sir James (**8** retire) from his directorship at Amical Assurance next year.'
'No, he (**9** retire), but a majority on the board has persuaded him to stay on. Personally I think he (**10** make) way for a younger man.'

'Did you know that Sir James (**11** speak) at o r political meeting, but couldn't because of a sore throat?'
'Really? You (**12** get) his son Toby to speak instead!'
'You (**13** not|make) jokes like that about poor Toby. I know he's not very bright, but then not everyone is born to be a politician.'

I'm surprised Ken lost to Willie at tennis last week. He (**14** win). They (**15** play) a return match yesterday, but it rained.

It rained solidly the whole day. I do think it (**16** stop) for Georgina's cousin's wedding! There (**17** be) a reception in the garden, but of course they had to move it indoors.

Marilyn (**18** return) from the United States at the end of this month, but she may have decided to prolong her stay. She (**19** not|delay) her return much longer, though, because her business over here in England needs looking after.

'What arrangement has Helen made with you?'
'I (**20** wait) for her at the end of the road, where she (**21** pick) me up in her car.'
'I think she (**22** offer) to call at your house instead of asking you to stand about in the cold.'

'Look at the filthy mess on this picnic site! I really do think people (**23** be) more careful where they throw their litter.'
'I agree. But in such a popular place as this the local council (**24** provide) litter baskets.'

'Zena (**25** not|leave) her alligator locked up in the bathroom for three weeks. No wonder it ate the soap.'
'Actually I (**26** feed) it for her while she was away, but she forgot to give me the keys.'

'Helen (**27** at least|invite) us to her party considering we invited her to ours.'
'Of course. We (**28** never|send) her an invitation.'

'There (**29** be) a company board meeting yesterday. Was there?'
'Yes, there was. And I hear there (**30** be) another one quite soon.'

11F   Use of *should* for suggestions, opinions, feelings etc.

Examples

WITHOUT *should*	WITH *should*
1 There was to be a party at Lady Blenkinsop's and Helen insisted *on my being* her partner for the evening.	There was to be a party at Lady Blenkinsop's and Helen insisted *that I should be* her partner for the evening.
2 I agreed *to our going* together.	I agreed *that we should go* together.
3 It was better *(for me) to go* with someone than with no one at all.	It was better *that I should go* with someone than with no one at all.
4 Then, quite suddenly, she suggested *asking* Willie to join us to make a group of three.	Then, quite suddenly, she suggested *that I should ask* Willie to join us to make a group of three.
5 I was put out. 'Why,' I asked myself, *'has* she *changed* her mind?'	I was put out. 'Why,' I asked myself, *'should* she *have changed* her mind?'
6 'I'm sorry (that) she *thinks* I'm an inadequate escort.'	'I'm sorry (that) she *should think* I'm an inadequate escort.'
7 But I soon recovered my equilibrium. After all, why *worry* about a girl like Helen?	But I soon recovered my equilibrium. After all, why *should I worry* about a girl like Helen?

Explanation

a In rather the same way as we use *would* or *could* for wishes (1Eb, c) we can use *should* for demands (1), consent (2), opinions expressed with *it is/was* + adjective (3), suggestions or recommendations (4) and feelings such as surprise (5), regret (6) and indignation (7).

b The effect of using *should* is to keep what may happen (1–4) or what has happened (5–7) as non-fact (1D, E), rather than let it join the world of possible or past fact. When, for example, we ask ourselves (5) 'Why *should* she have changed her mind?' we are not yet ready to accept the fact that she **has** changed it. Without the *should*, we have accepted it.

c The Examples show that a common use of *should* in this way is in *that* clauses which take the place of an *-ing* construction (1, 2, 4) or the infinitive with or without *for* (3). When used for feelings (5, 6, 7), *should* is an addition.

131

d There are some forms of rhetorical question* expressing surprise or
   indignation in which *should* is always used:

> She asked me where Denis was. How should I know?
> Who should walk in at that moment but Denis himself!

   Further examples of these occur in the Exercise.

e *Should* used in the way shown in these Examples and also after *in case* (**4Ad**)
   and *if* (**1Db**) is called putative *should*. It cannot be replaced by *would* or
   ought to, and cannot be contracted to *'d*. It may be regarded as a substitute
   for the present subjunctive, which although not common in modern
   English, occurs particularly in demands and suggestions (compare
   Examples 1 and 4):

> Helen insisted that I *be* her partner.
> She suggested that Willie *be asked* to join us.

   In verbs other than *to be* the present subjunctive is recognisable only in the
   third person singular:

> She suggested that Willie *join* us.

Exercise

Rewrite the following groups of sentences using *should* where it is
appropriate. As mentioned above (**d**), *should* is already in use in one or two
places in the Exercise.

1 Do you know what Denis's idea is? It is that we go into business with him in
   the hardware trade. I have told him it is essential for us to know exactly the
   extent of our commitment before we make up our minds. It is obviously
   better for us to be extremely cautious at this stage than to regret it later.

2 'Our stockbroker recommends that we buy as many Worthright shares as
   we can afford.'
   'Really? It's odd that he has suddenly changed his mind about them.'
   'Why is it odd? It's only right for a stockbroker to change his mind if the
   market itself changes. It seems that you mistrust his motives. I'm sure he
   intends us to make money, not lose it.'

3 'I'm sorry there was no one at the airport to meet you. I told Denis it was
   essential for him to be there by nine o'clock in case the plane was early.'
   'Don't worry. I naturally thought it strange there was no one there to meet
   me. But why should you take the blame?'

4 'I really don't see why some people get all the luck and others none at all.
   Why, after all, did Helen get the job when it ought to have been Sheila?'
   'The simple reason is that Helen's mother insisted on her daughter getting
   it. And Helen's mother is a woman of considerable influence.'

---

* A question which does not expect an answer.

'It makes my blood boil to think that she is able to influence things like that. I have already suggested to the committee that we change the appointments procedure at once.'
'I don't see why you are so upset about it. Helen's a very competent girl in her way. Why shouldn't she be up to the job?'

5 'I'm surprised that the railwaymen have gone on strike over the relatively small issue of overtime rates.'
'A small issue? Why is it a small issue? They are only suggesting that they be paid the same rate as people with comparable responsibilities. That you consider this a small issue astonishes me. I admit it's a pity they have to bring the matter to a head at a busy time of year like this — but then, after all, why not? If I had been in their shoes I would have done the same.'

6 Sir James was most anxious for the committee to give the matter its urgent attention and publish its findings. He said in Parliament it was better for the public to know the truth, however distasteful it might be. That he said this suggests to me that a political scandal is about to break.

12   Reported speech

12A   Word and tense changes: general review

Introductory note: When direct speech or thoughts are reported with a verb in the PAST tense (I *said/asked/told/thought* etc . . .) it is necessary to change some verb tenses and words. In the Examples below these **changes** are in *italics*; tenses that do **not** change are <u>underlined</u>. The rule for tenses is:

 i Tenses that express FACT (1B), since they are related to time, **change** by 'taking a step back' or, in the case of the future tenses, by converting *will/shall* to the conditional *would/should* (1D). The past perfect tense is an exception because it cannot 'take a step back'. The past tense is an occasional exception (see **h** on p. 136).

 ii Tenses, together with the subjunctive, that express NON-FACT (1D, E), are not directly related to time and so do **not** change.

This rule may be summarised with reference to the numbered Examples:

DIRECT SPEECH		REPORTED SPEECH	
present tense	⟶	*past tense*	1, 2, 3, 7, 9
present perfect tense	⟶	*past perfect tense*	8
past tense (FACT)	⟶	*past perfect tense*	8
future tense	⟶	*conditional tense*	9
future perfect tense	⟶	*conditional perfect tense*	
<u>past tense</u> (NON-FACT)*		<u>past tense</u>	4
<u>past perfect tense</u>		<u>past perfect tense</u>	8
<u>conditional tense</u>		<u>conditional tense</u>	4, 6
<u>conditional perfect tense</u>		<u>conditional perfect tense</u>	
<u>subjunctive</u>		<u>subjunctive</u>	6

Changes other than changes of tense are dealt with in the Explanation.

Examples

DIRECT SPEECH		REPORTED SPEECH	
1 '*I hope* to go to the States *next* month,' said Marilyn.	⟶	Marilyn said (that) *she hoped* to go to the States *the following* month/*in June* (etc.).	c, d

---

*In addition, the past tense does **not** change in idiomatic phrases like *had better* (1Fe) or *Did* (= Do) *you know that . . . ?*

2 'Who *are you* going with and how long *are you* staying?' I asked. ⟶ I asked her who *she was* going with and how long *she was* staying. **c, g**

3 '*I'm* not going with anyone,' she replied. 'It's a business trip. *I may* stay for as long as three weeks.' ⟶ She replied *that* she *wasn't* going with anyone, *as it was* a business trip, *and that she might* stay for as long as three weeks. **a, c, e**

4 '*I can't* stay any longer. If *I* <u>did</u> *I'*<u>d</u> start worrying about *my* business *over here*.' ⟶ *She said* (that) *she couldn't* stay any longer *because* if *she* <u>did</u> she'<u>d</u> start worrying about *her* business *in England* (etc.). **a, c, d, e**

5 '*Don't* give it a thought,' *said* Georgina's brother. 'Stay in America as long as *you need* to.' ⟶ Georgina's brother *told her* not *to* give it a thought *but to* stay in America as long as *she needed* to. **b, e**

6 'If *I* <u>were</u> running *your* business,' he said, '*I'*<u>d</u> spend more than three weeks over there.' ⟶ He said *that* if *he* <u>were</u> running *her* business *he'*<u>d</u> spend more than three weeks over there. **c**

7 'Whatever *you do*,' he said, '*don't* worry.' ⟶ He *told her*/said *that* whatever *she did she was*n't *to* worry. **b**

8 '*Have you* forgotten how *I* kept an eye on *your* Birmingham office the last time *you went* abroad?' he asked. 'And that *was*n't the first time *I'*<u>d</u> done it, *was it*?' ⟶ He asked *if/whether she'd* forgotten how *he'd* kept an eye on *her* Birmingham office the last time she'*d been/gone* abroad and *reminded her that* that *had*n't *been* the first time *he'*<u>d</u> done it. **f**

9 '*I'll* willingly do the same again,' he added, 'especially as *I'll* no longer have *my present* rather heavy business commitments by the time *you go*.' ⟶ He added *that he'd* willingly do the same again, especially as by the time *she went he'd* no longer have *the* rather heavy business commit-ments *he then had*. **d**

Explanation

In addition to the verb tense changes described above, the following changes take place in the reporting of speech:

a The auxiliaries *may* (3), *can, cannot* (4) change to *might, could, could not*, whatever their use (**11A, B, C**). (For possible changes in other auxiliaries, see **12B**.)

b The imperative (**11De**) changes either to:

  i the infinitive (5) introduced by *told* etc. (**12Cb**), or to:

  ii a construction (see **10Dd, 11De**) with *was/were (not) to* introduced by
    told etc. or *said* (7).

The first is the more common, but after a clause (*whatever she did*) only the
second can be used (**not** 'He told her that whatever she did not to worry').
The word order is therefore often reversed: 'He told her not to worry
whatever she did.'

c Personal pronouns such as *I* (1, 3), *you* (2, 5) and possessives such as *my* (4),
your (6) change according to context.

d Words relating to time and place like *next* (1) and *over here* (4) change
according to circumstance. (We may, after all, report the speech in a
different month and in a different country from those in which it was
spoken.) Sometimes these changes, as with *present* (9), need to be
considerable and involve word order.

e Suitable links such as *and* (3), *as* (3), *because* (4), *but* (5) are often inserted in
reported speech, where sentences are usually longer than in direct speech.

f Special features of spoken English (colloquialisms) such as question tags
(*was it?*) are omitted in reported speech but their effect may be partly
retained by the use of suitable introductory verbs such as *reminded* (8).

g Note the use in Example 2 of *who* (not *whom*) in both direct and reported
questions. The use of *whom* in questions ('With whom are you going? ⟶
I asked with whom she was going') is rare in modern English.

h If someone reports speech soon enough to use the same time references as
the speaker, a past tense expressing fact does not 'take a step back' to the
past perfect. Compare **i** and **ii**:

     'It happened yesterday/two days ago/on Sunday.' ⟶

  i She said it happened yesterday/two days ago/on Sunday. (Reported the
    same day or, for *on Sunday*, the same week.)

  ii She said it *had* happened the day before/two days before/the previous
    Sunday. (Reported days or weeks later.)

Time references for historical events are the same for both reporter and
speaker, and so her again the past tense does not change, even if a date is
not mentioned (see **1Ba**):

     'Thomas Edison invented the electric light bulb.' ⟶ Our teacher
     told us that Thomas Edison invented the electric light bulb.

In 1 in the Exercise the past tense may or may not change, depending on
whether the statement is reported within ten years of the event or later. In 2
it would be possible to keep the past tenses by regarding the events as
'history'. (In the Key only one alternative is given for 1 and 2.)

Exercises

Report the following direct speech in the way shown in the Examples. Use links (*and, because, which* etc.) to make not more than one sentence for each number and, in Exercise 3, to join some of these sentences together.

1

1 'When Brenda joined our firm ten years ago,' he said, 'she'd already worked in the same sort of business and had learnt a lot about it.'
2 'For the first eight years with us,' he said, 'she worked in the Sales Department, and was working there when I became the firm's Managing Director, but since then she's been working as my personal assistant.'
3 'Normally,' he went on to say, 'she works on the top floor in an office next to mine, but she isn't there at the moment because she's working in London on a special assignment.'
4 'I sincerely hope,' he said, 'that she'll go on working here until I retire, as over the last few years she's learnt as much about this business as I have. And that's quite a lot, I can tell you.' (Use link + *he assured me* . . . .)
5 'Who's she going to work for when you retire?' I asked. 'Perhaps,' I ventured to say, 'she can come and work for me, as she sounds an absolute gem.'
6 'Don't get the wrong idea and imagine we're talking about a young girl.' he said. 'She'll be well over fifty when I retire, and so will be retiring herself not long afterwards.'
7 'Is she going to retire to a cottage by the sea,' I asked, 'or do you think she's one of those who go on working till they drop?'
8 'I've heard her say she may set herself up as a business consultant,' he said. 'She'll certainly have had the right sort of experience for it.'
9 'But I think it would be better if you asked her about it yourself tomorrow. I expect her to be back from London then.' (Begin *However, he thought* . . .)
10 'If you look in in the afternoon I can introduce you to her,' he said. 'Don't come in the morning, though, because she may not be here until midday.'
11 'Incidentally, if anyone asks you who you've got an appointment with, tell them it's with me, not with her.' (Begin *He added* . . . .)
12 'I'd have liked to join you both tomorrow,' he said, 'but I don't think I'll have the time. Remember, though, that Brenda will be able to give you as much information about this business as I would.' (Begin *After explaining* . . . *he reminded.* . . .)

2

1 'Are you doing anything this evening?' I asked Willie one day. 'Would you like to go to a disco?'
2 'You may not believe this,' he replied, 'but I've never been to a disco in my life, as I'm afraid I just wouldn't be able to stand the noise.'

3 'It's clearly high time you went to one,' I said. 'I'd take you where you'd be surprised at the gentle, civilised atmosphere.'
4 'Sounds idyllic,' said Willie, 'but if I go out this evening who's to do all this work? It's got to be done by tomorrow morning.'
5 'Who are you doing it for?' I asked. 'Can't it wait? I had a lot of work myself the other day, but I didn't let it spoil my evening.' (Use *adding* . . . .)
6 'If my work spoilt my evenings,' Willie replied, 'I wouldn't be an architect, because I often have to work in the evening.'

3

1 He: I'd like to learn to play the piano. I wish I knew a good teacher who lived fairly near and who'd give me lessons.
2 She: Suppose I offered to give you lessons. What would you say?
3 He: I wish you would! I'd rather you taught me than anyone else.
4 She: I'll teach you provided you attend my lessons regularly and practise hard.
5 He: Did you know that you've got a good reputation as a teacher? It would have been nice if you'd been able to teach me last month, when I had quite a lot of free time.
6 She: Mind you, I'll never teach anyone who's not prepared to practise, no matter who they are. (Use *she emphasised that* . . . .)
7 He: I'd practise as if it were a matter of life and death. And I'd pay you what you wanted, even if it was more than you are getting at the music school, however much that is.
8 She: Good. It's time we started the first lesson, then. (Use *she expressed her satisfaction* . . . .)
9 He: I'd have liked to have started today, but unfortunately I can't. In the meanwhile we'd better settle the price, because if we didn't it would be unbusinesslike.
10 She: As you wish. I'd hate to start on the wrong note. (Use *she agreed* . . . .)

12B Possible changes in auxiliary verbs

will, shall, should
could, might
must, need not

Introductory note: In the Examples that follow, the auxiliary verbs that **change** are in *italics*; those that do **not** change are underlined; those that **may** and often do change if the speaker or writer so wishes are in <u>*underlined italics*</u>.

Examples

DIRECT SPEECH	REPORTED SPEECH	
1 'What'*ll* you do,' I asked Helen, 'if Ken's too late to drive you to the airport?'	⟶ I asked Helen what she'*d* do if Ken was too late to drive her to the airport.	a
2 'Sheila,' said Helen, 'what *shall* I do if your friend Ken is late?'	⟶ Helen asked Sheila what she *should/was to* do if her friend Ken was late.	b
3 'After all,' I said to Sheila, 'he might/could have trouble with his car.'	I reminded Sheila that he might/could have trouble with his car.	c
4 'Ken should/ought to be here in good time,' replied Sheila. 'He's seldom late.'	Sheila replied that Ken should/ought to be there in good time, as he was seldom late.	d
5 'You must have strange ideas about Ken to think that,' said Helen.	Helen told Sheila (that) she must have strange ideas about Ken to think that.	e
6 'You mustn't think Ken's always late,' I whispered to Helen.	I whispered to Helen that she mustn't think Ken was always late.	f
7 'I *must* catch that plane,' said Helen, 'whatever happens.'	⟶ Helen said (that) she *had to* catch the plane whatever happened.	g, h
8 'So if Ken's late,' she went on, 'I *must* order a taxi.'	⟶ She went on to say that if Ken was late she *would have to* order a taxi.	g, h
9 'You *must* tell me first,' said Sheila.	⟶ Sheila told Helen (that) she *had to/was to* tell her first.	g, h
10 'Helen *mustn't* order a taxi without telling me first,' she repeated to me.	⟶ She repeated to me that Helen *wasn't to* order a taxi without telling her first.	g, h
11 'Helen *needn't* worry,' she added. 'Ken won't be late.'	⟶ She added that Helen *didn't need to/have to* worry, as Ken wouldn't be late.	g, j
12 'You *needn't* worry if Ken's late,' I whispered to Helen, 'because I can take you to the airport.'	⟶ I whispered to Helen that she *wouldn't need to/have to* worry if Ken was late because I could take her to the airport.	g, j
13 'I *didn't need to* go back to my office after lunch, so I and my car are now at your disposal,' I said.	⟶ I told her (that) I *hadn't needed to* go back to my office after lunch, so that I and my car were now at her disposal.	k

14 'Well,' thought Helen, 'I <u>needn't have</u> worried after all.'	⟶	Helen then realised (that) she <u>needn't have</u> worried after all.	**k**
15 'I *couldn't* tell you before,' I said.	⟶	I told her (that) I *hadn't been able to* tell her before.	l
16 'You see, I didn't know whether I <u>could</u> take you or not.'		I pointed out that I hadn't known whether I <u>could</u> take her or not.	l

Explanation

a As already noted in **12A**, *will/shall*, which is commonly contracted to *'ll* (1), changes to *would/should*, which is commonly contracted to *'d*.

b **But** in questions asking for instructions or advice (2) and not just for information (1), uncontracted *shall* is used, which changes to uncontracted *should* or *was/were to*. This difference in usage allows us to distinguish between meanings. Compare Example 2 with the following:

Helen asked Sheila what she'd do if her friend Ken was late
(= 'Sheila,' said Helen, 'what'll you do if your friend Ken is late?').

c <u>Might</u> (**11Aa, e**) does not change (3). <u>Could</u> or <u>could not</u> does not change when it is used for possibility (3) or impossibility (**11Ae–g**).

d <u>Should</u> and <u>ought to</u> do not change (4) whether they are used for expectation (**11Ca**) or duty and advisability (**11Ea**).

e <u>Must</u> used for conclusions (**11Cd**) does not change (5).

f <u>Must (not)</u> used weakly with the meaning of *should (not)* to express advisability (6) rather than obligation does not change.

g *Must (not)* and *need not*, used respectively for obligation (**11Da**) and absence of obligation (**11Dg**), do not always change but very often do so, especially when what is reported is all in the past, or 'history'. These possible changes are given in Examples 7–12, where we may suppose that the reported conversation took place at least a few hours ago and that Helen has already either caught her plane or missed it. ('Helen said she must catch her plane' is likely to carry the idea that she has **not** yet caught or missed it.)

h The possible equivalents of *must (not)* in direct speech are *have (got) to* (**11Da, b, c**), *will have to* (**11Dc, d**) and *is/am* etc, *(not) to* (**11De**). It is these equivalents that, by 'taking a step back' (see **12A**, Introductory note), provide the changes in reported speech (7–10).

j Similarly, *need not* (**11Dg**) may be the equivalent of *does not need to/have to* or *will not need to/have to*, which provide the basis for the changes in reported speech (11, 12).

k Whereas *did not need to* changes to *had not needed to* (13), <u>need not have</u> does **not** change (14). (If you have forgotten the difference in use and meaning between these two forms of *need not*, see **11Dh**.)

l <u>*Could (not)*</u> often changes when it is the equivalent of the PAST tense meaning *was (not) able to* (15), but <u>could (not)</u> does **not** change when it is the equivalent of the conditional *would (not) be able to* (16) or the subjunctive *was/were (not) able to* (see **11Ad**):

    'If I couldn't (= wasn't/weren't able to) take you to the airport I wouldn't tell you I could (= was)' ⟶ He told her that if he couldn't take her to the airport he wouldn't tell her he could.

m Similarly, <u>could (not)</u> used for permission or prohibition does not change when it means *would (not) be allowed to* (**11Aa**) but may change when it means *was (not) allowed to* (**11Ab, c**):

    'At my school we couldn't keep pets' ⟶ He said that at his school they hadn't been allowed to keep pets.

Exercise

Report the following direct speech, making not only the **necessary** but also the **possible** changes, as shown in the Examples. Try and make one sentence for each number.

1. 'We must get rid of that new typist if she doesn't improve,' said Harry McArthur.
2. 'After all, we mustn't be too soft-hearted about her if we want an efficient firm,' he said. (Begin *He pointed out . . . .*)
3. 'It must be the third time I've told her about the petty cash,' he said. 'She should listen when I give her instructions.'
4. 'She must never take money out of the petty cash without my permission,' he said.
5. 'I think she might do it again,' said Georgina. 'What shall I tell her if she does?'
6. 'You needn't tell her anything,' answered Harry, 'because I'll deal with the matter myself.'
7. 'I couldn't ask Mr McArthur about the petty cash,' said the girl, 'because he'd gone out to lunch, and so I thought I could use my own discretion in the matter.'
8. 'The girl must be very stupid to say things like that,' said Georgina. 'Shall I tell her she's got the sack?'
9. 'No one must tell her anything,' replied Harry. 'She must come and see me.'
10. 'It looks very much as if we must tell her that her services are no longer required,' he said.
11. 'Regulations state that she must have at least two weeks' notice or salary in lieu,' he said.

12 'She's quite a nice kid,' remarked Harry, 'and one mustn't be too hard on her.'

13 'Although I'm afraid you must go,' he told her, 'you needn't worry too much because I'll give you quite a good testimonial.'

14 'Could I have the testimonial now?' asked the girl. 'Then I could start looking for another job at once.'

15 'Perhaps your father could help you find a job,' I said. 'You should pay him a visit.' (Begin *I suggested to her* . . . .)

16 'I might do just that,' she replied, 'although it would cost a lot.'

17 'Shall I book you a seat on this flight?' asked the travel agent. 'You needn't pay the whole of the fare now,' he added.

18 'I didn't need to pay the whole fare when I booked,' she told me later, 'so I needn't have worried so much about money.'

19 'I couldn't get through to my father last night to tell him of my plans,' she said. 'Could you phone him from your office for me?'

20 'She couldn't have arranged to come at a worse time,' said her father on the phone. 'I can't possibly meet her at the airport on Friday.'

21 'I'll have just come back from Canada,' he said, 'and there'll be several business matters I must see to before the weekend.'

22 'She couldn't warn you before,' I told him. 'What shall I tell her to do?'

23 'You shouldn't spoil the girl,' he said. 'She ought to be capable of coming to see me without all this help from strangers.'

24 'Shall I tell her what you said,' I asked, 'or would you rather I didn't?'

25 'Daddy couldn't have understood you,' the girl insisted later. 'I wish,' she added, 'that he was going to be at the airport to meet me, even if it was only to say "Hullo" before he went back to his business.'

12C   Requests and suggestions

Introductory note: So far in this section, requests have been limited to the use of the imperative or *must (not)*, and to their reporting with *told* or *said* followed by the infinitive, *was/were (not) to* or *had to* (**12Ab, Bg**). However, there are other ways of getting people to do or not to do things and of reporting them, varying from the gentle *ask* or *suggest* to the stern *order* or *warn*, and the more useful of these are given below. The words in italics in the Examples are those whose general sense and meaning correspond in direct and reported speech.

Examples

DIRECT SPEECH	REPORTED SPEECH	
1 *'Could* you,' *said* Sheila to a passing driver, 'give me a lift	$\longrightarrow$ Sheila *asked* a passing driver to give her a lift into town, as	**a**

into town? My car has broken down.'

her car had broken down.

2 'Hop in,' *said* the driver.   The driver *told her to hop in*.   **b**

3 '*What about* stopping for a ⟶ After a few moments, the
coffee?' *said* the man after a   man *suggested* stopping/that   **c**
few moments.   they should stop for a coffee.

4 'I *very much hope*,' said ⟶ Sheila *urged* the man to drive   **e**
Sheila, 'that you'll drive   straight on so she could keep
straight on so I can keep an   an important appointment.
important appointment.'

5 But the man stopped the car. ⟶ Having nevertheless stopped
'*If I were you*,' he *said*, 'I'*d*   the car, the man *advised*   **d**
hand over that bag of yours   Sheila to hand over her bag
without a struggle.'   without a struggle.

6 However, it was the man who ⟶ However, it was the man who
was soon struggling. '*For*   was soon struggling and
God's sake let me go!' he   *begging/imploring/entreating*   **e**
cried. 'You're breaking my   Sheila to let him go, as she
arm!'   was breaking his arm.

7 '*Now*,' *snapped* Sheila, 'you'*ll* ⟶ Sheila then *ordered* him to   **b**
drive me first to a garage and   drive her first to a garage and
afterwards to my weekly   afterwards to her weekly
appointment at the judo   appointment at the judo
school.'   school.

8 '*Whatever you do*,' she *said*, ⟶ She *warned him not to*   **f**
'*don't* try any more monkey   try/*against* trying any more
business.'   monkey business.

Explanation

a A more forcible alternative to *ask* (1) is *request*, but it is too formal to be
included among the above Examples:
> '*Please be sure* to be punctual at all my lectures,' she *told* her students.
> ⟶ She *requested* her students to be punctual . . . .

b A more forcible alternative to *tell* is *order* (7), or sometimes *command*.
Although *order* is more common in military and similar contexts, it may be
suitable in other contexts, such as this one. Instead of *order . . . not* we
generally use *forbid* (17A):
> '*No* talking!' *ordered* the headmaster ⟶ The headmaster *forbade*
> them to talk.

c When what we *suggest* (3) is based on a choice between things, or actions,
we may use *recommend*:
> '*Why don't you* try the Greek restaurant further up the street?' she
> said. ⟶ She *recommended* (our) (trying) the Greek restaurant . . . .

d For more serious matters, which may involve telling people **not** to do things, we normally use *advise* (5) instead of *suggest* or *recommend*.

e When we ask urgently, in order to try and persuade someone to do or not to do something, we use *urge* (4). If this is not strong enough, and we wish to convey anguish, pain or tears, we use *beg, implore* or *entreat* (6). *Beseech* (past tense *besought*) is also possible, but is literary.

f When someone *tells* or *advises* us **not** to do something wrong, imprudent or dangerous, the appropriate introductory verb is *warn* (8). This verb is also used with *that* to give us notice of possible danger or inconvenience:

'*Take care*,' he *said*, 'the roads will be icy.' ⟶ He warned (us) that the roads would be icy.

'*The trouble is*,' she *said*, 'the supermarket closes in half an hour.' ⟶ She warned (us) that the supermarket closed in half an hour.

Exercise 1

Report the following direct speech using the introductory verbs shown in the Examples or mentioned in the Explanation.

1 'Let's send away for this electric kettle advertised in the paper as a special offer,' said my wife.
2 It was about three weeks later that I said: 'Will you plug it in while I get the cups?'
3 'You mustn't,' I said, 'fill it with the switch on, whatever you do.'
4 'Stand back,' I cried, 'while I disconnect it!'
5 'Don't ever touch that kettle again,' I said. 'It's live.'
6 'Don't you think,' said my wife, 'we should get a lawn-mower the next time there's a special offer?'
7 'If I were you,' said the girl from next door, who'd just come in, 'I'd get the whole house rewired.'
8 'I do hope you'll follow such an excellent piece of advice,' said my wife.
9 'Mind your own business!' I snapped, still tense after the affair of the kettle.
10 'Don't ever speak to me like that again,' she said, 'if you want any more meals cooked.'
11 'I'm sorry, dearest,' I said. 'Please, please forgive me.'
12 'How about eating out this evening?' I then said, by way of a peace offering.
13 'Oh, yes!' said our neighbour. 'Why not go to the new Chinese restaurant? 'I've heard it's excellent.'
14 'Mind you,' she went on, 'you'll have to reserve a table.'
15 'And you'd better put on a tie,' she said, eyeing me disapprovingly.
16 'Yes,' said my wife, 'go upstairs and change into something decent.'
17 'You're not to come out with me looking like that,' she said.
18 'If I were you,' said our neighbour, 'I'd telephone the restaurant first.'

19 'Hurry up,' said my wife, 'whichever you do first.'
20 I suddenly felt a great need for peace and quiet. 'Look,' I said, 'why don't you two go out instead of me?'

Exercise 2

Oral practice (general revision): Without using the book yourself, get someone to say the following to you and then report, as if to a third person, what you have heard, beginning *She/He* as shown below. Since the reporting is immediate, do not change the reference to time such as *this morning* (see **h** on p. 136) or to place, such as *here*.

Excuse me for being late this morning; I was held up by the traffic.	⟶ *She asked me* to excuse *her* for being late this morning; *she said she was* held up by the traffic.
I'd have got here quicker if I'd come on a bicycle.	⟶ *She said she*'d have got here quicker if *she*'d come on a bicycle.
I should leave early this evening if I were you.	⟶ *She advised me to* leave early this evening.

 1 Where do you come from? Are you staying here long?
 2 Is this the first time you've been here?
 3 I've been living here for over a year and quite like the place.
 4 But I'd rather live in London. Wouldn't you?
 5 You must find this place rather dull compared with your home town.
 6 What can we do this evening if we decide to go out?
 7 We could go to the cinema if there are any good films on.
 8 How about going to a concert? Do you like music?
 9 You needn't decide now; you can let me know later.
10 Shall I come round to your house or wait for you here?
11 Will you be ready if I call for you at six o'clock?
12 Don't forget to bring an umbrella, as it may rain.
13 I wish my car was in order, so I could have given you a lift.
14 It's being repaired, and won't be ready until the end of the week.
15 I wish I knew more about cars than I do.
16 I could save a lot of money if I was able to do the maintenance myself.
17 I had to come here by bus this morning, as I'm without my car.
18 Did you walk or drive to work this morning?
19 You mustn't drive on the right here whatever you do.
20 If you've been to Japan, you'll know that they drive on the left there too.
21 Do you think I'd like your country if I visited it?
22 Tell me the things I should make a point of seeing.
23 I must try and save some money so that I can visit you.
24 I must go now, as I have to correct some homework.
25 You mustn't forget that you have some homework to do for tomorrow.

13 The passive

13A Subject formation from the active voice

Introductory note: You should already be fairly well acquainted with the English passive verb and should know how to form it from the corresponding active tenses, and this formation is not discussed here, although passive tenses are well illustrated in the Examples below (for the passive infinitive and gerund, see **10A, B**). What is discussed is the formation of the passive sentence as a whole and in particular the relationship between its grammatical subject and the grammatical object or objects in the active voice. An understanding of this relationship is the best way of knowing when and how to use the passive, since there is a connection between grammatical subjects and the subjects we like to talk or write about. The grouping of Examples and Explanations is as follows:

Formation from a single object
Formation from two objects
Formation of the auxiliary passive
Non-formation of the passive from two objects

Formation from a single object

Examples

ACTIVE		PASSIVE	
1 They arrested *Peter* two days ago.	⟶	*Peter* was arrested two days ago.	**a**
2 The Mercian press has declared *him* (to be) a spy.	⟶	*He* has been declared a spy by the Mercian press.	**a, c, e**
3 The authorities had clearly decided *to make an example of him.*	⟶	*It* had clearly* been decided by the authorities to make an example of him.	**a, b, e**
4 They've announced (that) *he'll be tried.*	⟶	*It* has been announced (that) he'll be tried.	**a, b**
5 They're not complying with *the law.*	⟶	*The law* is not being complied with.	**a, d**

* For the position of adverbs in the passive, see **2Bf**.

Explanation

a The subject of a passive sentence can be formed from the single object of almost any verb (1–5). The important exceptions are *have* and *get* in most of their meanings:

They have (= are holding) a lot of people in jail.   NO PASSIVE

The prisoners never get (= receive) our letters.   NO PASSIVE

But:

We all had (= experienced) a   ⟶ A good time was had by (us)
good time.   all.

Can they get (= make) the   ⟶ Can the room be got ready in
room ready in time?   time?

(See also **t** below.)

b The single object may be not only a noun or a pronoun (1, 2); it may be an infinitive phrase or a *that* clause (3, 4), which can become the subject of a passive sentence by the use of introductory *it* (**8Ap**). As already pointed out in **10Ac**, it is rare for an infinitive itself to stand first in a sentence as subject, and the same is true of a *that* clause.

c The single object may have a complement (2).* Although this may be a noun (*a spy*), you can see that it is not another object because (**i**) it can be linked to *him* by *to be* and (**ii**) it can be replaced by an adjective: 'The Mercian press has declared him insane.' It cannot therefore become the subject of a corresponding passive. The same is true of all complements, which you should be able to recognise even if (**i**) and (**ii**) do not apply:

They crowned him king.   ⟶ He was crowned king
                                          (**not** The king was crowned).

d The object (compare **p** below) of a verb used with a preposition (a prepositional verb) can usually become the subject in the passive (5). Exceptions occur with prepositional verbs of movement:

People very rarely *enter/go*   ⟶ These rooms are very rarely
into these rooms.   *entered* (**not** *gone into*).

Amundsen *reached/arrived at*   ⟶ The South Pole was *reached*
the South Pole on 14th   (**not** *arrived at*) by
December 1911.   Amundsen on 14th December
                                          1911.

When movement is not expressed, these verbs can be used in the passive:

The matter has been *gone into* very thoroughly.

No conclusion has yet been *arrived at*.

e Note that the subject of an active sentence is not represented in the passive unless it is of some significance (2, 3), when it appears as the agent (*by the Mercian press, by the authorities*). Whether there is an agent or not, we think

---

* Complements can be defined as nouns or adjectives that **complete** the way a verb is used (that is to say, the verb pattern) without being that verb's object. In 'He is a spy', *spy* is a complement, **not** an object, and of course this sentence has no corresponding passive.

in the passive more about the person or thing acted upon and about the action itself than about its source, which becomes remote or impersonal.

Formation from two objects

Examples

ACTIVE	PASSIVE	
6A A friend gave me *the information/the information* to me.	*The information* was given (to) me by a friend.	f, g, h
B A friend gave *me* the information/the information *to me*.	*I* was given the information by a friend.	
7A They've refused Peter *access to a lawyer*. ⟶	*Access to a lawyer* has been refused Peter.	f, g, h
B They've refused *Peter* access to a lawyer. ⟶	*Peter* has been refused access to a lawyer.	

Explanation

f Some verbs can have two objects, one usually a concrete or abstract thing (A), the other usually a person (B), although this too can be a thing: 'I gave *what she said* a lot of thought.' (See also **j** below.) For a list of the more common of these verbs, look at study list **17E**, where you will see that they fall into three groups.

g The first group (**i**) consists of verbs like *give* (6) and *refuse* (7), where **either** object can become the subject in a corresponding passive without it being necessary to introduce a preposition in the passive for object B.

h Most verbs in the first group are like *give* (6), which can be used alternatively with the preposition *to* in front of object B in both active and passive,* although there are a few verbs like *refuse* (7) with which there is no optional use of a preposition.

j The second group (**ii**) consists of verbs like *feed* or *build*, **either** object of which can become the subject in a corresponding passive but which, unlike those of the first group, **do** require a preposition for object B in the passive. This preposition (see **17E**) is usually *for* but may be *to* or *into*:

They fed the computer all the ⟶ All the available data were
available data/all the available   fed *into* the computer.
data *into* the computer.

---

* In British English the use of *to* in the passive is common, particularly in front of a noun as opposed to a pronoun: 'The information was given *to* the secretary of our committee by a friend.'

They've built it a special shed/a $\longrightarrow$ A special shed has been built
special shed *for* it.   *for* it.

k For verbs of the third group (**iii**), see **q, r, s** below.

Formation of the auxiliary passive

Examples

ACTIVE		PASSIVE	
8	A friend gave *me* the information/the information *to me*.	$\longrightarrow$ *I* had the information given (to) *me* by a friend.	**l**
9	They've refused *Peter* access to a lawyer.	$\longrightarrow$ *Peter* has had access to a lawyer refused *him*.	**l**
10	They never explain a citizen's rights *to prisoners*.	$\longrightarrow$ *Prisoners* never have a citizen's rights explained *to them*.	**m, n**
11	They'll confiscate *Peter's* cameras, of course.	$\longrightarrow$ *Peter* will have *his* cameras confiscated, of course.	**p**
12	And they'll carefully examine the photos *he* took, including that one of you.	$\longrightarrow$ And *he*'ll have the photos *he* took, including that one of you, carefully examined.	**p**

Explanation

l With verbs of the first or second group (see **g, h, j** above) there is a third
way of forming a passive, namely by the use of *have* (8, 9). You will see that,
although this is externally similar to causal *have* (**10Dc**), it is being used in a
passive, not an active (causal), sense. Compare these two sentences:

     Sheila has had her car repaired.   CAUSATION

     Sheila has had her car stolen.   AUXILIARY PASSIVE

In the first, the subject Sheila is in an active (causal) role; in the second, she
is in a passive role. Equivalent sentences could therefore be:

     Someone has repaired Sheila's car for her.

     Someone has stolen Sheila's car (**not** for her!).

Sentences using *have* can be passive or active in sense according to context.
Thus 'He had his head shaved' can refer to a man in a passive role subjected
to the indignities of prison life or to a free man actively following the latest
fashion.

m Although the auxiliary passive is quite often used with verbs like *give* (8)
and *refuse* (9), with them it is no more than an alternative to the passive

formed on object B (see **f–j** above), which has the advantage of being shorter than the auxiliary passive. With many verbs, however, such as *explain* (10), there is no object B without a preposition, and therefore no corresponding B passive with persons as subject (**not** 'They never explain prisoners a citizen's rights ⟶ Prisoners are never explained a citizen's rights'). Consequently with these verbs the auxiliary passive is very useful, since in everyday communication we tend to make persons and not things our subject, both in a social and a grammatical sense.

n Note the difference between (10) the PREPOSITIONAL OBJECT (*to prisoners*) of a verb such as *explain* and (5) the OBJECT (*law*) of a prepositional verb such as *comply with*. The first is dependent upon a verb with an object that can become the subject of a (non-auxiliary) passive:

A citizen's legal rights are never explained to prisoners.

The second, as we have seen, is an object that can itself become the subject of a passive ('The law is not being complied with').

p In addition to a prepositional object (10), the word in the active that provides the subject of an auxiliary passive may be (11) a possessive (*Peter's*) or (12) a noun or a pronoun (*he*) in a relative clause (**8**). Notice that the word, whichever it is, occurs **twice** in the passive in one form or another:

to prisoners	⟶	*Prisoners . . . to them* (10)
Peter's	⟶	*Peter . . . his* (11)
he	⟶	*he . . . he* (12)

Non-formation of the passive from two objects

Examples

	ACTIVE		PASSIVE	
13A	Many people wish Peter *luck*.		(none)	**q**
B	Many people wish *Peter* luck.		(none)	
14A	His fearless stand has won (for) him *a lot of sympathy*.	⟶	*A lot of sympathy* has been won *for* him by his fearless stand.	**r**
B	His fearless stand has won (for) *him* a lot of sympathy.		(none)	
15A	Freeing Peter now would save the authorities *a lot of trouble*.		(none)	**s, t**
B	Freeing Peter now would save *the authorities* a lot of trouble.	⟶	*The authorities* would be saved a lot of trouble by freeing Peter now.	

Explanation

q Passives cannot be formed from either object of **all** double-object verbs. A list of the more important of these exceptions appears under **17Eiii**. It includes verbs like *wish* (13), labelled **q** on the list, **neither** object of which can normally become the subject of a passive, although B objects can on occasion: 'They wished us a pleasant journey ⟶ We were wished a pleasant journey.'

r There are also verbs like *win* (14), labelled **r** in **17Eiii**, where object A but not object B can become the subject of a passive. This requires the use of the preposition *for*, optional in the active.

s Thirdly, there are a few verbs like *save* (15), labelled **s** in **17Eiii**, where the passive can be formed from object B but not from object A.

t Note that it is possible (see **a** above) to form passives from the **single** objects of these verbs:

> Freeing Peter now would   ⟶   A lot of trouble would be
> save a lot of trouble.   saved by freeing Peter now.

An exception on list **17Eiii** is *cost* (unless it means *estimate the price*). Thus 'It cost a fortune' has no passive.

Exercise

Transform the following into passives in which the grammatical subjects are formed from the words in *italics*. Where clauses are to become the subject (see **b** above), only *that*, and not the whole clause, is italicised.

1 I hadn't been with my firm for more than four months when they taught *me* the elements of marketing and made *me* a sales representative.

2 They recently increased *my* salary by thirty per cent. The trouble is that at the same time they reduced *my* expense allowance by nearly half.

3 Denis says his firm has offered *him* a job in Singapore, but that he won't take it because someone else has promised *him* a much better job in Japan.

4 Someone has lent *me* a book on computers and I now understand roughly how they work. No one had ever explained them *to me* before.

5 Last year they overtaxed *me* and now owe *me* quite a lot of money. I think that until they refund it *to me* they should pay *me* interest on it, don't you?

6 They should do away with *income tax* altogether. If necessary, they could put up *value added tax* by way of compensation. But unfortunately you can always rely on *this Government* not to do the right thing.

7 From the way people are speaking about *this Government*, one might think *that* they will not vote *it* back into power at the next election. However, the proverb 'Better the devil you know than the devil you don't' will probably decide *the result* in the Government's favour.

8 Over the years people have set up *various small, friendly shops* in this town, but they seldom survive long because the supermarkets force *their* prices down and drive *them* out of business. People have suggested *that* shop owners should combine in an advertising campaign, but this would probably lead to the supermarkets beating *them* yet again, this time in a propaganda war.

9 Have people ever stolen *your* washing when you've hung it out to dry? They have *mine*. In fact they've been stealing *mine* a bit at a time for the past month.

10 A couple of weeks ago they confiscated *Peter's* passport. They won't return it *to him* now he's been arrested.

11 The latest news is that they have charged *him* with conspiracy, refused *him* bail, and jailed *him*. They may forbid *you* any contact with him before the trial.

12 During the war they used to open *our* letters and censor them. They told *us*, of course, that the censors would never disclose or discuss *our* personal affairs.

13 Publishers were always rejecting the pieces *I* wrote, but now I am glad to say they are beginning to accept them. (Use **two** auxiliary passives, beginning *I. . . .*)

14 I thought they refused *children* admission to horror films, but the other day they allowed *my twelve-year-old niece* in to see that shocker at the Plaza.

15 Brenda Pearl's father left *her* a considerable sum of money but crafty lawyers took quite a lot of it *off her*.

16 They've endorsed *Ken's* driving licence again, I'm afraid. The next time they catch *him* for speeding they'll probably disqualify *him* from driving for a year.

17 My car broke down yesterday and they had to tow *it* to a local garage for repair. They'll charge *me* for the repair, of course, but not for the tow, as my membership of the Automobile Club covers *me* for that.

18 Someone onced showed *me* the way to the railway station, but I have now forgotten it, which is a pity, because people frequently ask *me* it.

19 People used to drum *into me* as a child *that* those were the best days of my life. (Begin *I* . . . and follow with introductory *it*.) They told *me* wrong.

20 They awarded the Nobel Peace Prize *to Martin Luther King* in 1964. In 1968 someone assassinated *him*.

21 Someone once taught *me* a Finnish song without telling *me* what it really meant. In fact they played a nasty trick *on me*, because when I sang it in Finland everyone blushed.

22 They've known for some time *that* if you feed penicillin *to the young of domestic animals* you significantly increase *their growth rate*.

13B   Passive constructions with the infinitive

Examples

ACTIVE | PASSIVE

1   They say (that) the country is ⟶ The country *is said to be* on   **a, b**
on the verge of civil war.   the verge of civil war.
2   People thought at first (that) ⟶ The President *was* at first   **a, b**
the President had been   *thought to have been*
murdered.   *murdered.*
3   One can't see a soul in the ⟶ There *isn't* a soul *to be seen* in   c
streets.   the streets.

Explanation

a   Instead of an active construction with *say, thought* etc. where *they* (1) or
people (2) refer to no one in particular, we sometimes, especially in written
English, use a passive construction with the full infinitive (see **17Be**). In
these constructions the infinitive itself may (2) or may not be (1) in the
passive.

b   Note (2) that the perfect infinitive (*to have been murdered*) is used only when
we wish to refer to time **before** that of the introductory verb (*thought*). This
time difference shows in the active as a tense difference (see **10Ag**).

c   There is also a particular type of construction (3), using *is/was* etc. to
correspond with *can/could* in the active (see **10Dd**), where the passive
infinitive is always used.

Exercise 1

Complete the sentence introduced in *italics* so that it has the same meaning as
the first sentence, as shown in the Examples.
1   People have known Willie stay up working in his office all night./*Willie* . . .
2   They say Willie's father was a chronic work addict too./*Willie's father* . . .
3   Unfortunately we cannot find his secretary anywhere./*Unfortunately his
secretary is* . . .
4   They say they saw her last in the Red Lion Hotel./*She* . . .
5   They know for certain she was at the meeting./*She* . . .
6   They found she was a very conscientious worker./*She* . . .
7   Last night they stopped Ken on the motorway and made him show his
licence./*Last night Ken* . . .
8   It appears that they did not detain him./*He* . . .
9   They say that both Helen and Sheila were with him at the time./*Both* . . .
10   Some people think he is a dangerous driver./*He* . . .

11 They believe he has had his licence endorsed twice./*He* ...
12 Many people consider that Willie's father was one of the best artists of his generation./*Willie's father* ...
13 It seems that most of the art critics ignored him./*He* ...
14 People said that he had insulted the critics in some way or other./*He* ...
15 Can one trust such people?/*Are* ... ?
16 They presumed the man was waiting for them outside./*The man* ...
17 They could not see him anywhere./*He was* ...
18 They should have made him pay the extra cost himself./*He* ...
19 One is not meant to use that kind of paint on walls./*That* ...
20 One can seldom find real craftsmen nowadays./*Real craftsmen are* ...

Exercise 2

Oral practice (13A, 13B): Without looking at the book yourself, get someone to say the following to you and then repeat in the passive what you have heard, taking care to keep the same tense. Make *she* the subject of each sentence.

Someone should advise her to apply for the job.	⟶ She should be advised to apply for the job.
Have they rejected her application?	⟶ Has she had her application rejected?

1 They're considering her for the job.
2 They may interview her tomorrow.
3 They won't tell her the result until next week.
4 They're not likely to give her the job.
5 Did they pay her last month?
6 Do they usually pay her by cheque?
7 No one's paid her anything yet.
8 They'll tell her what to do.
9 Someone should have explained it to her already.
10 They made her look pretty foolish.
11 People were talking about her behind her back.
12 They say she did her work carelessly.
13 They saw her running out of the room.
14 Someone had insulted her.
15 Someone had even pulled her hair.
16 They're treating her disgracefully.
17 They've cancelled her sabbatical leave.
18 They're going to cut her salary.
19 They're going to make her apologise to the Principal.
20 They should have allowed her the chance to explain herself.

14 Inversion of subject and verb

Introductory note: Subject-verb inversion occurs as standard in questions. Otherwise its use in English is largely optional, its purpose being to alter emphasis within the sentence, which may in turn result in heightened dramatic effect. As an advanced learner you should try to acquire the additional variety and power of expression that comes from this optional inversion. (You will at the same time be safeguarding yourself against its popularity in some English examination questions.) It is introduced by certain lead words, which are classified and dealt with in **14A**. Section **14B** deals with some of the lead words that introduce established sentence patterns (*No sooner ... than* etc.).

14A Types of lead word

Examples

STANDARD FORM		INVERTED FORM	
1 My friend Sherlock Holmes (the famous detective) has *never* been so intrepid as he was in the case of the Green Face.	⟶	*Never* has my friend Sherlock Holmes (the famous detective) been so intrepid as he was in the case of the Green Face.	**a**
2 His powers of deduction have *never* been better used *either*.	⟶	*Nor/Neither* have his powers of deduction ever been better used.	**a**
3 I *well* remember the night we lay in wait for the Green Face.	⟶	*Well* do I remember the night we lay in wait for the Green Face.	**d**
4 I have had reason to be grateful for my umbrella *many* times, and so it was then.	⟶	*Many* is the time I have had reason to be grateful for my umbrella, and so it was then.	**d**
5 For we had *hardly* hidden ourselves among the bushes when it began to rain.	⟶	For *hardly* had we hidden ourselves among the bushes when it began to rain.	**b**
6 I have *seldom* known the hours pass so slowly.	⟶	*Seldom* have I known the hours pass so slowly.	**b**

155

7   It was *only* when a cold grey ⟶ *Only* when a cold grey dawn   **b**
    dawn had begun to break in   had begun to break in the
    the east that the fearful   east did the fearful spectre
    spectre appeared.   appear.

8   I was *so* terrified/My terror ⟶ *So* terrified was I/*Such* was   **c**
    was *such* that I tried to hide   my terror that I tried to hide
    under my umbrella.   under my umbrella.

9   Silently and mysteriously, ⟶ Silently and mysteriously,   **h**
    and only a few yards away, a   and only a few yards away,
    face of the most horrible   *there* came into view a face of
    appearance and ghastly   the most horrible appearance
    colour imaginable came into   and ghastly colour
    view.   imaginable.

10 (none)   'Here comes our foe,   **f**
                                    Watson,' whispered my
                                    companion, drawing his
                                    sword-stick, 'and there he
                                    goes!'

11 With these words Holmes ⟶ With these words *up* sprang   **f, j**
    sprang *up* and lunged – and   Holmes and lunged – and *pop*
    the Green Face went *pop*!   went the Green Face!

12 The miserable rubber ⟶ *At our feet* lay the miserable   **g**
    remnant of the terror that   rubber remnant of the terror
    had haunted Abbey Grange   that had haunted Abbey
    for years lay *at our feet*!   Grange for years!

13 'If you (*should*) ever see the ⟶ '*Should* you ever see the   **l**
    Green Face again,' said   Green Face again,' said
    Holmes grimly, sheathing his   Holmes grimly, sheathing his
    sword, 'you'll know what to   sword, 'you'll know what to
    do.'   do.'

14 If you saw/*were* to see the ⟶ *Were* you to see the Green   **m**
    Green Face, would you know   Face, would you know what
    what to do?   to do?

15 If I *had* known it was only a ⟶ *Had* I known it was only a   **n**
    balloon I would of course   balloon I would of course
    have used my umbrella.   have used my umbrella.

Explanation

LEAD WORDS, TYPE I (Examples 1–8):

a negative adverbials like *never* (1)*, *nor* or *neither* (2), *not since* (*last March*
   etc.), *not for (ten years* etc.), *on no account* and *not only* or *no sooner* (see
   14Ba);

* Note that *never* as a lead word is used in an emphatic, total sense. As a non-emphatic substitute for
not in a sentence like 'We expected to see Willie at the party but he never came' it could not be used
as a lead word.

b near-negative (= restrictive) adverbs such as *scarcely* or *hardly* (5), *rarely* or *seldom* (6), or *only* when used with other words to complete a phrase like *only by working hard* or to introduce a clause (*when . . . break*) as in Example 7;

c *so* or *such* (8) used with *that* to express result (**3Ac,d**), and *so* meaning *too* as in '*So do I* (= I do too)';

d a small number of adjectives and adverbs like *well* (3), *many* (4) and *little* (**14Ba**), restricted to certain expressions.

e After this type of lead word, inversion
   i always occurs;
  ii is of the same form as it is in questions, involving only the verb *to be* and the auxiliaries *do, have* etc.;
 iii occurs in all tenses;
  iv involves both nouns (1, 2, 4, 7) and pronouns (3, 5, 6, 8).

LEAD WORDS, TYPE II (Examples 9–12):

f adverbs indicating position or movement like *here* (10), *up* (11);

g phrases indicating position or movement like *at our feet* (12);

h the word *there*, which, as well as being used in the familiar *there is/are*, can combine with a few verbs of position and movement in expressions like *there stands a monument on a hill, there came into view* (9), but which unlike the adverb *there* is not stressed (compare 'there **came** into **view**' with 'and **there** he **goes**' in Example 10);

j one or two words, expressing noise like *bang* or *pop* (11), used generally with the verb *go*.

k After this type of lead word, inversion
   i does not always occur (*up sprang Holmes* or *up Holmes sprang*);
  ii involves the main verb, which usually corresponds in meaning to the lead word, that is to say is a verb of position (12) or movement (9–11);
 iii normally occurs only in the simple present, past and future tenses;
  iv involves (see Example 10) nouns like *foe* but not pronouns like *he* (**not** 'and there goes he').
There is an exception to the last rule when *there* or *here* is used with the verb *to be*:
    Here am I, slaving away, while you're doing nothing!

LEAD WORDS, TYPE III (Examples 13–15):

l *should* (13), which, as we have seen (**1Db**), may be used in certain conditional sentences, can act as a lead word, eliminating *if*;

m the subjunctive *were* (14), which may occur in certain conditional sentences (**1Db**), can act as a lead word, eliminating *if*;

n the auxiliary *had* (15), which occurs in certain conditional sentences (1Dc), can act as a lead word, eliminating *if*.

Exercise

Rewrite as many as possible of the following sentences using subject-verb inversion based upon the lead words they may contain or (see Examples 2, 9, 13, 14) that may be added. Leave any sentences that you do not think can be rewritten in this way as they are.

1 The starter's gun went bang and the runners went off at a good pace.
2 They'd scarcely covered the first lap when the leading runner, Roger Baines by name, slipped and fell.
3 A runner called Plunger was behind him at the time.
4 Although he tried hard, Roger Baines never made up the distance he had lost.
5 At the start of the last lap he was last; our friend Ken was second from last.
6 The time had come for Ken to make one of his famous sprints, so there we were, cheering our heads off!
7 The rest of the spectators sat around the track, silent but expectant.
8 We had hardly started cheering when Ken responded: he shot forward, like a bolt from the blue!
9 I well remember Plunger's look when Ken passed him ten metres from the tape!
10 I've rarely seen anyone judge his final sprint so well.

11 The thieves had hardly got round the corner when the engine of their car stalled.
12 They jumped out and ran off up the street.
13 Just at that moment a couple of police cars drove up.
14 Windows flew open all along the street and a lot of heads popped out to watch the chase.
15 A church stands at the top of the street; one of the fugitives darted into it.
16 Nothing like this had ever happened in our street before.
17 If I hadn't seen it with my own eyes I wouldn't have believed it.

18 The Blenkinsops' thirtieth wedding anniversary was being celebrated at Blenkinsop Hall.
19 Lady Blenkinsop sat at the head of the table, Sir James at the foot.
20 'I haven't eaten a dinner as good as this since my wedding day,' said Sir James to himself.
21 In replying to the guests' toast, he said: 'A man begins truly to appreciate the qualities of a wife like mine only after thirty years of marriage.'
22 'If I had another chance,' he said, eyeing his wife, 'I'd choose the same woman.'
23 The said woman was so overcome with emotion that two large tears rolled down her cheeks.

24 A loud guffaw came from the middle of the table. 'There goes my son,' thought Sir James. 'Disorderly and disrespectful as usual. **He** mustn't be allowed to make a speech on any account!'

25 A vision of his son Toby in twenty years' time, idle and useless, presiding over the death of the Blenkinsop family, suddenly appeared before Sir James's eyes.

26 'The social pressures to make one smoke are so strong that few can resist them.

27 'I have been made tragically aware of this fact many times.'

28 I was so amazed by what I had heard that I stood there speechless.

29 I hadn't heard such nonsense for a long time.

30 If you ever hear anyone say the same sort of thing, don't believe them for a moment.

31 'I shall never, never trust a man again!' cried Helen.

32 'One can have peace in this life only by avoiding them altogether,' she said.

33 'A truer word has seldom been spoken,' I said. 'But who wants peace?'

14B Established sentence patterns

Not only . . . but
No sooner . . . than
Little . . . think/know/realise etc.

Examples

1 *As soon as* I was in the shower someone must have entered my hotel bedroom. ⟶ *No sooner* was I in the shower *than* someone must have entered my hotel bedroom.

2 I had *no idea*, as I dried myself, what a shock was in store for me. ⟶ *Little* did I *know*, as I dried myself, what a shock was in store for me.

3 All my money had disappeared, *and* my clothes had gone *as well*. ⟶ *Not only* had all my money disappeared, *but* my clothes had gone (as well).

Explanation

a These lead words (*Not only* etc.) combine with other words (*but* etc.) in effective and relatively common subject-verb inversions that are worth practising. Note, however, that *No sooner . . . than* (1) is not used for future events ('Immediately my passport is ready I'm leaving') and that *Little . . .* (2) is seldom used for pleasant events ('She had no idea she had won all that money').

b *Hardly/Scarcely* (**14Ab**) *. . . when* is an alternative, but perhaps less forceful, sentence pattern to *No sooner . . . than*.

Exercise

Where possible rewrite the following using the appropriate form of inversion shown in the Examples. Leave as they are any sentences like those mentioned in the Explanation as unsuitable for inversion.

1 As soon as I come home in the evening I switch on the television.
2 I watch it all evening and I have it on for breakfast as well.
3 As soon as I have time I'm going to get rid of the damned thing.

4 As soon as they made the announcement share prices began to rise.
5 Share prices rose and the dollar recovered as well.
6 Of course we had had no idea we were going to make a fortune.

7 Robert's father owns half the land in the village and has bought three small hotels as well.
8 Immediately a hotel in the area comes up for sale he buys it.
9 And as soon as he buys it he starts making money out of it.

10 Zena gave him the use of her flat and lent him her car as well.
11 She had no idea he was a man on the run from the police.
12 Immediately you have any news of him get in touch with her.
13 He may pinch her car and he may ransack her flat into the bargain.
14 We never thought he was that sort of fellow.

15 It was a long way, and it was a rough, winding road as well.
16 Immediately we got to the hotel we collapsed, dead tired, into our beds.
17 We had no idea that there was worse in store for us the next day.
18 Just after we left it started to come down in buckets.
19 There was now extensive flooding as well as a bad surface to contend with.
20 We little suspected when we started our holiday that it would be like this!

15 Dependent prepositions

Introductory note: The prepositions that are dependent on certain words are, together with phrasal verbs (16), particularly the problem of the advanced learner. They form one of the last barriers to mastery of the language, which is why they receive a lot of attention here. There are altogether 300 words with their dependent prepositions in this section. How many you know already you can establish the first time you do the Exercises. Those you do not know you can learn with the help of study lists 17F, before repeating the Exercises until you are satisfied with your knowledge.

Exercises

For each number provide a preposition, but before doing so run your eye over each group of sentences in order to grasp the general meaning and context.

1

Sheila is very strict (1) the children in her class. She is particularly strict (2) punctuality. However, her relationship (3) the children is a happy one.

We think that Brenda's system of office filing is a great advance (4) the old system. We should benefit a lot (5) it. Yes, it definitely has a lot of advantages (6) the old system.

I can't possibly agree (7) your demands. Unless you are prepared to compromise we'll never be able to agree (8) a sensible way to deal with the problem of your monthly allowance. Why can't you learn to agree (9) me sometimes – especially (9) my ideas for your future? They are in your interest, you know.

Nowadays there is no advantage (10) being a woman. In the old days a clever woman could take advantage (11) being female. But now the rules of social conduct apply (12) men and women alike.

Denis is always boasting (13) his success as a salesman. His behaviour is typical (14) the social upstart. He is quite incapable (15) showing a bit of modesty.

Things have changed considerably (16) the worse, I am afraid. There has been a serious deterioration (17) the economic situation. The key (18) recovery lies in our export trade.

Ken has been charged by the police (19) dangerous driving. He has pleaded guilty (20) driving without due care and attention. He says he is not guilty (21) dangerous driving.

The man confessed (22) stealing food, pleading that his children had been suffering (23) malnutrition and might well have died (24) starvation.

Many people say nuclear power stations are a potential danger (25) the local population and have little confidence (26) the so-called safety measures. They are very concerned (27) what might happen in an emergency.

These revelations have done a lot of damage (28) Sir James's political reputation. It is difficult to be critical, though, (29) what he did. Everyone is very curious (30) what he will do next.

2

Marilyn's father is a dealer (1) antiques. He has a great reputation (2) honesty. He is an expert (3) eighteenth-century porcelain.

Helen was very jealous (4) her sister's popularity. Her sister was very popular (5) the teachers at school. She impressed them (6) her work and her personality.

What are this year's figures (7) road accidents? There has been a slight increase (8) the total number of casualties. But there have been fewer actual deaths (9) road accidents this year.

The members of the local garrison are confined (10) barracks during the week. But at the weekends the town swarms (11) soldiers. I am glad to say that on the whole they make a good impression (12) the inhabitants.

Toby and his father differ a lot (13) their views on life. They have very different attitudes (14) work. Toby disapproves strongly (15) working any harder than he feels like working.

We should not discourage Helen (16) being an actress. We would only prejudice her (17) us. And it certainly would not cure her (18) stage fever.

I'm very surprised (19) your doing a thing like that. Personally, I never interfere (20) other people's affairs. And so I'm rather disappointed (21) your behaviour.

'Denis objects strongly (22) being called a nutcase. He absolutely insists (23) an apology. An apology might be preferable (24) a fight.'
'I never called him a nutcase; I never even hinted (25) it. Denis is famous (26) his wildly inaccurate statements. He has apparently fooled you (27) believing one of them.'

Sheila need have no doubts (28) passing the exam. She can be absolutely confident (29) success. I have complete faith (30) her ability to pass.

3

Sheila is very good (1) handling children. Yes, she is indeed very good (2) children. What is the secret of her appeal (3) children?

It's a wonderful opportunity (4) Marilyn. One doesn't often get such a good opportunity (5) seeing the world. She shouldn't miss the chance (6) a trip like that.

That TV serial they showed last year was an insult (7) one's intelligence. I had every intention (8) writing and protesting (9) the producer about it, but never had the time.

Helen is always fishing (10) compliments. I am fed up (11) paying her compliments. Personally I am not in the habit (12) complimenting people.

There's going to be an improvement (13) the weather. The weather has a great influence (14) my mood. There's a definite relationship (15) my mood and the weather.

My new secretary is very pretty but is sadly lacking (16) powers of concentration. She seems to be unable to concentrate (17) anything for more than two minutes at a time. I shall clearly have to deal (18) the important matters myself and leave her to deal (18) the visitors.

Marilyn has been ill in bed for three days (19) influenza. There is little hope (20) her getting up tomorrow. It all depends (21) what the doctor says.

I am full of admiration (22) Sheila's mother. Her life has been one continual struggle (23) illness or poverty. But she has never surrendered (24) despair.

Zena feeds her alligator once a week (25) raw eggs and scraps. There is little likelihood (26) its getting fat on that. Perhaps one day it will avenge itself (27) its owner.

The War of Independence ended in victory for the USA (28) the British. In 1812 the USA itself declared war (29) Britain. What are your views (30) British policy at the time?

4

I hear they suspect Denis (1) taking the money. Are you yourself suspicious (2) Denis? I can't say that I would have trusted him (3) all that cash.

Ken says he will make another attempt (4) beating the 400-metre record. In fact he is making an attempt today (5) the record. He has gained enormously (6) self-confidence, you know.

The country is very poor (7) natural resources. It is trying to become self-sufficient (8) food. The Government has had finally to decide (9) a definite agricultural policy.

You seem to be terribly envious (10) your sister's wealth. There's little point (11) being envious. Money isn't essential (12) happiness.

I would like to congratulate you (13) your cooking. You have certainly succeeded (14) turning out a wonderful meal. You'd have no difficulty (15) finding a first-class job as a chef.

Robert says he is not going to sacrifice his ambitions as a footballer (16) a safe, conventional career. Future security, he says, is no substitute (17) present success. He adds that the great thing about football is that it is independent (18) wealth or social status; anyone can join in.

Ken's gaining (19) us rapidly in his Bangmobile. He has the reputation (20) being a reckless driver. I'm going to try and prevent him (21) passing.

Denis has virtually accused me (22) cheating him. He says I cheated him (23) two hundred pounds in a business deal. I take the strongest exception (24) his accusation.

Sir James succeeded (25) the hereditary title in 1969. His father died (26) injuries received in a road accident. Although Sir James takes pride (27) his ancestry, he is no snob.

Once a year in the British navy the officers wait (28) the seamen at table. This custom seems to be good (29) discipline, not bad. Is the custom peculiar (30) the British navy?

5

My wife now usually compliments me (1) my taste (2) clothes. She is very particular (3) my appearance, which she says is a great improvement (4) what it was.

Sir James is always very honest (5) his dealings (6) us. He is always very honest (7) all of us. There is never any question (8) a limit being set (9) what he tells us.

Am I eligible (10) this insurance scheme? Would it insure me fully (11) illness? Personally, I think this insurance scheme is superior (12) anything else on the market. Do you know (13) any better?

What was Sheila so angry (14) yesterday? She was angry (15) Ken (16) keeping her waiting. She was also angry (17) being told to be more patient in future.

Sheila's sister has grown (18) a lovely girl. For a moment I mistook her (19) Sheila herself. Then I noticed how she differs (20) Sheila. For one thing, I don't think that Sheila's sister has grown much (21) wisdom.

Sir James ended his speech (22) rather an extravagant attack (23) the Government. He said nothing was safe (24) the Government's pernicious influence. He blamed it (25) all our economic ills. He even seemed to blame the bad weather (26) it too.

Marilyn has made herself familiar (27) modern electronic gadgetry. She has equipped her office (28) the latest (29) electronic calculators. In fact she has made her office (30) a kind of laboratory.

6

Zena is devoted (1) her pet alligator and says she would never part (2) it. Personally I do not know what she sees (3) the creature. It seems to be concerned only (4) eating and sleeping.

Denis is never very free (5) his own money but he makes free (5) other people's. The other day he helped himself (6) most of my cigars. I have a good mind to charge him (7) them.

Willie seldom takes people (8) his confidence, but last week he confided (9) me. He told me he was keen (10) Sheila.

The snow storm resulted (11) most people being late at work. Sheila excused her children (12) being late for class that morning. And she excused them (13) attending afternoon school.

I am disappointed (14) Sir James. He says he is entering (15) some sort of political agreement with the Liberals. I am opposed (16) any deal of that kind.

Helen said she was now mercifully free (17) Denis. What did she mean (18) that strange remark? It sounds as if their flirtation has ended (19) a row.

Sir James won the last Parliamentary election (20) only a hundred and seven votes. He says his party will soon be forced by circumstances (21) an alliance with the Liberals. He says both parties could profit (22) the experience.

At one time Helen was thinking (23) becoming a model like Zena. Now she is interested (24) the stage. In any case she has a taste (25) the bright lights.

Contrary (26) many people's expectations, Lady Blenkinsop's farm is proving a success. This year she is planting one field (27) maize, and is turning two more (28) a vineyard. The area for grazing is being reduced (29) half, (30) a little over twelve hectares.

7

Sir James said we should guard (1) any restrictions (2) our freedom. Yet he did not mention that many of us are threatened (3) the loss of our jobs. The threat (4) unemployment is a threat (5) our freedom.

Sir James's son Toby is certainly living (6) his reputation as a ne'er-do-well. He lives entirely (7) his wits and (8) credit. They say he is living (9) the day his father dies.

What she said about Toby was news (10) us. She obviously had a very low opinion (11) him. I think she should have kept her opinions (12) the subject (13) herself. There were one or two people there who were highly indignant (14) her remarks.

We had heard that Lady Blenkinsop had been robbed (15) her jewels. So we listened (16) news of the robbery on the radio. And we watched (17) it on television too. But no one mentioned it on either.

You say we are a country rich (18) tradition. Surely that is true (19) most countries. What is important (20) us is that we should remain true (21) our best traditions.

I am not convinced (22) the general value of a university education. It is clearly an advantage (23) some, but its benefits (24) others can be very limited. What is important is that it should not be restricted (25) those who can afford it.

Helen is greedy (26) praise. Mind you, I don't hold this (27) her, because I'm fully aware (28) the difficulties she has had to face in her life. I really feel quite friendly and well disposed (29) her. Feelings of animosity are foreign (30) my nature.

8

Sheila is applying (1) a headmistress's post. She may well get it, since her aunt has influence (2) the educational authorities. Also Sheila is well qualified (3) the post in her own right.

The international relief organisations have appealed (4) the public (5) aid (6) the victims of the earthquake. They hope to provide everyone (7) adequate shelter by winter. To allow the homeless to remain in tents is to condemn them (8) death. One naturally has a lot of sympathy (9) the people in their terrible plight. I shall certainly contribute (10) the fund.

Martyrs are people who suffer (11) their beliefs and sometimes die (12) them. They are not prepared to bargain (13) their persecutors (14) their lives. Nor do they expect people to have pity (15) them. There is therefore little danger (16) the world becoming crowded (17) martyrs.

Some people think that universal, formal education is an obstacle (18) an individual's full mental development. Others think that without it there is no hope (19) society's future. No one can afford to be indifferent (20) the problem.

According to Darwin's Theory of natural selection there is a struggle (21) survival (22) individuals and (22) species. It seems to me that *Homo sapiens* has to struggle mainly (23) his own nature. There are times when his prospects of survival do not look too good (24) me.

Sheila is noted (25) her success (26) young children. She cares (27) them as individuals, not as playthings. They do not have to conform (28) some preconceived notion of what a child should be. Sheila devotes a lot of her own time (29) the children at her school, especially (29) those deprived (30) parental affection.

9

I am usually in complete sympathy (1) Sir James's views, but you cannot expect me to feel sympathetic (2) him when he speaks (3) wishing to lead his party (4) an alliance with the Liberals.

I do not approve (5) his son's recent activities either. Do you know that Toby Blenkinsop's debts now amount (6) over twenty thousand pounds? I'm sorry I consented (7) his using my name in a job application.

When I come home from the office I change (8) casual clothes. I then feel free (9) the restraints of my working life. My mood, in fact, changes (10) the clothes I wear.

Ken is competing (11) some of our best local runners (12) the Athletic Club Trophy. I have warned him (13) the dangers involved (14) competing (15) this event, as some of the runners will resort (16) all sorts of dirty tricks in order to win. In particular I have warned him (17) a fellow called Plunger who specialises (18) jabbing his opponents with his spiked shoes. I carry a scar that resulted (19) that fellow's attentions.

Zena says that if one is patient (20) alligators and does not interfere (21) them or their habits they behave very well. She says they are very sensitive (22) changes (23) the environment. I should have thought that Zena's alligator would find her flat a great change (24) the swamps of Florida.

Willie is an architect. At present he is working (25) a town development scheme. He works very hard (26) his job and seems to find great pleasure (27) puzzling (28) the problems of his profession. Sometimes he is so occupied (29) his work that he is scarcely conscious (30) the passage of time.

10

Willie beat Ken (1) tennis the other day. Ken is now determined to have his revenge (2) Willie (3) his defeat, and says he will show no mercy (4) Willie in their next match. Willie, for his part, says he will have no mercy (5) Ken either. He says a good racket is essential (6) victory, and has fitted his (7) a special grip.

As a public figure, a Member of Parliament is responsible not only (8) his constituents but (8) the public at large (9) his conduct. I am glad to say that Sir

James is an MP who has never been concerned (10) any scandal at all.

Robert has now decided (11) university and football in favour of the latter. He says he can't share his time or his enthusiasm for football (12) anything else. It's impossible to reason (13) him (14) the subject, as he has clearly made up his mind (15) it. Robert's father, who until recently was ignorant (16) his son's decision, seethed (17) anger when informed (18) it.

A few people may criticise modern domestic gadgetry, but most of us are highly satisfied (19) it. Things like a washing machine give relief (20) drudgery, so that we can attend more (21) our own interests, while television and hi-fi can provide the intellectual stimulation that is often missing (22) the daily round.

Since it is important (23) many parents that their children should be provided (24) after their own deaths, a large part of their time is spent (25) finding ways round the inheritance laws. They do not see why they should not invest (26) their children's future if they want to.

The firm that supplies us (27) nuts and bolts say that they are having production difficulties and that we must allow (28) considerable delays (29) delivery when we order. Is there any possibility (30) our getting them anywhere else?

16 Phrasal verbs

Introductory note: Phrasal verbs are a vital, expressive part of the language, particularly of the colloquial, everyday sort. A good knowledge of them goes a long way towards being a good knowledge of English itself. Their grammar is dealt with in **16A**. The Exercises in **16B** give further practice in this grammar while aiming principally to extend your vocabulary of phrasal verbs and of their more formal synonyms (which are mainly Latin-derived). The study lists in **17G** will help you to this end.

16A   Type, meaning and word order

Examples

PHRASAL VERBS: WORD ORDER	TYPE		MEANING **k**
The boy who (1) *brings round* our newspapers/*brings* our newspapers *round* was run over by a car when he was	ADVERBIAL	**a, c**	delivers
(2) *bringing* one *round* for me and knocked unconscious. Luckily I was able to give first	ADVERBIAL	**a, d, f**	delivering
aid and (3) *bring* the lad *round* before the ambulance arrived.	ADVERBIAL (SPLIT)	**a, h**	revive
The Government has started (4) *bringing in* new tax regulations. I'm glad it isn't	ADVERBIAL	**a, c**	introducing
(5) *bringing* them all *in* at once, because it gives me time to	ADVERBIAL	**a, d, e**	introducing
think of ways of (6) *getting round* them. Most people feel	PREPOSITIONAL	**b, g, j**	evading
like me; if there's any further tax increase, they just won't (7) *put up with* it.	PREPOSITIONAL	**b, g, j**	tolerate

Explanation

a In its narrow definition, a PHRASAL VERB (1–5) is a verb consisting of a VERB (*bring*) and an ADVERBIAL PARTICLE (*round, in*).

b In its broader definition, as used here, a phrasal verb (6, 7) is also a VERB (*get, put*) which combines with a PREPOSITION (*round*), or with an ADVERB (*up*) AND A PREPOSITION (*with*), to form a phrase which, like many adverbial phrasal verbs, has a meaning of its own, distinct from that of the separate words.

c In the adverbial type of phrasal verb, the particle may come either before or after a noun object (1), although it usually precedes a noun object when this consists of several words (4).

d However, the adverbial particle always comes *after* the object when this is a personal pronoun such as *me, it, them* (5) or the indefinite pronoun *one*, standing for a noun used with *a/an* (2).

e Although it precedes nouns, *all* (5) directly follows personal pronouns and so must also precede an adverbial particle, unlike *all of*, which can follow it: 'I'm glad it isn't bringing in all of them at once.'

f Similarly, *one* (2) as a NUMBER can follow the adverbial particle: 'How many bottles does the milkman deliver? – He usually brings round one.'

g In a prepositional phrasal verb the preposition always comes **before** the object, whether or not this is a pronoun (6) and whether or not it is combined with an adverbial particle (*up*) in a three-word phrasal verb (7).

h Conversely, there are some adverbial phrasal verbs in which the particle **always** follows the object, even if it is a noun (3). This can help to distinguish it from a similar phrasal verb of a different meaning (1, 2) in which the particle may, as usual, precede the object. These split phrasal verbs are identified in lists **17G** by the use of *sb./sth.* (= *somebody/something*): *bring round = deliver; bring sb. round = revive sb.*

j Distinguishing between adverbial and prepositional phrasal verbs so as to know where to put a personal pronoun is not difficult. For one thing, **all** three-word phrasal verbs (*put up with* etc.) are prepositional; for another, the prepositions that occur most in two-word prepositional verbs (*at, into, through*) rarely or never occur as particles in adverbial verbs (see **17G**).

k Many phrasal verbs have Latin-derived synonyms like the verbs *deliver, revive, introduce, evade, tolerate* shown in the Examples, and a good way of increasing your knowledge of English is to learn the correspondence between the more colloquial phrasal verb and its more formal or literary counterpart (see **16B**). Note, however, that this correspondence can depend on the context. Thus in the Examples (4, 5) *introduce* is *bring in*, but to *introduce* person X to person Y is **not** to *bring in* X to Y.

Exercises

Read or write out each of the following sentences **twice**, first with the NOUN OBJECT, then with the PRONOUN OBJECT, thus:

Has your secretary fixed up (the interview/it) yet?

⟶ 1 Has your secretary fixed up the interview/fixed the interview up yet?
2 Has your secretary fixed it up yet?

I take back (all the rude things I said/them all).

⟶ 1 I take back all the rude things I said.
2 I take them all back.

I wish I could get out of (going to his wedding/it).

⟶ 1 I wish I could get out of going to his wedding.
2 I wish I could get out of it.

1

1 As an actor Zena's father *looked down on* (ordinary mortals/them).
2 He *put on* (a superior air/one) to impress people.
3 But it didn't *take in* (people/them).
4 You must admit he was a marvellous mimic; he could *take off* (some of our public figures/them) brilliantly.
5 His wife *gave up* (her own career/it) for his sake.
6 He *got through* (all her money/it all) in no time.
7 She had *put by* (quite a tidy sum/it) for a rainy day.
8 Why on earth did she *put up with* (the man/him)?
9 She was afraid of *letting down* (her husband/him) at the peak of his career.
10 She *turned down* (all offers of help/them all).
11 She *laughed off* (one outrageous episode after another/them all).
12 I can't *make out* (why she did so/it).
13 He never *owned up to* (treating her badly/it).
14 Well, he certainly didn't *get away with* (the way he behaved/it) in the end.
15 Why are you always *running down* (the man/him)?
16 You don't expect me to *stick up for* (the man/him), do you?
17 I think you *make up* (most of these stories/them).
18 Zena will *bear out* (what I've said/it).
19 She *takes after* (her father/him) in many ways.
20 I gently *pointed out* (the fact/it) to her.

2

1 They want to *do away with* (the British monarchy/it).
2 They *look on* (the monarchy/it) as outdated.
3 They aim also to *bring down* (the Government/it).
4 They'd like to *hold up* (this Government's legislative programme/it).

5 They hope to *win over* (all the workers/them all).
6 They say that if they won power they'd *let off* (the workers/them) their taxes.
7 They'd *wipe out* (all opposition/it all).
8 They'd *take over* (all the mass media/them all).
9 They'd *try out* (their new social system/it) on us.
10 They don't realise how long it takes to *build up* (a social system/one).
11 You can't just *think out* (a social system/one) overnight and expect it to work in the morning.
12 People should think more than twice before *setting about* (the task of reforming society/it).
13 But they mean to *carry out* (their so-called reforms/them).
14 They've *drawn up* (a political manifesto/one).
15 Their stated aim is to *set up* (a republic/one).
16 They say they've *worked out* (how to do it/it).
17 Now, they say, they're *getting down to* (the practical details/them).
18 They threaten in the next election to *put up* (a candidate/one) in each constituency.
19 If they do that, we can't *rule out* (the possibility of their winning a seat or two in Parliament/it).
20 Well, well! I don't believe a word you say! But as Home Secretary I'd better *look into* (the matter/it).

16B Meaning and use of selected verbs

Exercises

For each number in brackets replace the words in *italics* by one of the phrasal verbs given at the top in each Exercise. The same verb can sometimes be used more than once in an Exercise, and sometimes there is a choice of verbs. Follow **16Ac–j** in the matter of word order, remembering that the phrasal verbs you are asked to use are both adverbial (**16Aa**) and prepositional (**16Ab**). Remember (see **16**, Introductory note) that in making these substitutions you are changing the style from a formal to a less formal and more natural one. If you have much difficulty with the Exercises it is advisable to spend time on study lists **17G**, aided by a dictionary, and to return to the Exercises later. ·

1 VERBS WITH *about, after, at, away*

bring about	set about	fly at	die away
come about	take after	get at	do away with
hang about	drive at	go at	get away with

'Robert has been saying that exams are unfair and should be (1) *abolished*. He won't (2) *avoid severe criticism for* a remark like that in his family. I don't know what's (3) *caused* this sudden change of attitude.'
'His attitude hasn't changed; he's never liked hard work. He (4) *resembles* his mother in that respect.'
'How do we (5) *take steps towards* reforming him, then?'

'Charles was on his way home from school yesterday when a dog (6) *attacked* him and took a piece out of his trousers.'
'He was no doubt (7) *loitering* in some backstreet.'
'What are you (8) *implying*? That it was Charles's fault?'
'Not necessarily. But I know from experience that man-against-dog situations usually (9) *arise* because the man interferes with the dog and not vice versa.'

The conductor raised his baton and conversation (10) *became fainter and then ceased*; there was silence in the concert hall.

2 VERBS WITH *down*

bring down	get down to	let sb. down	run down
cut down	go down	look down on	tone down
die down	hand down	put down	turn down
get sb. down	lay down	put sth. down to	

Toby Blenkinsop often (1) *strongly criticises* the aristocracy and appears to (2) *despise* the titled people he knows. Sir James Blenkinsop, who cherishes the title which has been (3) *transmitted* from father to son for many generations, feels that Toby has (4) *failed* the family.

'There's a general air of gloom in this firm that is beginning to (5) *depress* me.'
'It shouldn't. The management's directive (6) *stipulates* quite clearly what we should do.'
'I don't see how we can possibly (7) *reduce* our overhead expenses.'
'We can if we (8) *work really hard at* the task. I (9) *attribute* our past failure *to* lack of real determination.'

The railwaymen's strike could have (10) *caused* the Government *to fall*. The Transport Minister's remark that their revolt should have been (11) *suppressed* at once (12) *was* not well *received* [change passive to active], with the result that they (13) *rejected* the last wage offer. However, now that the Minister has (14) *moderated* his criticism of the railwaymen, the excitement has (15) *abated* and agreement may soon be reached.

3 VERBS WITH *by, in, into*

get by	stand by	call (in) at	check in
put by	bring in	call (in) on	drop in at

drop in on	go in for	put in	come into
fall in with	join in	run sb. in	go into
get in with	keep in with	take in	look into
give in	let sb. in for	take sb. in	run into

I don't think you (1) *really understood* all she said. Amongst other things she said that you should (2) *report your presence* at the flight desk by six-thirty.

Why don't you (3) *submit* your insurance claim at once? Otherwise you may (4) *involve* yourself *in* extra expense.

I shouldn't (5) *yield* to the child's entreaties if I were you. If the other children are playing games, she should be made to (6) *participate*. If you take a firm line with her, I'll (7) *support* you.

I try as a matter of principle to (8) *remain on good terms with* my relatives, and so sometimes I find myself (9) *agreeing to* the maddest of plans. The other day, for instance, I (10) *happened to meet* my cousin Georgina, and have now accepted an invitation to go pot-holing with her.

Our solicitor is (11) *investigating* the matter of our late grandfather's will. His affluent life style had led us to think that we would (12) *inherit* a fortune, but it is now clear that we were (13) *deceived*, because by the time he died he had (14) *incurred* debts [use singular *debt*]. He should have been able to (15) *manage* easily on his income, and even to (16) *save* some of it, because his investments alone (17) *yielded* more than £15,000 a year. However, in his middle age he unfortunately (18) *became friendly with* a pretty wild set who (19) *had as their hobbies* fast cars and fast women. My parents told me that one Sunday they were expecting him to (20) *visit* them but that on the way he got (21) *arrested* for speeding and had to (22) *visit* the police station instead.

4 VERBS WITH *off*

break off	get off	let sb. off	show off
bring off	give off	make off	strike off
call off	go off	put off	take off
come off	laugh off	put sb. off	tell off
cut sb. off	lay off	see sb. off	wear off
fall off			

Trade between the two countries has (1) *decreased* drastically, and several of our firms have had to (2) *dismiss* workers *temporarily*. Now diplomatic relations have been (3) *suspended* and the proposed meeting between the two Foreign Ministers has been (4) *postponed* indefinitely, in other words (5) *cancelled*. Our Government had the chance of (6) *achieving* a diplomatic victory there, but now nothing it plans ever seems to (7) *succeed*.

A stink bomb (8) *exploded* in the lecture theatre and (9) *emitted* a most foul odour. When discovered, the culprit tried to (**10**) *make light of* the episode, clearly expecting to (**11**) *escape* with just a warning, but I see his name has been (**12**) *deleted from* the faculty list, which serves him right, because he has (**13**) *deterred* a lot of people *from* going to lectures.

'Why does young Charles always (**14**) *go away quickly* at the sight of his headmaster?'
'Because Charles used to (**15**) *mimic* him. One day the headmaster heard him and (**16**) *reprimanded* him. He told Charles that if he wanted to (**17**) *demonstrate how clever he was* in front of the other boys he needed more practice.'

Our tutor has (**18**) *excused* us our weekly seminar so that we can (**19**) *bid farewell to* Christine at the airport. I'm afraid she'll feel terribly (**20**) *isolated* from her friends once the novelty of being in a strange country (**21**) *passes away*.

5 VERBS WITH *on*

carry on	get on for	keep on	press on
come on	go on	look on/upon	put (it) on
get on	have sb. on	pass on	take on

'Your father told me he was (**1**) *approaching* eighty.'
'He was (**2**) *deceiving* you! He's only sixty-eight. He sometimes likes to (**3**) *feign* an air of venerable old age.'
'He's lucky! I don't need to (**4**) *pretend*. I'm younger than he is, but I feel old age (**5**) *beginning*, I can tell you! And unlike your father, I (**6**) *regard* old age as a tragedy!'

The Board chairman said that the firm would not (**7**) *engage* any more staff but would (**8**) *proceed rapidly* with automation. He asked me to (**9**) *convey* the information to my department so that everyone would know what was (**10**) *happening*. He then (**11**) *proceeded* to deal with the question of redundancy. He (**12**) *continued* talking about it until the end of the meeting.

Willie is (**13**) *progressing* well with his Japanese. He is now able to (**14**) *conduct* an everyday conversation in it, and says that he will (**15**) *persevere* with it until he reaches examination standard.

6 VERBS WITH *out*

back out	get out of	pass out	think out
be sth. out	give out	point out	try out
bear out	grow out of	put sb. out	wear sb. out
carry out	have it out	rule out	wipe out
cut out	iron out	stand out	work out
fall out	make out	stick out	

When we (1) *calculated* the weekly figures at the office yesterday we found we (2) *were in error by* over three hundred pounds in our accounts. We just could not (3) *understand* what was wrong. You can imagine how (4) *disconcerted* we were when Denis (5) *drew attention to* a simple mistake in our calculations.

Helen claims that it was Denis and not Brenda who (6) *planned in detail* the new filing system which has (7) *eliminated* so much unnecessary work at the office, and that several people are prepared to (8) *corroborate* what she says. She is apparently determined to (9) *decide the issue one way or another* with Brenda herself sooner or later.

Helen (10) *exhausts* people with her continual arguing. It's a childhood habit that she has never (11) *left behind her*. Adults should be able to (12) *resolve* their differences in a civilised way, but it looks as if Helen and I are going to (13) *become enemies*.

After saying they would all support the scheme, some of them (14) *withdrew their support*, so it is now going to be difficult to (15) *put the scheme into effect*. However, one should not (16) *exclude* the possibility of its eventually being (17) *given a trial* at least on a small scale.

Her son's infantry platoon was (18) *killed to a man*. They (19) *announced* the news on the radio. When she heard it she (20) *fainted*. Apparently he could have (21) *avoided* serving overseas if he had wanted to.

He (22) *was conspicuous* everywhere by reason of his height. I am afraid I am conspicuous only because my stomach (23) *protrudes*.

7 VERBS WITH *over, through*

blow over	talk over	be through	go through
get over	think over	with	with
get sth. over	throw over	fall through	run through
make over	tide sb. over	get through	see through
take over	win over	go through	see sth. through

He (1) *spent* an awful lot of money in his youth. He was engaged to the local heiress, but (2) *rejected* her for a cabaret singer, whereupon his father demanded to see him. The son, who naturally wanted to (3) *have done with* the interview as soon as possible, feigned repentence, but the father (4) *was not deceived by* [change passive to active] his little game. He had (5) *suffered* a lot because of his son and (6) *had had enough of* him; so he (7) *transferred* the property in his will to a nephew. The scandal (8) *was* soon *forgotten*. [Change passive to active.] The heiress (9) *recovered from* the shock and married a hotel owner.

The bank has offered us a million-pound loan to (10) *keep us going* until business recovers. After (11) *carefully considering* the offer and (12) *discussing* it amongst ourselves, we have decided to accept it. We should be able to (13) *gain the support of* the shareholders, since they will not want our plans to

(14) *come to nothing* and another firm to **(15)** *gain control of* us any more than we do. We are sure that, like us, they will think that once you start something you should **(16)** *persevere and complete* it.

8 VERBS WITH *up*

be up to	give up	make up for	set up
beat up	have sb. up	own up to	size up
blow up	hold up	pick up	snap up
bring up	land up	pull up	stand up for
build up	look up	put up	stick up for
do up	look up to	put up with	take up
draw up	make up	run up	(get) worked up
end up	make it up		

He **(1)** *developed* the business himself from scratch, **(2)** *acquiring* the necessary technical knowledge as he went along. Now he is **(3)** *establishing* a branch in Manchester. The local authorities are **(4)** *providing* some of the capital. Negotiations were **(5)** *delayed* for a long time by red tape, but the contract has been **(6)** *prepared* at last.

If these business premises are for sale, our firm should **(7)** *buy* them *at once*. We could **(8)** *redecorate* them quite cheaply. Our offices would not **(9)** *occupy* all the available space and we could let the rest. I'll **(10)** *raise* the matter at the directors' meeting tomorrow.

We have **(11)** *accumulated* a lot of debts in the last few years, but now business seems to be **(12)** *improving*, and so we may not **(13)** *find ourselves* in the bankruptcy court after all. Let us hope that good times are coming to **(14)** *compensate for* times past.

'My boss can get terribly **(15)** *excited* over very little. Once, when he was speeding, a police car ordered him to **(16)** *stop* at the kerb. He jumped out of the car and started to **(17)** *assault* one of the policemen. Of course he was **(18)** *prosecuted* for assault and battery and for resisting arrest as well as for exceeding the speed limit.'
'How can you **(19)** *tolerate* that sort of thing? I can only work for people I can **(20)** *respect*. I think it **(21)** *behoves* a person in your boss's position to set a good example. When he is criticised, why do you **(22)** *defend* him?'
'He's not as bad as you think. Although he and his wife often quarrel, they always **(23)** *become reconciled*. And in the office he soon **(24)** *abandoned* trying to bully me because he saw I could **(25)** *defend* myself. When he **(26)** *severely reprimanded* me for being late once, I gave him as good as I got. It did not take me long to **(27)** *form an opinion about* him and to realise I **(28)** *was* more than *capable of* the job of being his secretary.'

'I'm not **(29)** *inventing* these stories, you know.'
'You wouldn't **(30)** *admit* it if you were.'

17 Study lists

17A   The past tense of certain verbs (with past participle)

Note: These are the verbs used in the Examples and Exercises in 1A. Not all of them are irregular verbs, since regular verbs (e.g. *flow, lay, raise, stroke*) can also cause difficulty through confusion with irregular ones (*fly, lie, rise, strike*). Pronunciation, when given, is in brackets (   ).

arise	arose	arisen	
bet	bet	bet	
bid	bid	bid	not *bid, bade, bidden* = *ask* (literary)
bind	bound	bound	(rhymes with *find, found*)
bleed	bled	bled	
broadcast	broadcast	broadcast	
deal	dealt	dealt	(*dealt* rhymes with *felt*)
dig	dug	dug	
fall	fell	fallen	
feed	fed	fed	
feel	felt	felt	
flee	fled	fled	
flow	flowed	flowed	(rhymes with *slow(ed)*)
fly	flew	flown	(*flew, flown* rhymes with *blue/blew, blown*)
forbid	forbad(e)	forbidden	(*forbade* = [fə' bæd] or [fə' beɪd])
grow	grew	grown	(rhymes with *throw, threw, thrown*)
hit	hit	hit	
hurt	hurt	hurt	
lay	laid	laid	(*laid* rhymes with *made*, **not** *said*)
lie	lay	lain	
quit	quit	quit	(rhymes with *slit, split*)
raise	raised	raised	([reɪz(d)] = *rays(d)*)
rise	rose	risen	([raɪz], [rəʊz], [rɪzn])
saw	sawed	sawn/sawed	([sɔː(d)])
seek	sought	sought	(*sought* = [sɔːt] = *sort*)
sew	sewed	sewn/sewed	(pronounced like *sow* below)
shed	shed	shed	
shine	shone	shone	(*shone* rhymes with *John*)
skid	skidded	skidded	
slit	slit	slit	
sow	sowed	sown/sowed	(*sow* = [səʊ] = *so*)
speed up	speeded up	speeded up	**not** *speed, sped, sped* = *hasten* (literary)

split	split	split	
spread	spread	spread	(rhymes with *bread*)
stick	stuck	stuck	
strike	struck	struck	
stroke	stroked	stroked	(rhymes with *joke(d)*)
sue	sued	sued	(may rhyme with *few(d)* or *foo(d)*)
swell	swelled	swelled/swollen	(*swollen* rhymes with *stolen*)
tread	trod	trodden	(*tread* rhymes with *bread*)
wake	woke	woken	([weɪk], [wəʊk], [wəʊkn])
weave	wove	woven	([wiːv], [wəʊv], [wəʊvn])

17B   Verbs and phrases followed by the plain infinitive (see 10Aa)

can/could
dare **a**
do (AUXILIARY)
had better **b**
help **c**
know (= have experience of) **d**
let **e**
make **e**

may/might
must
need **f**
shall/should
will/would
would rather . . . than **g**
would sooner . . . than **g**
why (not) . . . ? **h**

Notes

a In sentences beginning with *how* that do not expect an answer (rhetorical questions), *dare* is always used as an auxiliary verb like *can, will* etc., that is to say, without auxiliary *do* and without the third person ending in -*s*:

How dare she say that about me!

In negative sentences or in true questions, *dare* may be used either as an auxiliary verb or as a main (non-auxiliary) verb with a plain or a full infinitive:

Dare he ask/Will he dare (to) ask?
No, he daren't ask/doesn't dare (to) ask/won't dare (to) ask.
Dared he do it/Did he dare (to) do it, I wonder?
No, he dared not do it/didn't dare (to) do it.

In affirmative constructions, which are less common than the above, *dare* is normally used with a full infinitive (**10Ab**):

One day he may dare *to ask* her.

The -*ing* form of *dare* is always followed by the full infinitive:

He stared at her, not daring *to say* a word.

For *dare* meaning *challenge*, see **17C**.

b For the use in context of *had better*, see **1Fe**.

c *Help* may also be used with a full infinitive, either alone or after an object:

I helped (them) (to) *carry* the injured outside the building.

For *can't help* meaning *can't stop*, see **17D**.

d *Know* may be used with the plain infinitive (after an object) only in the present perfect tense, meaning 'have had the *experience* of':

I have known *Willie* (to) *stay up* all night working.

In its usual meaning of 'have the *knowledge* of' *know* is used with a *that* clause or a full infinitive:

I know (that) Willie sometimes stays up working all night.
I know Willie to be/(that) Willie is a chronic work addict.

e   *Let* and *make* are most often used with the plain infinitive after an object:
   I'll let *you know* in good time.
   You made *me realise* how foolish I'd been.
   However, they are both used with the infinitive alone in one or two special phrases:
   Let go (of) the rope!
   We'll have to *make do* (= manage) with the money we've got.
   In the passive, however, *make*, like **all** verbs except *let*, takes a **full** infinitive:
   I *was made to realise* how foolish I'd been.
   Let, in one of its rare uses in the passive, takes a plain infinitive:
   A remark *was let slip* at the meeting that made everyone sit up.

f   *Need*, like *dare* (see **a** above), can be used interrogatively or negatively either as an auxiliary
   with the plain infinitive or as a non-auxiliary:
   Need she leave/Does she need to leave straightaway?
   She needn't worry/She doesn't need to worry about being late.
   But unlike *dare*, *need* as a non-auxiliary or main verb (**i**) always takes the full infinitive, as
   the above examples show, (**ii**) is not always used interrogatively or negatively in the same
   contexts as auxiliary *need/need not* (see **11Df, g, h**) and (**iii**) is often used affirmatively (see
   10Ce).

g   With *would rather/sooner . . . than*, there may be two plain infinitives:
   I'd rather *fly* than *go* by train.
   But since it is not necessary to repeat a verb, *than* may be followed by other words besides
   an infinitive:
   I'd sooner *go* by car than *(by) train*.
   For the use of *would rather* with the past tense or subjunctive to express wish, see **1Eg**.

h   *Why (not)* + plain infinitive is used in suggestions and invitations. It has an equivalent
   longer form **only** when used with *not*:
   Why not come/Why don't you come by car with us?
   Why waste (**not** Why do you waste) money on a train ticket?

j   For those verbs followed by the plain infinitive or *-ing* (present participle) according to use
   or meaning, see **10D**.

17C   Verbs followed by an object + full infinitive (see 10Ab)

aid	depend on **b**	inspire	rely on **b**
allow	enable	instruct	remind
appoint	encourage	intend	request
ask **a**	entitle	invite	stimulate
assist	entreat	lead	teach
beg **a**	expect **a**	oblige	tell (= order)
cause	forbid	order	tempt
challenge	force	permit	trust
command	implore	persuade	urge
compel	incite	prompt	warn
dare (= challenge)	induce	provoke	wish **a, c**

Notes

a *Ask, beg, expect, wish* can also be followed **directly** by a full infinitive, as in 'We asked to see the director/He begged to be allowed to stay/She wishes to leave.' Alternative active/passive constructions are often possible:

I'm expecting *a friend to meet* me at the airport.
I'm expecting *to be met* at the airport *by a friend*.

b *Depend on* and *rely on* are prepositional verbs and (see **10C**) can also be followed by *-ing* (gerund):

She relies on me to wake her every morning.
She relies on me/my waking her every morning.

c For *wish* used with a past or conditional tense for non-fact, see **1E**.

d There are a number of verbs like *believe, consider, know, prove, show, think* that may be followed by an object + *to be* but which have not been included in this list because (i) they are more commonly used with a *that* clause and (ii) after most of them *to be* can be omitted:

   i They *knew/showed* etc. the theory to be wrong ⟶ They *knew/showed* etc. (that) the theory was wrong.
   ii They *believed/considered/proved/thought* the theory (to be) wrong.
   For the use of some of these verbs in the passive, see **13B**.

e For verbs that may take an object + full infinitive or *-ing* depending on use or meaning, see **10Cb, e** and **10Db, c**.

17D   Verbs and phrases followed by *-ing* (gerund) (see **10Bb**)

admit   c
advise   b
anticipate   c
appreciate
avoid
begrudge
cannot bear (= cannot tolerate)   a
cannot help (= cannot stop)
carry on (= continue)
consider (= contemplate)
contemplate
continue   a
delay
deny
detest
dislike
endure (= tolerate)
enjoy
entail
envisage
escape (= avoid)
excuse (= forgive)   d
fancy
finish
foresee   c

forgive   d
give up (= stop)
grudge
have difficulty (in)
imagine   c
include
intend   a, b
involve (= entail)
it is no good
it is no/little *etc*. use
it is (not) worth
justify
keep (on) (= persist in)
mention   c
mind (= object to)
miss
necessitate
pardon
postpone
practise
prevent   e
propose (= intend)   a
propose (= suggest)   c
put somebody off (= deter)
put off (= postpone)

181

recall   c
recollect   c
recommend   **b**
report   c
require (= be in need of)
resent
resist

risk
stand (= tolerate)
stop (= prevent)   **e**
stop (= cease)   **f**
suggest   c
there is no   **g**
tolerate

Notes

a   *Cannot bear, continue, intend, propose* (= *intend*) can also be followed by an infinitive **without** any change of meaning:
    She clearly intends *marrying/to marry* the man.
For verbs that take the gerund or infinitive **with** a change of meaning, see **10C**.

b   *Advise, recommend, intend* are normally used with a (pro)noun + infinitive instead of a (pro)noun/possessive + -*ing* (**10Bd, e**):
    She clearly intends *him to marry* her (instead of *him/his marrying* her).
This can be replaced by a *that* clause after *recommend* and *intend*:
    She clearly intends (that) he should marry her.*
Advise used with *that* means *inform* (formal English): 'Our agent has advised us that the goods have already been despatched.'

c   *Admit, anticipate, foresee, imagine, mention, propose* (= *suggest*), *recall, recollect, report, suggest* can all be used directly with a *that* clause:
    The girl admitted *being*/(that) *she was* the smuggler's accomplice.
This usually replaces a (pro)noun/possessive + -*ing* after *admit, propose* (= *suggest*), *report, suggest*:
    The smuggler admitted (that) *she was* his accomplice (instead of *her being* his accomplice).

d   *Excuse, forgive* can take a (pro)noun/possessive + -*ing* or a (pro)noun + *for* + -*ing*:
    Please excuse me/my being late.
    Please forgive me for being late.
In the meaning of *let off* or *exempt, excuse* is used with a (pro)noun + *from*:
    The Government excuses foreign students from paying taxes.

e   *Prevent, stop* can take a (pro)noun/possessive + -*ing* or a (pro)noun + *from* + -*ing*:
    What is there to prevent him/his marrying her?
    What is there to stop him from marrying her?

f   *Stop* meaning *cease* also takes -*ing*, but this may be left out as something understood, so that *stop* can be directly followed by an infinitive of purpose (**4Aa**):
    Has he *stopped* (going ahead with his plans) *to think* what the consequences might be?

g   *There is no* + -*ing* occurs in a few common phrases such as:
    There's no knowing what he may do.
    There's no accounting for tastes.

* For the use here of *should*, see **11Fa**.

17E Verbs used with two objects*

i Verbs where **either** object can become a subject in a corresponding passive, *italicised* verbs being those that are used alternatively with *to* in both active and passive (see 13Af–h):

award sb. a prize
bring sb. sth. (used also with *for*)
deal sb. a card
deny sb. sth.
do sb. good, harm
find sb. a job, accommodation
    (used alternatively with *for*)
forbid sb. alcohol, use of a car
forgive sb. his bad behaviour
give sb. sth.
grant sb. permission
hand sb. sth.
leave sb. money (in a will)
lend sb. sth.

offer sb. sth.
owe sb. money
pay sb. money
play sb. a trick (used alternatively with *on*)
promise sb. sth.
quote sb. a share price
recommend sb. a hotel
refuse sb. a request
repay sb. money
send sb. sth.
set sb. an example, a task
teach sb. sth.
tell sb. sth.

ii Verbs similar to the above but requiring in the passive the prepositions given in brackets (see 13Aj):

build sb. sth. (for)
buy sb. sth. (for)
cook sb. sth. (for)
cut sb. a piece (for)
do sb. a favour (for)
draw sb. a plan (for)
feed sth. (an animal, a computer) sth. (to,
    into)
order sb. a meal, a complete rest (for)

paint sb. a picture (for)
pass sb. the butter, a note (to)
read sb. a poem (to)
sell sb. sth. (to)
show sb. sth. (to)
take sb. sth. (to, for)
throw sb. a lifeline (to)
write sb. a letter (to)

iii Verbs where one or both objects can **not** become subjects in corresponding passives (see 13Aq–s for key):

allow sb. privileges s
ask sb. a question s
bear sb. a grudge q
cost sb. £300, her life q
earn sb. money, a reputation (for) r
envy sb. sth. q
get sb. sth. (for) r
keep sb. a seat (for) r
leave sb. a key, a message (for) r

make sb. an offer s
make sb. sth. (for) r
save sb. the expense, trouble s
spare sb. a moment, a pencil q
stand sb. a drink s
strike sb. a blow s
win sb. support (for) r
wish sb. luck, a happy birthday q

* sb. = somebody; sth. = something. The other objects given are typical but are not the only possible ones.

17F   Dependent prepositions

This is a list of the dependent prepositions in **15**, Exercises 1–10. It is divided into:

  i prepositions dependent on adjectives and nouns, and

  ii prepositions dependent on verbs.

It is not a complete list, but one selected for the advanced learner. For example, you will not find in it *listen to* or *wait for*, which you will know already, but you will find *listen for* and *wait on*, which you may not know. Sb. = somebody; sth. = something; *-ing* = a construction with the *-ing* form or gerund (see **10Bb**).

i Prepositions dependent on adjectives and nouns

admiration for

advance on

advantage in sth./*-ing*

      over sb./sth.

      to sb.

aid for

angry about sth.

    at *-ing*

    with sb. for *-ing*

appeal to

attack on

attempt at *-ing*

     on sth.

attitude towards

aware of

benefit to

chance of

change from sb./sth. (= substitution)

      in sb./sth. (= alteration)

concerned about sb./sth. (= anxious)

      in sth. (= involved)

      with sth. (= occupied)

confidence in

confident of

confined to

conscious of

contrary to

convinced of

critical of

crowded with

curious about

damage to

danger of *-ing*

    to sb.

dealer in

dealings with

death from

delay in

deprived of

deterioration in

devoted to

difficulty in *-ing*

disappointed at sth.

      by / in/with sb./sth.

disposed towards

doubt about

eligible for

envious of

essential for sb./sth. (purpose)

      to sb./sth. (need)

exception to

expert in/on

faith in

familiar with

famous for

fed up with

figure(s) for

foreign to

free from sth. (usually abstract)

    of sb./sth. (concrete)

    with sth. (money etc.)

good at sth./*-ing*

    for sb./sth. (= beneficial)

    with sb./sth. (= skilled)

greedy for

guilty of

habit of

honest in one's dealings etc.

      with sb.

hope for sb./the future

     of sth./*-ing*

ignorant of

ill (in bed) with
important for sb./sth. (purpose)
   to sb. (need)
impression on
improvement in sb./sth.
    on sb./sth. (= better than)
incapable of
increase in
independent of
indifferent to
indignant at
influence on sb./sth. (= effect)
   over sb./sth. (= domination)
   with sb. (= power)
insult to
intention of
interested in
involved in
jealous of
keen on
key to
lacking in
latest in
likelihood of
limit to
mercy on sb. (see *have* in ii below)
   to(wards) sb. (see *show* in ii
      below)
missing from
(be) news to
noted for
obstacle to
occupied with
opinion about/on sth.
  of sb.
opportunity for sb.
   of sth./-*ing*
opposed to
particular about
patient with
peculiar to
pity on (see *have* in ii below)
pleasure in
point in
poor in

popular with
possibility of
preferable to
pride in
qualified for
question of
relationship between sb./sth.
    with sb./sth.
relief from
reputation for honesty etc.
   of being honest etc.
responsible for sth.
   to sb.
restricted to
restrictions on/to sth.
revenge for sth.
  on sb.
rich in
safe from
satisfied with
self-sufficient in
sensitive to
strict about sth.
  with sb.
struggle against/with sb./sth.
   between/among sb.
   for sth.
substitute for
success with
superior to
surprised at
suspicious of
sympathetic towards
sympathy for sb. (see *have* in ii below)
   with sb. (see *be* in ii below)
taste for sth.
  in sth. (plural)
threat of sth.
  to sb./sth.
true of sb./sth.
  to sb./sth. (= faithful)
typical of
victory over
views on

ii Prepositions dependent on verbs

accuse sb. of
agree on a plan etc. (jointly)*
     to a proposal etc. (= consent)
     with sb./sb.'s views etc. (= concur)
allow for
amount to
appeal for sth.
     to sb.
apply for sth. (= ask)
     to sb./sth. (= concern)
approve of
attend to
avenge oneself on
bargain for sth.
     with sb.
be in sympathy with
beat sb. at a game etc.
benefit from
blame sb. for sth.
     sth. on sb.
boast about/of
care for
change for the better/the worse
     into sb./sth.
     with time etc.
charge (sb.) for sth. (commercial)
     sb. with sth. (legal)
cheat sb. out of
compete against/with sb.
     for a prize etc.
     in a race etc.
compliment sb. on
concentrate on
condemn sb. to
confess to
confide in
confine sb./sth. to
conform to
congratulate sb. on
consent to
contribute to(wards)
convince sb. of
cure sb. of
deal with
decide between
     on sb./sth.
declare war on
depend on
deprive sb. of

devote oneself/time etc. to
die for one's beliefs etc.
     from injuries etc. (= external cause)
     of a disease etc. (= internal cause)
differ from sb./sth.
     in sth.
disapprove of
discourage sb. from
end in
     sth. with
enter into an agreement etc.
equip sb./sth. with
excuse sb. for sth. (done)
     sb. from (doing) sth.
feed (sb./sth.) on
fish for
fit sb./sth. with
fool sb. into
force sb. into
gain in sth.
     on sb.
grow in strength etc.
     into sb./sth.
guard against
have mercy on
have pity on
have sympathy for
help oneself to sth.
hint at
hold sth. against sb.
impress sb. with
inform sb. of/about
insist on
insure against
interfere in sth.
     with sb./sth.
invest in
involve sb. in
keep sth. to oneself
know of
lead sb. into
listen for
live by sth. (means)
     for sb./sth. (purpose)
     on sth. (food, salary)
     up to one's reputation etc.
look to (= seem)
make sb./sth.into
make up one's mind about

*In this meaning, *agree* is being increasingly used without a preposition as a transitive verb.

mean sth. by
mistake sb./sth. for
object to
part with
plant sth. with
plead guilty to
prejudice sb. against
prevent sb./sth. from
profit from
protest to
provide for sb./sth.
    sb./sth. with
puzzle over
reason with sb. on sth.
reduce sth. by
    sb./sth. to
resort to
restrict sth. to
result from (= be caused by)
    in (= lead to)
rob sb. of
sacrifice sb./sth. for/to
see sth. in sb./sth.
seethe with
share sb./sth. with
show mercy to(wards)

speak of
specialise in
spend time in -ing
struggle against/with
succeed in sth./-ing
    to the throne etc.
suffer for one's beliefs etc.
    from a disease etc.
supply sb. with
surrender to
suspect sb. of
swarm with
take advantage of
take sb. into one's confidence
think of
threaten sb. with
trust sb. with
turn (sb./sth.) into
warn sb. about sb./sth.
    sb. against -ing/sb.
    sb. of the dangers etc.
wait on
watch for
win (sth.) by
work at a job etc.
    on a project etc.

17G   Phrasal verbs

Listed below are the 165 phrasal verbs that occur in **16**, Examples and Exercises. They have been chosen, from the many hundreds that exist, as a useful selection for the advanced learner (some of the more common ones being omitted). They are divided into (i) adverbial phrasal verbs (**16Aa**) and (ii) prepositional phrasal verbs (**16Ab**).

i Adverbial phrasal verbs

For the majority of the verbs below, in which the adverbial particle can either precede or follow an object (**16Ac**), a typical object in *italics* similar to that used in the Exercises is given after the particle. For verbs that take no object like *back out* or for split verbs (**16Ah**) like *cut sb. off* the approximate meaning or a typical phrase is given in brackets. Verbs like *check in*, which can be used with or without an object, are given with a possible object in brackets. (Sb. = somebody; sth. = something.)

back out (= withdraw one's support)
be sth. out (= be in error by 3 cms etc.)
bear out *what sb. says*
beat up *sb. one dislikes*

blow over (= be soon forgotten)
blow up *an employee (for being late)*
break off *relations*
bring about *a change*

bring down *a government*
bring in *new regulations*
bring in *£15,000 a year*
bring off *a victory*
bring round *our newspapers*
bring sb. round (= revive sb.)
bring up *a matter*
build up *a business*
call off *a meeting*
carry on *a conversation*
carry out *a scheme*
check in (*one's baggage*)
come about (= arise, happen)
come on (= begin)
come off (= succeed)
cut down *expenses*
cut sb. off (*from her friends*)
cut out *unnecessary work*
die away (= become fainter and then cease)
die down (= abate)
do up *premises*
draw up *a contract*
end up (*in court*)
fall off (= decrease)
fall out (= become enemies)
fall through (= come to nothing)
fix up *an interview*
get by (= manage)
get sb. down (= depress sb.)
get off (*with a warning*)
get on (= progress)
get sth. over (= have done with sth.)
give in (= yield)
give off *a smell*
give out *the news*
give up *trying*
go down (*well* or *badly*)
go off (= explode)
go on (= continue, happen, proceed)
hand down *a hereditary title*
hang about (= loiter)
have sb. on (= deceive sb.)
have it out (*with Brenda*)
have sb. up (= prosecute sb.)
hold up *negotiations*
iron out *one's differences*
join in (*the games*)
keep on (*with one's studies*)
land up (*in court*)
laugh off *the episode*
lay down *what one should do*
lay off *workers*
let sb. down (= fail or disappoint sb.)
let sb. off (= excuse sb.)
look up (= improve)

make off (= go away quickly)
make out *what is wrong*
make over *one's property*
make up *stories*
make it up (= become reconciled)
pass on *information*
pass out (= faint)
pick up *knowledge*
point out *a mistake*
press on (= proceed rapidly)
pull up (= stop)
put by *some money*
put down *a revolt*
put in *a claim*
put off *a meeting*
put sb. off (= deter)
put on *an air*
put it on (= pretend)
put sb. out (= disconcert)
put up *the capital*
rule out *the possibility*
run down *the aristocracy*
run sb. in (= arrest sb.)
run up *a lot of debts*
see sb. off (= bid farewell to sb.)
see sth. through (= persevere with sth.)
set up *a business*
show off (= show how clever etc. one is)
size up *one's boss*
snap up *an opportunity*
stand out (= be conspicuous)
stick out (= project)
strike off *a name* (or strike *a name* off *a list*)
take back *what one said*
take in *all she said*
take sb. in (= deceive sb.)
take off *the headmaster*
take on *more staff*
take over *a firm*
take up *space*
talk sth. over (= discuss sth.)
tell off *young Charles*
think out *a new filing system*
think sth. over (= consider sth.)
throw over *one's fiancée*
tide sb. over (*a difficult period*)
tone down *one's criticism*
try out *a scheme*
turn down *an offer*
wear off (= pass away)
wear sb. out (= exhaust sb.)
win over *the shareholders*
wipe out *a platoon of soldiers*
work out *figures*
(get) worked up (= become excited)

ii Prepositional phrasal verbs

Unlike adverbial phrasal verbs, prepositional phrasal verbs must by definition **always** be followed by objects, and typical examples of these, similar to those used in the Exercises in **16**, are given below in *italics*. (Sb. = somebody; sth. = something.)

be through with *his son*
be up to *sb. (to do sth.)*
be up to *a job*
call (in) at *the police station*
call (in) on *my parents*
come into *a fortune*
do away with *exams*
driving at (*What are you* . . . ? Used only in progressive question form.)
drop in at *the police station*
drop in on *my parents*
fall in with *her plans*
fall in with *a wild set*
fly at *sb.* (= attack sb.)
getting at (*What are you* . . . ? Used only in progressive question form.)
get away with *a remark like that*
get down to *a task*
get in with *a wild set*
get on for *eighty*
get out of *serving overseas*
get over *a shock*
get round *the regulations*
get through *a lot of money*
go at *sb/sth.* (= attack sb./sth.)

go in for *fast cars*
go into *the matter*
go through *a lot* (= suffer)
go through *a lot of money*
go through with *a project*
grow out of *a habit*
keep in with *one's relatives*
let sb. in for *extra expense*
look down on *sb.*
look into *the matter*
look (up)on *old age as* . . .
look up to *sb.*
make up for *times past*
own up to *a deed*
put sth. down to *lack of* . . .
put up with *that sort of thing*
run into *sb.* (= happen to meet sb.)
run into *debt*
run through *a lot of money*
see through *his little game*
set about *reforming him*
stand by *sb.* (= support sb.)
stand up for *oneself*
stick up for *sb. else*
take after *one's father*

Subject index

References are similar to those used in the text, namely to numbered (1 etc.) and lettered (A etc.) sections and to entries (a etc.) under their respective Explanations.

Word index

References are similar to those used in the text, namely to numbered (1 etc.) and lettered (A etc.) sections and to entries (a etc.) under their respective Explanations.

Key to exercises

Contracted verb forms ('s, *don't* etc.) are not used in the Key to sections 1 and 2. Elsewhere they are used when they are appropriate to the context so long as they do not interfere with clarity (see Introduction, 'Style and usage').

1A Exercise 1
1   The car *skidded* nearly thirty metres.
2   The driver *trod* on the accelerator because he thought it was the brake.
3   Yes, the accelerator *stuck* wide open.
4   The car *hit* a lamp-post.
5   They *bound* the driver's wound with a piece of shirt.
6   The passenger's nose *bled* for quite a long time.
7   The passenger *lay* down on the pavement.
8   The driver *woke* up in hospital.
9   They *laid* the blame on the other driver.
10 They *sued* him for twenty thousand pounds.
11 He *quit* his job straight after the accident.
12 He *fled* the country to escape the law.
13 No, no one *shed* any tears when he left.
14 He *sought* refuge in Australia.
15 Yes, he *dug* for gold there.
16 He *struck* hardly any gold.
17 No, he *grew* grass.
18 He *sowed* grass wherever he could.
19 He *sawed* down trees to make a fence for sheep.
20 He *fed* the sheep on bananas, of course!

Exercise 2
1   Sheila's lip *swelled* up because a wasp stung her.
2   Ken *split* his trousers climbing over a fence.
3   Yes, Toby *bet* that Ken could not sew them up himself
4   Yes, Ken *sewed* them up himself.
5   Helen *slit* the envelope open with her enormously long fingernail.
6   Marilyn *speeded up* her typing by going to evening classes.
7   Zena *bid* a couple of hundred for the Chinese vase.

8   She *fell* going down the stairs.
9   She *felt* terrible about breaking the vase.
10 Yes, she *hurt* her wrist.
11 The water *flowed* downstairs.
12 Helen *flew* out of the room in a rage because of what her father said.
13 Her father *forbade(e)* her to go out with Denis.
14 Her father *dealt* with her by stopping her monthly allowance.
15 Denis *stroked* Helen's hand to try and calm her down.
16 Helen's friends *spread* the rumour that she was going to get married.
17 Marilyn *wove* her rugs on the looms over there.
18 She *raised* her prices by fifteen per cent.
19 The question of a bank loan *arose* at the directors' meeting.
20 They *broadcast* the news just now, on the BBC.

1B Exercise 1
1   joined
2   had been working/had worked
3   had acquired
4   worked/was working
5   was working
6   became
7   has been working/has worked
8   has proved
9   works
10 is working
11 laid
12 had been fighting
13 had won
14 had lost
15 was
16 was
17 had led
18 was
19 did not survive/had not survived
20 (had) surrendered
21 was
22 is always ringing
23 happened
24 did not answer
25 learnt/learned
26 had rung

27 offered/had
   then offered
28 have just told
29 is
30 (have) missed
31 have you been
   doing
32 have not seen
33 have been
34 saw
35 were you
36 did you do/
   were you doing
37 did/was doing
38 have already
   told
39 am working
40 is it going/has it
   been going
41 hope/am hoping
42 lives
43 was living/
   lived*
44 wrote
45 invited
46 have had
47 am wondering/
   wonder

48 have also had
49 applied
50 was
51 have
52 am I doing
53 am babysitting
54 have gone
55 are
56 was babysitting
57 started
58 are being
59 is eating
60 gave
61 left
62 have found
63 are happily
   painting
64 assure/have
   assured
65 have done
66 had
67 hope
68 are telling/have
   told
69 has got
70 have been
   trying

Exercise 2

1 will still be
   working
2 retires/will be
   retiring
3 will then be
4 will have been
   working/
   will have
   worked
5 will have
   qualified
6 is going to work/
   will work
7 will probably
   earn
8 is coming
9 will/shall
   introduce
10 Shall I tell
11 will/shall be
   seeing/see

12 will/shall tell
13 will be
14 are you going to
   do/will you do/
   are you doing
15 Are you going
   to/Will you
   prepare
16 am
17 leave/am
   leaving
18 does/will not
   give
19 will need
20 do I meet/am I
   meeting
21 am
22 means/will
   mean
23 is not/will not
   be

24 Are you
25 am I
26 is going
27 is she going to
   do/is she doing
28 is going to
   promote/is
   promoting
29 is she going to
   do/is she doing
30 is going to
   demonstrate/is
   demonstrating
31 will do
32 will have been
   married
33 are celebrating/
   are going to
   celebrate
34 will be
35 will be
36 are going (to go)
37 will have left
38 will go
39 will/shall be
   working/am
   working
40 Are you going
41 will be
42 is definitely
   going to be
43 will probably
   be
44 will win
45 will win

46 is going to/will
   lose
47 will/shall be
   taking
48 will/shall do
49 will/shall give
50 am not going
51 am staying/am
   going to stay
52 (am) going/go
53 will be
54 is going to snow
55 will soon be
56 was going to fly
57 will not get
58 will/shall spend/
   be spending/
   am going to
   spend
59 will you be/are
   you doing
60 am going
61 are you going to
   do
62 am going to do
63 will/shall visit
64 will you be
65 am flying
66 will surprise
67 are going to get/
   are getting
68 will/shall
   believe
69 will not last
70 will soon start

Exercise 3

1 was driving
2 went
3 was passing
4 was
5 did not have
6 are still using/
   still use
7 fall
8 will/shall not
   drive
9 will/shall have
   been
10 will/shall have
   lived/been

living
11 are going to
   celebrate/are
   celebrating
12 (have) invited/
   are inviting
13 are
14 have already
   said
15 are/will be
   coming/are
   going to/will
   come

* Whether we use *was living* or *lived* depends on whether we regard living as an activity or state. Over longer periods it normally 'sinks' into the category of state: 'I've lived (= been) here all my life.' For shorter periods living usually claims our attention as an activity: 'Sheila's living with her mother now, I hear.'

16 are/is not (being)
17 have/has declined
18 had
19 had been
20 (had) got
21 (had) done/did
22 are
23 (have) naturally sent
24 have so far refused/are so far refusing/so far refuse
25 was not
26 landed
27 was
28 were walking
29 (were) chatting
30 were watching
31 (were) listening
32 had ever happened
33 think
34 will ever happen
35 do you say
36 has/had ever happened
37 have been visiting/have visited
38 began
39 are hovering
40 (are) watching
41 are doing
42 was walking
43 saw

44 had definitely not come/ definitely did not come
45 think
46 had been drinking
47 was not
48 have seen
49 have seen
50 have reported
51 am going to write/will/shall write
52 am going
53 have been/am thinking
54 are you doing
55 are you
56 was/was going to be
57 have changed
58 wants/wanted
59 have you/do you have/did you have
60 is
61 Have you ever seen
62 saw
63 have never seen
64 will/shall go
65 will/shall book
66 Shall I ask
67 will be working
68 is always working
69 works
70 will have

1C
1 has gone
2 will not be
3 saw
4 was looking
5 went
6 does not remember
7 is/will be
8 has been
9 is continually urging
10 will pay
11 refuse
12 has not yet

shown/does not yet show
13 does
14 will/shall not lend/am not lending/am not going to lend
15 is going
16 is
17 will/is going to keep/is keeping
18 has helped

19 trusts
20 is not
21 has been going/has gone
22 thinks
23 go/have gone
24 have (had)
25 do/have
26 Does this mean
27 is thinking
28 does
29 succeeds
30 will have done/will be doing
31 (has) always wanted
32 had
33 doubt
34 will get
35 does not improve
36 left
37 goes
38 works
39 will accept
40 will find
41 prefers
42 has continued
43 will consider
44 trains
45 lies
46 are talking
47 takes
48 does
49 tends
50 spends
51 will not become
52 dreams
53 chooses
54 will clearly have to/ clearly has to
55 find
56 feel
57 costs
58 will go
59 means/will mean
60 is
61 will be

62 has been studying/has studied
63 will be taking/ takes/is taking
64 passes
65 will then specialise
66 will take
67 will not be
68 is
69 will then have been studying/have studied
70 will have earned
71 has been working/has worked
72 has been supporting/ has supported
73 is expecting
74 will soon be giving up/is soon going to give up/will soon give up
75 will live/are going to live
76 is no longer working/no longer works
77 are not worrying/do not worry
78 has never felt
79 is going to/ will qualify
80 takes
81 work/have worked
82 earn/have earned
83 have qualified
84 suffer
85 is
86 keep
87 is certainly not/will

certainly not
be

88 have lost
89 ceases
90 are
91 does not
occur/has not
occurred
92 will have
passed

93 proves
94 will always
be/is always
95 will/shall
come
96 (will) drive
97 do
98 will/shall
99 think
100 am going

1D

would be?

1 are
2 is/will be
3 will/shall call
4 have just
suggested
5 would not
have
suggested
6 was/were/
had been

Wanted 7 had wanted
8 would be/
would have
been
9 would be/
would have
been
10 would be
11 taught
12 are
13 wins
14 was/were
15 would never
do
16 would not go
17 did not like
18 needed
19 was/were not
20 would agree
21 would live
22 needed
23 did/were to
do
24 would/could
I justify
25 did
26 would have
to
27 went
28 would be
29 get
30 expect/am

am going to

31 expecting
will/shall
keep
32 had
33 would not be
34 has
35 is
36 (will/shall)
continue
37 get
38 would/could
fly
39 had
40 would/could
41 would be
42 had
43 would not be
44 lived
45 would need
46 chewed
47 would also
need
48 do
49 fitted
50 could we not
do
51 would be able
52 had
53 could not do
54 would use
55 had not been
56 made
57 would now
drive/be
driving
58 do
59 is
60 had had
61 would now
be/have been
62 would not
have fallen

63 would have
spent
64 leave
65 count
66 will/shall call
67 have
68 count
69 call
70 knew
71 would realise
72 do you not
mind
73 did
74 would be
75 am taking
76 would it be
77 could show
78 went
79 do not know
80 leaves/is
leaving/will
be leaving
81 is
82 will be
83 are/will be
84 do you mind/
would you
mind

1E

1 would get
2 would
3 was/were
4 realised
5 acted
6 could get
7 would/could
learn
8 did not want
9 thought
10 think
11 ask
12 could call
13 can
14 will/shall let
15 had left
16 had
17 would/should
have given
18 would
19 was/were
20 was/were
21 would/should
then spend
22 learnt/learned

85 come/came/
were to come
86 allowed/were
to allow
87 would have to
88 got
89 would now
be working/have
been working
90 had
91 would almost
certainly
have lost
92 might have
93 might not
(have)
94 had got
95 would now
be working/
now have
been working
96 has broken
97 would not be
98 was/were
99 would not be/
not have been
100 had done

23 told
24 would not
always criticise
25 became
26 knew
27 would realise
28 would stop
29 got
30 began
31 worked
32 would adopt
33 had chosen
34 had done
35 had listened
36 had/were to
have
37 would choose
38 had been born
39 would not/
should not have
had to
40 would/should
have (had)
41 could have
migrated

42	had wanted	45	would be/would
43	came		have been
44	had been		

1F

1	had	43	is coming
2	would be	44	would be/
3	would/should		would have
	like/have liked		been
4	bought	45	was
5	learnt	46	would/could
6	would be		finish/have
7	was/were not		finished
8	would/should	47	will/shall be
	have to	48	would gladly
9	enjoy		give
10	ran	49	would not laugh
11	put	50	had hit
12	would do	51	would not be
13	would not pay		sitting/would
14	said		not have been
15	finished		sitting
16	would/should	52	had not been
	be	53	would have
17	discovered		been
18	were	54	Would
19	would	55	took
20	will/shall leave /	56	did/were to
	am going to	57	could have
	leave	58	have
21	gets	59	would/should
22	would stop		be
23	thought	60	could/would
24	could	61	would be
25	cannot	62	could spend
26	had worried	63	is/has been
27	was	64	did
28	would not have	65	will/shall
	done		punish
29	would	66	is
30	speak	67	have
31	was/were	68	had not warned
32	is not	69	is
33	left	70	will know
34	have	71	had seen
35	learnt/learned	72	were
36	had finished	73	would you
37	was		believe
38	helped	74	would
39	wanted	75	do not believe
40	would happen	76	had seen
41	would become	77	would/should
42	will/shall have/		tell
	are going to	78	thought
	have	79	had seen

80	had	85	had said
81	had warned	86	would not melt
82	met	87	did not look
83	had	88	would think
84	would have	89	did
	taken	90	would do

2A Exercise 1

1 He smiled bitterly.
2 The dollar has fallen drastically.
3 The Stock Exchange reacted quite calmly.
4 To a European, Chinese sounds strange.
5 These almonds taste bitter.
6 Why did she look at me sternly?
7 Try and answer me intelligently.
8 You acted in a cowardly way.
9 The boy limped slightly.
10 The little girl looked rather sad.
11 Her mother had slapped her hard.
12 She moved clumsily.
13 She walks in an ugly way.
14 But she plays tennis well.
15 The sports committee meets every month/ once a month/monthly.
16 What they said affected me deeply.
17 The room looked nice and cosy.
18 The flowers smelt/smelled fragrant.
19 I talked to her in a fatherly way.
20 I said that she had behaved in an extremely silly way.
21 She glanced at me slyly.
22 It would be advisable to start early.
23 I'm sure her parents will welcome me warmly.
24 You are not arguing logically.

Exercise 2

1	direct	19	tightly
2	loud	20	light
3	deeply	21	clean
4	strong	22	lightly
5	high	23	deep
6	widely	24	closely
7	wide	25	highly
8	short	26	hard
9	loudly	27	slow
10	sharp	28	right
11	wrong	29	sharply
12	wrongly	30	strongly
13	Faintly	31	flat
14	faint	32	flatly
15	hardly	33	directly
16	tight	34	closer
17	shortly	35	badly
18	rightly	36	right

2B Exercise 1

1 to work *by car* on most days

2 Sometimes, *though*, he/behind, *though*, and/by bus, *though*

3 would *never* drive

4 Sheila, *too*, usually/usually drives to work *too*

5 She *only* has/has *only* to drive/to drive *only* a few miles

6 there and back *quicker* by bicycle

7 still *seriously* considering

8 *recently* changed

9 will *probably* join

10 may *then* be closed/may be closed *then*

11 will *only* be closed/be closed *only* temporarily

12 *Unfortunately* Lady B's son/a job yet, *unfortunately*

13 she *no longer* considers

14 seems *slowly* to/be *slowly* getting

15 will *easily* win/in October *easily*

16 do not *always* entirely agree

17 *However*, I/quite agree, *however*, with/on Friday, *however*

18 *entirely* by herself

19 because *eventually*/father *eventually*/ money *eventually*

20 Sheila, *too*, invested/in Marilyn's business *too*

21 *Already* Marilyn/is *already*/again *already*

22 *In the beginning* she . . . but *in the end* she/ went bankrupt *in the beginning* . . . succeeded *in the end*

23 behaves *very sensibly*

24 *Very sensibly* she/She *very sensibly* leaves

25 weekends *quietly*

26 would *almost certainly* have succeeded

27 She *clearly* has

28 *At present* she/is *at present*/USA *at present*

29 treated *very hospitably*

30 *Strangely enough* she/the other day, *strangely enough*

Exercise 2

1 The car skidded *badly*, *only just* missed a lamp-post, and *finally* came to a halt *in the butcher's.*

2 *Unfortunately* my car was *also badly* damaged *in an accident the other day.*

3 It was *definitely*/*Definitely* it was not my fault *in any way.*

4 The other driver *very stupidly* jammed on his brakes *right in front of me.*

5 He *possibly* thought/*Possibly* he thought

the traffic lights had *just* changed *from green to red.*

6 *Luckily enough* Willie was with me *at the time* and *fully* confirmed everything I said.

7 *Apparently* he had/He had *apparently* returned *from an architects' conference in the States only the day before.*

8 Did you know that Willie can *sometimes accurately* estimate the height of a building/estimate the height of a building *accurately by eye alone*?

9 I had *hardly* got home *in my car last night* when it *suddenly* started to snow.

10 It is *still* snowing *quite hard today*/Today it . . .

11 It is *already* lying *at least twenty centimetres deep*/Already it . . ./It . . . *deep already.*

12 If it is *still* snowing *at six o'clock* I shall *probably* stay *comfortably at home by the television the whole evening.*

13 Transport has *already* been *seriously* affected *throughout the country.*

14 *In fact* it has/It has *in fact* been brought *practically* to a standstill/It has been . . . standstill, *in fact.*

15 The local authorities are *clearly* not *adequately* equipped to deal *efficiently* with *such* heavy falls/*Clearly* the . . .

16 It will *very likely*/*Very likely* it will snow *tomorrow as well.*

17 *Frankly* I have/I have *frankly never much* liked snow/liked snow *much.*

18 *However*, children/Children, *however*, *evidently* adore it because they *immediately* rush out *into it.*

19 *Presumably at your age* you would/*At your age* you would *presumably* rather stay *snugly indoors.*

20 *Surprisingly enough* I would *much* prefer to run about *energetically outside.*

21 *Luckily* I *only rarely* want to do the things I *obviously* couldn't do.

22 *In fact* my age *seldom* prevents me from doing *exactly* what I want to do.

23 I *occasionally*/*Occasionally* I *still* go for long walks *alone through the woods*/I *still* . . . *occasionally.*

24 *Sometimes* I *also* like/I *sometimes also* like to row *gently about the lake in the park in the early autumn.*

25 The leaves are *then just* turning and the grapes are *fully* ripe.

26 *In the old days* we *very often* used/used

very often to take a trip *up into the mountains at that time of year.*

27 *Of course* things have/Things have *of course* changed *unbelievably since then*/ *Since then, of course,* things have changed *unbelievably.*

28 *On the whole, though,* they have not changed *for the worse in this part of the world.*

3A

1 The lecturer spoke *so* fast *that* I found it difficult to make any notes.

2 *As* he also spoke with a strong accent(,) I didn't understand all he said.

3 Mr McArthur's a very keen fisherman, *so* (he) spends a lot of time by the river.

4 Mrs McArthur, *knowing* that fishing is in his blood, doesn't try to stop him/*Knowing* that fishing is in his blood, Mrs McArthur doesn't try . . .

5 Many of the roads are flooded(,) *because* . . ./*Because* there was a lot of rain last night(,) many . . .

6 The weather forecast is for more rain, *so* I think we should postpone our trip.

7 Two years ago there was a very bad drought, *so that* the wells in our village began to dry up.

8 Soon there was *such* a (great) shortage of water *that* we had to ration it.

9 *Since* the plane didn't leave until the evening(,) they . . ./*They* decided to spend the afternoon sightseeing(,) *since* . . .

10 However, there was *so* little to see *that* they soon returned to the airport.

11 I felt rather nervous, *for* I'd never talked to a film star before.

12 *Knowing* how I felt, she soon put me at my ease.

13 My car wouldn't start *and so* I had to take a taxi.

14 *Realising* I'd be late for an appointment, I phoned my secretary.

15 *Having* heard nothing from my husband for over a week, I was getting rather worried.

16 Ken, *being* a friend of his, was getting worried too.

17 *Because* Willie had sprained his ankle(,) he found walking painful/Willie found walking painful(,) *because* he'd sprained his ankle.

18 However, he's *such* a reticent sort of

fellow *that* he said nothing about it.

19 My father's health was poor, *so* he retired early.

20 *Finding* himself short of money(,) he gave up smoking.

21 The Reds were determined to capture the city, *for* it was a vital communications centre.

22 The Whites, *fully aware* of its importance, were equally determined not to surrender it/*Fully aware* of its importance, the Whites were equally . . .

23 Many children have *so* much homework to do *that* they have very little leisure during the week.

24 *Since* this is the case(,) many families have to confine all their recreational activities to the weekend.

25 My son had *such* a bad cough *that* I kept him home from school this morning.

26 *So* few of the children are well enough to perform in the school concert *that* they've cancelled it.

27 Young David was deprived of parental love, *so* (he) naturally sought affection elsewhere.

28 *Since* Mrs McArthur was able to provide that affection(,) David became more attached to her than to his own mother.

29 *As* I'll be out quite late tonight(,) I'm . . ./I'm going to take a front-door key with me(,) *as* . . .

30 My father made a lot of/a terrible/a great fuss about my coming in late last night. I *therefore* told him I'd go and look for somewhere else to live.

3B Exercise 1

1 The lecturer spoke *too* fast *for* me to take any notes.

2 My dictionaries are *too* heavy (*for* me) to bring to class.

3 It's *too* difficult a subject (*for* us) to go into now.

4 He said that no one was *too* old to work/for work.

5 Sir James is *too* intelligent a politician to have made a remark like that.

6 The coffee Zena served at her party was rather *too* strong *for* my liking.

7 The swimming-pool was *too* shallow to dive into/for diving.

8 Those antique chairs are *too* valuable to sit on.

9 Do you mean they're *too* valuable to

use/for use/to be used?

10 If razors are *too* blunt to shave with, they have to be thrown away.

11 As an architect, Willie's far/much *too* much of a perfectionist to be responsible for the error on the plan.

12 It's *too* important a matter to leave to anyone but him.

13 The lighting in the room was *too* dim to read by/for reading.

14 The woman was sitting *too* far away *for* us to see who it was.

15 She looked rather *too* plump to have been Zena.

16 I'm wondering whether there's *too* much difference/*too* great a difference in our ages *for* our marriage to be a success.

17 It's *too* good an opportunity *for* Marilyn to miss.

18 She's *too* smart a businesswoman to miss a chance like that.

19 Ken's far/*much too* much of a Philistine to like classical music.

20 Helen's *too* outspoken *for* most people's liking.

Exercise 2

1 He was old *enough* to have been her father.

2 She was stupid *enough* to go and marry him.

3 He wasn't man(ly) *enough* to speak up in his own defence.

4 He didn't have *enough* sense even to realise what his rights were.

5 She was honest *enough* not to try to deny all responsibility for the accident.

6 She was also lucky *enough* to have the services of a very good lawyer.

7 Don't you think she sang (quite) well *enough* to have become a professional?

8 Her husband was undoubtedly a good *enough* guitarist to have become a professional.

9 I was idiot(ic) *enough* to throw away an opportunity of going to university.

10 I didn't have *enough* patience even to consider staying at school for the extra study required.

11 I haven't *enough* time to make a hotel reservation before I leave.

12 Would you be kind *enough* to book a room for me?

13 There are not *enough* experienced political figures left *for* the President to (be able to) form an effective government.

14 Ken has (quite) *enough* athletic talent to be very good indeed if he was well trained.

15 Marilyn didn't have *enough* money of her own to start a business by herself.

16 Sheila did well *enough* in the oral to make up for rather a poor paper in the written examination.

17 The country has *enough* natural resources to be practically self-sufficient in the event of war.

18 There's not *enough* of the green paint left *for* us to finish the wall (with).

19 My place of work isn't far *enough* away from my home *for* me to qualify for a travel allowance.

20 These people are fanatical *enough* in their cause to stop at nothing to gain their ends.

Exercise 3

1 The lecturer didn't speak slowly *enough* *for* me to take any notes.

2 The swimming-pool wasn't deep *enough* to dive into/for diving.

3 If razors aren't sharp *enough* to shave with, they have to be thrown away.

4 The lighting in the room wasn't bright *enough* to read by/for reading.

5 The woman wasn't sitting close/near *enough for* us to see who it was.

6 She didn't look slim *enough* to have been Zena.

7 Although it's an hour after sunset, it's still not cool *enough* for comfort, is it?

8 The coffee wasn't quite weak *enough* for my liking.

9 Some people are foolish *enough* not to realise/are not sensible *enough* to realise it is to their own advantage that others should not starve.

10 However, there are very few who are mean *enough* not to give/who are not generous *enough* to give at least a little of their money to charity.

4A

1 We're going to the coast *(in order/so as) to* get some photos of sea birds.

2 Don't go climbing up the cliff *in case* you fall.

3 We'll have to climb the cliff *(in order/so as) to* get good photos.

4 We're leaving early *so as not/in order not* to (have to) hurry.

5 We're going to drive slowly *so as not/in order not* to skid on the wet roads/*in case* we skid on the wet roads.

6 We're taking food with us *in case* we're home late.

7 We'd better take our waterproofs with us *in case* it rains.

8 And leave the heating on *so that* the house won't get cold while we're out/*in case* the house gets cold while we're out.

9 And put the food away *so that* the cat can't/won't get it/*in case* the cat gets it.

10 I won't shut the front door *in case* the cat wants to come in.

11 We're going to cut a hole in the back door *so that* the cat can get in and out as it likes.

12 Hadn't you better cut a hole in the front door *in case* it wants to get in and out that way as well?

13 I'm not taking my holiday next week after all *in case* I have to fly to Milan on business.

14 I'd better come into the office on Sunday *(in order/so as)* to prepare the necessary papers.

15 My assistant Brenda will keep in touch with you *so that* you'll know where I am.

16 I've drained the water out of my car *in case* it freezes tonight.

17 Why don't you put antifreeze in it *so as not/in order not* to have to bother about such things?

18 Please talk quietly *so as not/in order not* to wake the baby/*in case* you wake the baby.

19 Personally I always keep my baby up late *so that* he'll be really tired by the time I put him to bed.

20 I'm sure Denis is marrying Helen only *(in order/so as)* to have an influential father-in-law.

21 Yes, and Helen's trying to get a job as a teacher just *(in order/so as)* to impress Denis.

22 When I'm away I shall telephone my husband every evening *so that* he won't think/*in case* he thinks I'm having too good a time.

23 Let me know when you're going *so that* I can keep your husband company if he's lonely.

24 Sir James tried to persuade his son Toby to enter the family business *so that* he could eventually take it over.

25 He would also have liked him to learn Arabic and Chinese *so that* he could have been a real asset to the firm.

26 Zena gave me the key to her flat *so that* I could feed her alligator while she was away.

27 I shouldn't have gone near it if I'd been you *in case* it had snapped my hand off.

28 Where can I find Harry McArthur *(in order/so as)* to give him an important message?

29 You'd better go down to the river *in case* he's fishing.

30 He sometimes goes straight there from work *(in order/so as)* to save time.

4B

1 Please send me some samples of your firm's products *(for me) to show* (to) my customers.

2 When we go out we always leave our dog at home *to guard it* for us.

3 Sheila lent her sister a skirt *to wear* at Helen's party.

4 Marilyn is bringing some magazines with her this afternoon *for me to take* to my aunt in hospital.

5 If you're going out, buy some postcards *for us to send off* before we leave Rome tomorrow.

6 I'll get you a basket *to carry* all those things *in*.

7 Give me a nail *to hang* this picture up *with*.

8 Put the salmon in the freezer *for us to eat* next weekend.

9 I'm going to put this notice here *for everyone to see* as they walk in.

10 We're gathering our old toys together *for Sheila to give* to orphan children next Christmas.

11 As I'm arriving at the airport in the early hours of the morning, my wife's leaving our car there *for me to drive* home *in*.

12 I didn't put that book there *for you to pinch* but *for Willie to have a look at* during lunch.

13 When we go to town we always leave our children in the municipal playground *to amuse* themselves on the swings and roundabouts.

14 We also leave them there *so as* (to be able) *to do* the shopping undisturbed.

15 I've asked my secretary to stay at the office *to cope* with visitors while I see to the arrangements for the banquet over here.

16 I'll get her over here later *to help* me with the arrangements.

17 In the meanwhile I'm leaving her there *so as to be* free to concentrate on things over here.

18 Our parents sent us all to Britain when we were quite young *to learn* English.

19 They sent us *so as* (to be able) *to learn* English from us afterwards.

20 Personally I think they sent us there *to learn* to stand on our own feet.

5

1 *Although* I've been ... life, I've always ...

2 Cars are ... life and limb, *yet* advertisers ...

3 *Much as* Topal would have liked ... Britain, his tight schedule ...

4 His schedule may be tight, *but* he really should find time ...

5 *Even though* there is ... my parents' ages, it has been ...

6 What you say ... your parents' case. I think ... than the rule, *though*/I think, *though*, it's ... than the rule.

7 *Though* Sheila's pupils ... only a year, some of them ...

8 Sheila ... in Spain. *Even so* she has acquired ...

9 *Much as* I like Willie, I cannot ...

10 He may be unbusinesslike, *but* you must admit ...

11 We've never met Helen. *However*, we've heard ...!/... a lot about her, *however*!

12 We'd have (very much) liked to go to her party. I'm afraid we can't, *though*, because ...

13 Ken ... to life, *yet* he's no fool.

14 Fond *as* he is of Sheila, he's not ...

15 I suppose ... a brilliant politician. He makes a splendid country gentleman, *though*.

16 He has had ... time now. *Nevertheless*, he has managed ...

17 *Even though* Denis ... employee, he has ...

18 Don't you realise that, *although* he is junior to you, he's ...?

19 Helen's father ... Denis. Now, *however*, they're .../Now ... thieves, *however*.

20 *Though* Mr Elkins is ninety-three, he's ...

21 Old *as* he is, he still ...

22 He's a little hard of hearing. *Even so* he's ...

23 *Much as* I admire him, I'd never ...

24 You may (very much) dislike ... old. *Nevertheless*, the chances ...

6

1 *In spite of/Despite* Harry McArthur's good qualifications for the job, he ...

2 Perhaps ... it *because of* his scruffy appearance.

3 No, I ... was *because of* his failure to do ...

4 Some ... driving licences *because of* short sight.

5 What can I do *to make* the examiner give/ *to persuade* the examiner to give me my licence?

6 I can no longer ... test, *in spite of/despite* all my efforts/attempts/endeavours to take care of my eyes.

7 Helen ... chocolates *to prevent* anyone else (from) eating them.

8 *In spite of/Despite* my/a partiality to good chocolates, I ...

9 *Because of* these suspicions of hers, she ...

10 They ... fuel tanks *to give* it a greater range.

11 They ... this *to make* it a better commercial proposition.

12 However, *because of* the increase in weight/its increased weight, it will ...

13 My cousin ... she lives *because of* the lack of social life.

14 Her husband ... early *to allow/to enable* her to get ...

15 *In spite of/Despite* his efforts/attempts/ endeavours to help her, she continues ...

16 The flight was postponed *because of* a telephone(d) warning about ...

17 They ... out of service *to allow/to enable* the security personnel to search it.

18 *Because of* this delay, I ...

19 We ... promoted *because of* our lack of technical qualifications.

20 Ah, but ... programme *to allow/to enable* you to attend ...

21 They're ... courses *to give* the staff the chance ...

22 Exports ... now, *because of* the recent devaluation of the currency/the recent currency devaluation.

23 However, business . . . bad, *because of* the basically unstable economic situation.

24 We . . . country, *in spite of/despite* the absence/lack of sun.

25 Willie, *despite/in spite of* appearances, is . . .

7

1 *After* paying/*Having paid*/*When*/*After* I had paid at the cash desk . . . way, I left . . .

2 *On* checking/*When* I checked my change outside, I found . . .

3 *After* checking/*Having* checked/*When*/*After*/*Once* I had checked it again very carefully, I went back . . .

4 *As*/*When* Harry was getting into bed the other night, his wife said . . .

5 *Putting* on his dressing gown, he went downstairs.

6 *Going* into every room, he had a good look round, but . . .

7 *After* going/*Having* gone/*When*/*After* she had gone through her handbag three times, she (finally) found . . .

8 *On* putting/*When* she put the key in the lock, she found . . .

9 *As*/*While* she tried . . . the door, she thought . . .

10 *Chancing* to look up at the door number, she realised . . .

11 *On* touching/*When* I touched the handle of the fridge, I got . . .

12 I called out to my husband in the garage, *telling* him . . .

13 *As soon as*/*Immediately* he heard me, he came into the house.

14 *After* making/*Having* made/*When*/*After*/*Once* he had made sure all the current was switched off, he carefully . . .

15 *On* examining/*When* he examined one of the connections, he discovered . . .

16 *Uttering* a startled exclamation, he rushed . . .

17 *While* (he was) driving/*As* he was driving to the airport, Georgina's brother suddenly . . ./*As*/*While* Georgina's brother was . . . he suddenly . . .

18 *Drawing* up at the side of the road, he emptied . . .

19 *Seizing* his jacket off the back seat, he searched . . .

20 *As soon as*/*Immediately* he (had) got to the airport, he dashed off . . .

21 He spoke to his secretary at the office, *telling* her . . .

22 *While* (he was) waiting for her reply, he happened . . .

23 'Eureka!' he shouted into the phone, *waving* . . .

24 *On* hearing/*When* they heard him at the other end, they thought . . .

25 *When* he told them what had happened, they thought . . .

8A

1 Our neighbours . . . Lady Blenkinsop, *who* . . . Hall, *which* . . . grounds *that*/*which* . . .

2 Last Saturday . . . party, *where* . . . Chambers, *whom* . . .

3 Willie, *who* . . . architects (*that*/*which*) I . . . day, was . . .

4 It was . . . party *that* . . . Sheila, *whom* . . .

5 I told her that *what* . . . good, *which* . . .

6 Sheila . . . teachers (*whom*/*that*) I know *who*/*that* . . . voices, *which* . . . ability (*that*/*which*) children . . .

7 The blond fellow (*whom*/*that*) you . . . Ken, *whom* . . .

8 Incidentally, our athletic club, *whose* . . . council, are . . . Blenkinsops *who*/*that* . . .

9 At the stroke . . . Blenkinsop, *who* . . . bizarre, rode . . . staircase, a feat *that*/*which* . . .

10 It . . . occasions *when* . . . damage, *which* . . .

11 The time (*that*/*which*) I . . . was *when* . . . chandelier(,) the chain *of which* . . . table(,) *that*/*which* . . .

12 All *that* . . . trousers, *which* was hardly *what* . . .

13 *What* . . . Helen, *who* . . . party, is . . . about *what* . . .

14 Marilyn, *whom* . . . about, is . . . firm (*that*/*which*) she . . .

15 I . . . October, *when* . . . and *when* . . . contracts, *which* . . .

16 The first . . . India, *whose* . . . people *who*/*that* . . . business, *which* . . .

17 India is *where* . . . holiday (*that*/*which*) I . . . but *which* . . .

18 I . . . passport, *which* . . . date, at . . . consulate, *whose* . . .

19 My grandmother, *who* . . . birth, was . . . sisters, *which* . . .

20 Actually . . . one *who*/*that* . . . first, *which* . . . looks, *which* . . . man *who*/*that* . . .

21 It . . . today *that* . . . yesterday, *when* . . . office, I . . . something (*that*/*which*) I . . .

22 I bought *what* . . . home, *where* . . . the

decorators(,) *whom* ... week. These men
... it was I *who* ...

23 It ... 1945 *that* man committed *what* ...
Hiroshima *that/which*. ... That *which* ...

24 The ... terrain, *which* ... hilly, and ...
bomb, *which* ...

25 The atomic bombs *that/which* ...
kilotons, *which* ... bombs *that/which* ...
megatons, *which* ...

26 These ... bombs, *which* ... countries
that/which ... powers, are ...

27 A hydrogen bomb ... splitting, *which* ...
fusion, *when* two nuclei, *which* ...
hydrogen, come ...

28 Nuclear fission, *which* ... stations,
results ... residues *that/which* ... fusion,
which ... sun, has ...

29 The problem (*that/which*) scientists ...
temperatures *that/which* ... but *which* ...
fission *that/which* ...

30 Our greatest benefit ... nature, *which* ...
do, but ... ourselves, *which* ... by *what*

8B

1 New Zealand, *which* is situated between
latitudes 34°S and 47°S, consists
principally of two islands, of *which* the
southern is the larger but the northern
(is) the more highly populated.

2 The Maoris ... eighteenth century, *when*
the country began to be colonised by the
British, *whom* the Maoris, *whose* valour
and physique have been much admired,
resisted fiercely at times.

3 The Maoris, *who* at one time were
divided into many tribes *that/which* were
often at war with each other, are now a
peaceable people among *whom* the tribal
system scarcely exists.

4 The Maoris, *whose* name means
'indigenous', have a tradition according
to *which* they originally came from an
island called Hawaiki, *which* some people
have identified with Hawaii.

5 I fly ... twenty-second, *which* will give
me ten days there, after *which* I fly to
Singapore, *where* I plan to spend four
days before going on to Japan, *which* I
should reach on the twenty-seventh.

6 In India ... New Delhi, *where* the shade
temperature can reach 45°C in June, after
which it drops a bit because of the
monsoon.

7 India has many wonderful buildings, the

most famous of *which*/of *which* the most
famous is undoubtedly the Taj Mahal,
which the Emperor Shah Jehan built for
his favourite wife Mumtaz Mahal, *whose*
body lies ...

8 The Taj Mahal, *which* took twenty-two
years to complete and *which* is built of
white marble, exquisitely carved and
inlaid in places with semi-precious
stones (many of *which*/of *which* many,
incidentally, have been stolen), is one of
the greatest buildings in the world.

9 India, *which* after China is the most
populated country in the world, has over
half a billion people, a fact *that/which*
weighs heavily on its rulers, *whose* birth-
control policies have met with varying
success.

10 Singapore, *which* is an island off the coast
of Malaysia, to *which* it is linked by a road
and rail bridge but from *which* it seceded
politically in 1965, has grown from
practically nothing in the early
nineteenth century, *when* it was leased
from the then owners by a British
trading company, into an independent
Republic(,) *whose* present prosperity is
proverbial.

11 Japan, *where* so many of our consumer
goods are now made, deliberately cut
herself off from the outside world from
the early 1600s until 1853, *when*
Commander Perry of the United States
re-established communication, as a result
of *which* Japan has not only caught up
industrially with the West but has
overtaken it in some respects.

12 George Bernard Shaw, a photo of *whom*
smiles impishly at me from the wall of
my study, was an Irish playwright(,) *who*
audaciously set himself above
Shakespeare, *whom* in one outrageous
statement he said he despised as much as
he despised Homer.

13 Shaw was, in fact, something of an
intellectual clown, *which* did not prevent
... language *that/which* shows itself to
the full in the prefaces (*that/which*) he
wrote to most of his plays.

14 GBS ... London, *where* he spent a lot of
time ... politics, *which* led ...
playwright, a role in *which* he did not
fully establish himself until his forties.

15 In 1860 Abraham Lincoln ... the United
States, as a result of *which* a war soon

broke out between the North and South(,) *that/(which)* cost half a million lives and *(which)* ruined the South, *whose* slaves, *who* were set free, had been the basis of much of the economy.

16 The two best known generals . . . Grant and Sherman, *who* have both . . . after them, while on the Southern side . . . Lee and Jackson, after *whom*, to the best of my belief, no military equipment has been named, *which*, since Lee is usually held to be the greatest of the four, is rather ironic.

17 The turning point of the American Civil War, *which* went quite well for the South at first, came in 1863 at Gettysburg, a battle in *which* General Lee's troops were defeated and after *which* Abraham Lincoln made a speech(,) *that/(which)* is perhaps the most famous (speech) in American history.

18 The best known book . . . 'Gone with the Wind', *whose* authoress/the authoress of *which*, Margaret Mitchell, was herself brought up in the South, *where* she heard first-hand accounts of the struggle, many of *which* she . . .

19 Powered flight, *which* is perhaps . . . century, began with the two Wright brothers, *who* first achieved it on 17th December 1903, *when* each of them . . . aeroplane 'Kitty Hawk', *which* is now . . .

20 Their achievement . . . Otto Lilienthal, a German *who* designed . . . gliders(,) in one of *which* he unfortunately met his death in 1896 while . . .

21 The next stage in the development of the aeroplane, *which* was greatly stimulated by the Wrights' achievements, took place largely in France, *where* Bleriot . . . in 1909, after *which* governments were forced to take the flying machine seriously.

22 Unlike most of the aeroplanes of the time, *which* were biplanes, Bleriot's machine was a monoplane, a type of *which* he was the pioneer and *which* has since proved itself . . .

23 The problem of how to support a single wing, *which* Bleriot had overcome with wires from a central post, was not fully solved until the 1930s, *when* the use . . . stronger wings *that/which* needed no external support, *which* soon led . . .

24 Another epoch-making flight . . . 1919,

when two Britons . . . Ireland, *where* they landed in a bog after flying . . . in an open plane of military type(,) *that/(which)* had . . .

8C Exercise 1

1 Marilyn has lost a purse *containing* . . .
2 Anyone *finding* . . .
3 (Unchanged)
4 Marilyn, *smiling* . . . face, has . . .
5 (Unchanged)
6 Willie, *a young architect*, has . . .
7 His client, *a Japanese*, cannot . . .
8 Willie, *anxious* not to lose his client, is . . .
9 Lady Blenkinsop, *a woman* of considerable enterprise, is . . .
10 (Unchanged)
11 Now Lady Blenkinsop, *full of enthusiasm* for her new life, gets . . .
12 I tell those friends of mine *with* sedentary jobs that . . .
13 (Unchanged)
14 Anyone *buying* a second-hand car should . . .
15 (Unchanged)
16 Several young mothers, all *with* babies in their arms, waited . . .
17 There are many people *just not patient enough* to wait . . .
18 Anyone *thinking* of taking the exam should . . .
19 (Unchanged)
20 (Unchanged)
21 No, that's Zena, *a fashion model with* a pet alligator.
22 (Unchanged)
23 It is one of the few houses *not up* for sale.
24 (Unchanged)
25 On the left there is an oak tree *with* branches *stretching* right across the road.
26 Sir James, *realising* . . . a layabout, has . . .
27 Toby, *(with)* a note of sarcasm in his voice, asked . . .
28 I envy people *with* no family ties . . .
29 (Unchanged)
30 (Unchanged)
31 A working mother *with* four young children has her hands full.
32 (Unchanged)
33 I notice that some of those *applying* for the post have . . .
34 Any motorist *wishing* to take advantage . . .
35 (Unchanged)

Exercise 2

1 Our neighbours . . . grounds *open* to the public in summer.
2 Sir James, *a Radical Member of Parliament*, is . . . Blenkinsop Hall, *left* him by his father, and live in something *with* a less aristocratic image.
3 Sheila is one of the few teachers *able* to control . . . voices, *an ability* that . . .
4 New Zealand, *situated* between latitudes 34°S and 47°S, consists principally of two islands, the southern *being* the larger but the northern (*being*) the more highly populated.
5 The Maoris, at one time *divided* into many tribes often *at war* with each other, are now a peaceable people among whom . . .
6 The atomic bombs *dropped* . . . twenty kilotons, *equal* to that of 20,000 tons of TNT, whereas some of the bombs *developed* since then are said . . . forty-five megatons, *equal* to that . . .
7 These more powerful bombs, *now included* in the arsenals of all countries *calling* themselves nuclear powers, are known . . .
8 A hydrogen bomb . . . or splitting, *the basis* of the atomic bomb, but on nuclear fusion, when two nuclei, in this case *nuclei* of 'heavy' hydrogen, come together . . .
9 Nuclear fission, the *source* of energy of atomic power stations, results in . . . residues *difficult* to dispose of, whereas nuclear fusion, *the source* of energy of the sun, has . . .
10 The problem scientists are faced with . . . the high temperatures *found* in the sun but so far *produced* artificially only by the nuclear fission *providing* the 'trigger' mechanism . . .

9 Exercise 1
1 like
2 so/as
3 than
4 Whereas
5 than
6 as
7 as
8 as
9 in
10 from
11 to
12 as
13 as
14 like
15 as
16 as
17 like
18 such
19 as
20 as
21 as/like
22 as

23 as
24 except/other than
25 like
26 as
27 as
28 The
29 the
30 the
31 in
32 whereas/while/ but
33 such
34 whereas/while/ but
35 than
36 whereas/while/ but
37 like
38 as
39 to
40 as
41 than
42 like
43 than
44 besides
45 like
46 like
47 whereas/while/ but
48 as
49 like
50 like
51 like
52 than
53 to
54 than
55 as
56 as
57 like
58 The
59 the
60 as
61 as
62 than
63 as
64 so/as
65 as

Exercise 2

1 The sitting room has more chairs in it than the dining room.
2 Downstairs the ceilings are higher than they are upstairs.
3 This house is better built/built better than the one next door.
4 We expected to arrive earlier than we did.
5 It was much noisier at the airport than it is here.
6 We'd like to live nearer the town than we do.
7 We should have done more homework than we have.
8 Tokyo's a bigger city than London.
9 The Mediterranean's saltier than the Atlantic.
10 India's more densely populated than Russia.
11 Chinese is a harder language than Arabic.
12 The Japanese are better at judo than we are.
13 Saturn's farther/further from the sun than Jupiter.
14 On the whole northerners are fairer than southerners.
15 In the north of England people are more friendly/friendlier than they are here.

16 You thought there was less petrol in the tank than there is.
17 Mosquitoes are more of a nuisance than flies.
18 Salmon are scarcer now than they were twenty years ago.
19 Last year inflation was worse than it is this.
20 People think being rich is more of an advantage than it is.

Exercise 3
1 We don't work as/so hard as our grandparents did.
2 They didn't have such a high standard of living as we do.
3 We don't live as/so far from the town as they do.
4 We haven't as/so little money as they have.
5 They haven't as/so much confidence in the future as we have.
6 Old people aren't nearly as/so active as young people.
7 They haven't as/so few responsibilities as we have.
8 Pets aren't such a/as/so much of a responsibility as children.
9 Cats aren't such a/as/so much of a nuisance as dogs.
10 They don't greet us in such a friendly/in as/so friendly a way as they used to.
11 We usedn't/didn't use to see them as/so often (as we do).
12 We don't speak the language as well as they do.
13 English hasn't (got)/doesn't have such a complicated/as/so complicated a grammar as German.
14 I didn't expect her to have as/so little self-confidence.
15 He usedn't/didn't use to smoke as/so much (as he does).
16 We shouldn't eat as/so much (as we do).
17 The present generation doesn't behave as/so badly as we did in our youth.
18 I didn't think the house would be as/so well furnished (as it is).
19 Ours isn't such a good/as/so good a table as this (one)/Our table isn't as/so good as this (one).
20 Inflation isn't nearly as/so bad this year as last.

10A

1	to brush up	19	get
2	stay	20	(to) compete
3	practise	21	win
4	to open	22	to be working
5	turn	23	to be gardening
6	suspect	24	fishing
7	to be travelling	25	to have had
8	be accused	26	to have been injured
9	interfere	27	to believe
10	(to be) searched	28	(to be) stopped
11	to be going	29	(to) find
12	be	30	to have typed
13	to be told	31	(to) have
14	to pick up/to have picked up	32	to let
15	give/given	33	know
16	to be	34	to do
17	have	35	to be working
18	fall	36	(to be) living

10B Exercise 1

1	watching	14	me/my taking
2	them/their doing	15	going
3	being watched	16	happening; me/my going
4	me/my being	17	learning; reading
5	being kept	18	Learning; learning
6	being mistaken	19	having
7	fooling about	20	being called up
8	talking	21	having had
9	you/your telling	22	him/his apologising
10	me/my mentioning	23	standing
11	lending; paying	24	her standing
12	Being; you/your treating		
13	being treated		

Exercise 2
1 Helen suggests *(us/our) going* ...
2 Is it necessary *to be* ...?
3 The last time I went I managed *to get in* ...
4 Ken's ... and so we're unlikely *to have* ...
5 Do you fancy *going* ...?
6 Don't ... that will put her off *going*.
7 Will your mother mind *you/your taking* ...?
8 She allows me *to use* ...
9 It's not worth *going* ...
10 You risk *being stopped* ...

11 A blowout in one of the front tyres caused Ken *to lose* control . . .
12 I always avoid *driving* . . .
13 I've given up *counting* . . .
14 Why don't you forbid him *to use* . . . ?
15 It's no use *him/his pleading* . . .
16 He doesn't deserve *to get away* . . .
17 Denis denies *breaking* . . .
18 Can you imagine *him/his* ever *admitting* . . . ?
19 It's impossible for my secretaries/My secretaries find it impossible *to cope* . . .
20 It enables them *to do* . . .
21 I miss *being* able . . .
22 Denis is usually the last *to arrive* . . . is seldom the first *to leave* . . .
23 I'm surprised *to hear* . . .
24 I dare you *to tell* . . .
25 He's certain *to ask* . . .
26 Yes, you can always rely on Denis *to ask/ asking* . . .
27 I can't afford *to make* . . .
28 I've put off *going* . . .
29 Leaving tomorrow would involve (*me/ my*) *missing* . . .
30 Ken and I have arranged *to meet* . . .
31 We're considering *hiring* . . .
32 I enjoy *messing about* . . .
33 I intend *to get/getting* . . .
34 I strongly resent *paying* . . .
35 I'm trying to persuade Willie *to come* . . .
36 I keep *telling* . . .
37 His own doctor has advised him *to have* one.
38 He has warned him *not to overwork/ against overworking.*
39 My doctor recommends *taking/one to take* . . .
40 Willie must be made *to see* sense.
41 How much longer do you expect Marilyn *to stay* . . . ?
42 She plans *to return* . . .
43 Her American friends are probably encouraging her *to stay* longer.
44 They're so hospitable that she may find it hard to resist *staying* . . .
45 But I can't foresee *her staying* . . .
46 Some Americans have difficulty *(in) understanding* . . .
47 By the way, she mentioned *meeting* . . .
48 She happened *to be staying* . . .
49 Getting to know Toby well would necessitate *sharing* . . .
50 That's not something I propose *to do/ doing.*

10C

1	criticising	28	writing
2	to think	29	posting
3	doing	30	to get
4	to do	31	trying
5	to say	32	to convince
6	applying	33	to say
7	looking after	34	changing
8	to think	35	to think
9	skiing/to ski	36	going
10	to turn	37	criticising/to criticise
11	(to) become		
12	to interest	38	to think
13	trying	39	to cut
14	to tell	40	cutting
15	giving up	41	to interest
16	to form	42	giving
17	to think	43	to be
18	eating	44	modernising/ to be modernised
19	(to) take		
20	to stop		
21	snoring	45	to lock
22	sleeping	46	to do
23	being	47	to tell
24	being	48	talking
25	to keep	49	to have/to have had
26	smoking/to smoke		
27	to deteriorate	50	to ring

10D

1	reading	21	go
2	do	22	say
3	open	23	saying
4	lying	24	to say
5	to be suffering	25	to see
6	to finish	26	sightseeing
7	standing	27	fishing
8	holding	28	to mean
9	getting	29	working
10	to get	30	write
11	to lend	31	watching
12	running	32	click
13	fishing	33	approaching
14	to meet	34	stop
15	to use	35	beating
16	borrowing	36	loitering
17	running	37	to tell
18	to find	38	to be
19	voting	39	creeping
20	do	40	to know

11A

1 I remember our parents *could* be very strict . . . they *could* control us . . .

2 We certainly *couldn't do* ... *Can* your children do ...?

3 Mankind *may have* ... if it *can't* mend ...

4 What they said *may not have* been true, but we *couldn't* ignore it.

5 *May/Might/Could* I use ...? I *may/might/could have* left ...

6 I *couldn't* possibly pay back ... *Couldn't* you let ...?

7 Did ... noise? I think the clock *may have* fallen ... *Could* you go and see?

8 I *can't* go ... I *can't* leave ...

9 Mary and Harry McArthur have at last been able to do (unchanged) ... Unfortunately Christine *couldn't* go ...

10 I *can't* usually get ... but I was able to get (unchanged) ...

11 When ... you *could* park .... But you *can't* do ...

12 You *can* spend .... The other day, when I was able to find (unchanged) ...

13 'Under ... *can* my daughter marry ...! He *can't* go ...!'

14 'You/One *can't* adopt .... You should know you *can't* stop ...'

15 '*May/Might/Could* I make ...? *Couldn't* we at least show ...?'

16 'He *may* after all not be ... When you've been able to form (unchanged) ... we *can* think again.'

17 Later ... Helen was able to convince (unchanged) ... they *could* ask ...

18 'All right ... you *can* ask ... I *can* confirm ...'

19 You/One *couldn't* criticise ... Denis ... and he certainly *can* turn it on ... he *could* say ...

20 You *can* fool ... but you *can't* fool ...

11B

1 Willie *would spend* ... *wouldn't often* play ...

2 He ... they *would tease* ...

3 When ... he *(woul)d smile* and *say* nothing.

4 He *used to be* very shy ... he *(wi)ll* accept ...

5 In fact he *(wi)ll tell* people that he *used to keep* himself to himself so as to be able to ...

6 He *may have* kept quiet on the subject, *but* he always knew ...

7 Denis and Helen's father *usedn't to be/ didn't use to be* on speaking ...

8 Yes, Denis *would* know how ...!

9 He *may* be the boss's future son-in-law, *but* I'm damned if ...

10 You *will criticise* ...

11 Charles, why *will* you *interrupt* ...? Why *won't* you wait ...?

12 Charles *wouldn't* admit ... He *may* be a nice boy, *but* he can be ...

13 I ... your cat *(wi)ll* lie about ... *Used* it *to be/Did* it *use to be* more active?

14 Oh yes, she *used to be* .... You ... kitten, when she *wouldn't keep/(woul)d never keep* still ... But ... cats *will grow up*, *won't* they?

15 People *will leave* their litter .... This picnic site *used to look* quite tidy ...

16 There *usedn't to be/*There *didn't use to be* anything ... a few people *(woul)d come* ...

17 When ... she replied: 'Robert *would*! He *may pretend* ... sporting type, *but* actually he's ...'

18 I ... who *(wi)ll* sit in cafés ...

19 Robert *would* go and spoil ...

20 I ... Robert *would say* ... He *may have* said that, *but* has he ...?

11C

1 'll be going	14 must have
2 won't be going	cancelled
3 'll be enjoying	15 must have gone
4 must have	16 won't have gone
forgotten	17 'll be sitting
5 should have	18 must be
6 should be	19 should be
7 'll be/must be	20 can't drink
8 'll be looking	21 will still be
forward	22 should be
9 will have taken	23 must have
off	passed
10 should be	24 can't have
11 must have	25 won't know
missed	26 will have got
12 'll know/should	27 should have
know	28 'll be
13 'll be	29 can't be
	30 must have had

11D

1 don't need to/	worried
have to lock	5 needn't pay
2 have to lock	6 must
3 didn't need to/	7 don't need to/
have to wait	have to get up
4 needn't have	8 have to get up

9   wouldn't need to/have to get up
10 'd have to pay
11 needn't have turned off
12 must finish
13 won't need to/have to go on
14 will/shall
15 Did you have to call
16 didn't
17 won't need to/have to have
18 'll need to/have to have
19 didn't need to/have to buy
20 had to buy
21 needn't have worried
22 has to/must worry
23 didn't need to/have to take
24 'll have to/must take
25 have to report
26 must let
27 needn't drive/doesn't need to/have to drive
28 don't need to/have to be
29 needn't be
30 must try

11E

1   could have/might have apologised
2   shouldn't/oughtn't to behave
3   was to go
4   was to take
5   should keep
6   could have/might have told
7   should have/ought to have told
8   is to retire
9   was to have retired
10 should have/ought to have made
11 was to have spoken
12 should have/ought to have got
13 shouldn't/oughtn't to make
14 should have/ought to have won
15 were to have played
16 could have/might have stopped
17 was to have been
18 was to return
19 shouldn't/oughtn't to delay
20 'm to wait
21 's to pick
22 should have/ought to have offered
23 could/might be
24 should have/ought to have provided
25 shouldn't have/oughtn't to have left
26 was to have fed
27 could/might at least have invited
28 should never have/ought never to have sent
29 was to be
30 is to be

11F

1   ... It is that we *should* go into business .... I have told him it is essential *that we should know* .... It is obviously better *that we should be* extremely cautious ... than *(that we should)* regret it later ...
2   Our stockbroker recommends that we *should* buy .... Really? It's odd that he *should have* suddenly changed .... Why *should* it *be* odd? It's only right *that a stockbroker should change* .... I'm sure he intends *that we should make* money, not lose it.
3   I'm sorry (that) there *should have been* .... I told ... essential *that he should be* ... in case the plane *should be* early .... I naturally thought it strange (that) there *should be* ...
4   I really don't see why some people *should* get .... Why, after all, *should* Helen *have got* ...? The ... Helen's mother insisted *that her daughter should get* it .... It makes my blood boil to think that she *should be* able .... I have already suggested to the committee that we *should* change .... I don't see why you *should be* so upset ...
5   I'm surprised that the railwaymen *should* have gone .... Why *should it be* a small issue? They ... suggesting that they *should* be paid .... That you *should* consider ... astonishes me. I admit it's a pity (that) they *should* have to bring ... but then, after all, why *shouldn't* they?
6   Sir James was most anxious *that the committee should give* .... He said ... that it was better *that the public should know* .... That he *should have* said ....

12A Exercise 1

1   He said (that) when Brenda *had* joined *their* firm ten years *before* she had already worked ... and had learnt ...
2   He said *that* for the first eight years with *them* she *had* worked in the Sales Department, and *had been* working there when he *had* become the firm's Managing Director, but *that* since then she *had* been working as *his* personal assistant.
3   He went on to say *that* normally she *worked* ... next to *his*, but *that* she *was* not there *then*/at *that* moment because she *was* working ...
4   He said (that) he sincerely hoped (that)

215

she *would* go on working *there* until he *retired*, as over the *previous* few years she *had* learnt as much about *the* business as *he had, which, he assured me, was* quite a lot.

5 I asked *him* who she *was* going to work for when *he* retired, and ventured to *suggest* (that) she *could*/and said that perhaps she *could* come and work for me, as she *sounded* an absolute gem.

6 He *told me* not *to* get the wrong idea and imagine we *were* talking about a young girl, *as/since/for/because* she *would* be well over fifty when he *retired*, and so *would* be retiring . . .

7 I asked *whether/if* she *was* going to retire . . . or *whether/if he thought* she *was* one of those who *went* on working . . .

8 He *replied that* he *had* heard her say (that) she *might* set herself up as a business consultant, for *which* she *would* certainly have had the right sort of experience.

9 *However, he thought* (that) it would be better if *I* asked her about it *myself* the *next/following day, when he expected* her to be back from London.

10 He said that if *I looked* in in the afternoon *he could* introduce *me* to her, *but told me* not *to* come in the morning, because she *might* not be *there* until midday.

11 He added *that* if anyone *asked me* who *I had* (got) an appointment with, *I was to* tell them (that) it *was* with *him*, not with her.

12 *After explaining that* he would have liked to join *us* both the *next/following day* but *did* not think (that) *he would* have the time/*After explaining that, although* he . . . *day, he did* not think . . . time, *he reminded me* that Brenda *would* be able to give *me* as much information about *the* business as *he* would.

Exercise 2

1 I asked Willie one day *whether/if he was* doing anything *that* evening and *whether/if he* would like . . .

2 He replied *that, although I might* not believe it, *he had* never been to a disco in his life, *as/since/because/for he was* afraid *he* just wouldn't be able to stand the noise.

3 I said (that) it *was* clearly high time *he* went to one *and that* I'd take *him* where *he* would be surprised . . .

4 Willie replied that *it sounded* idyllic but *asked* who; if *he went* out *that* evening, *was* to do all *the* work *which/that had* (got) to be done by *the next/following* morning.

5 I asked *him* who *he was* doing it for *and whether/if* it *could* not wait, *adding that* I *had* had a lot of work myself *a few days before*, but *had* not let it spoil my evening.

6 Willie replied *that* if *his* work spoilt *his* evenings *he* would not be an architect, because *he* often *had* to work in the evening.

Exercise 3

1 He *said* (that) *he* would like to learn to play the piano and *that he wished he* knew a good teacher who lived fairly near and who would give *him* lessons.

2 She asked (him) what *he* would say if *she* offered to give *him* lessons,

3 *and when* he *exclaimed that he wished she* would, *as* (etc.) *he* would rather *she* taught *him* than anyone else,

4 she *replied that she would* teach *him* provided *he attended her* lessons regularly and *practised* hard.

5 He *asked* (her) *whether/if she* knew (that) *she had* a good reputation as a teacher, *adding that* it would have been nice if *she* had been able to teach him *the previous* month, when *he had* had quite a lot of free time.

6 She *emphasised that she would* never teach anyone who *was* not prepared to practise, no matter who they *were*,

7 *to which* he *replied that he would* practise as if it were a matter of life and death, and *that he would* pay *her* what *she* wanted, even if it was more than *she was* getting at the music school, however much that *was*.

8 *When* she *expressed her satisfaction, saying* (that) it *was* time *they* started the first lesson,

9 he *replied that although he* would have liked to have started *that* day *he* unfortunately *could* not, *adding that* in the meanwhile *they had* better/*suggesting that* in the meanwhile *they should* settle the price, because if *they* did not it would be unbusinesslike.

10 (To this) She *agreed, declaring that she* would hate to start on the wrong note.

12B

1 Harry McArthur said (that) *they would have to* get rid of *the* new typist if she *did* not improve.

2 He *pointed out that they* must not be too soft-hearted about her if *they wanted* an efficient firm.

3 He said (that) it must be the third time *he had* told her about the petty cash, *and that* she should listen when *he gave* her instructions.

4 He said (that) she *was* never *to* take money out of the petty cash without *his* permission.

5 Georgina said (that) *she thought* she might do it again, *and asked* what she *should/was to* tell her if she *did*.

6 Harry answered *that she did* not *need to/have to* tell her anything, because *he would* deal with the matter *himself*.

7 The girl said (that) *she had* not *been able to* ask Mr McArthur about the petty cash because he had gone out to lunch, and (that) *she had therefore* thought *she* could use *her* own discretion in the matter.

8 Georgina said (that) the girl must be very stupid to say things like that, *and asked whether/if she should/was to* tell her she *had* got the sack.

9 Harry replied *that* no one *was to* tell her anything *and that* she *had to/was to* come and see him.

10 He said (that) it *looked* very much as if *they would have to* tell her that her services *were* no longer required.

11 He said (that) regulations *stated* that she *had to* have at least . . .

12 Harry remarked *that* she *was* quite a nice kid and that one must not be too hard on her.

13 He told her *that* although *he was* afraid *she would have to* go *she would* not *need to/have to* worry too much because *he would* give *her* quite a good testimonial.

14 The girl asked *whether/if she* could have the testimonial *straight away* so that *she* could start looking for another job at once.

15 I *suggested to her that* perhaps *her* father could help *her* find a job and *that she* should pay him a visit.

16 She replied *that she* might do just that, *but added that* it would cost a lot.

17 The travel agent asked (her) *whether/if he should* book *her* a seat on the flight (in question), *adding that she did* not *need to/have to* pay the whole of the fare *then*.

18 She told me later (that) she *had* not *needed to/had to* pay the whole fare when *she had* booked, *and* so need not have worried so much about money.

19 She said (that) *she had* not *been able to* get through to *her* father the night *before/previous* night to tell him of *her* plans, *and asked* (me) *whether/if* I could phone him from *my* office for *her*.

20 Her father said on the phone (that) she could not have arranged to come at a worse time and *that he could* not possibly meet her at the airport on *the* Friday.

21 He said (that) *he would* have just come back from Canada and *that* there *would* be several business matters *he would have to* see to before the weekend.

22 I told him (that) she *had* not *been able to* warn *him* before, *and asked* (him) what I *should/was to* tell her to do.

23 He said (that) *I* should not spoil the girl, *and that* she ought to be capable of *going* to see *him* without all *the* help *she was getting* from strangers.

24 I asked *whether/if* I *should/was to* tell her what *he had* said or *whether/if he* would rather I did not.

25 The girl insisted later *that her father* could not have understood *me*, *adding that she wished* that he was going to be at the airport to meet *her*, even if it was only to say 'Hullo' before he went back to his business.

12C Exercise 1

1 My wife *suggested* sending away/that we should send away for *an* electric kettle advertised . . .

2 It was about three weeks later that I *asked* her to plug it in while I got the cups.

3 I *warned* her not to fill/against filling it with the switch on.

4 I *ordered* her to stand back while I disconnected it.

5 I *warned* her never to touch/against ever touching *the* kettle again, *as* it was live.

6 My wife *suggested* getting/that we should get a lawn-mower the next time there was a special offer.

7 The girl from next door, who'd just come in, *advised* us to get the whole house rewired.

8 My wife *urged* me to follow such an excellent piece of advice.

9 I, still tense from the affair of the kettle, *told* her to mind her own business.

10 She *warned* me never to speak/against ever speaking to her like that again if I wanted any more meals cooked.

11 I apologised and *begged/implored/entreated* her to forgive me.

12 Then, by way of a peace offering, I *suggested* eating/that we should eat out that evening.

13 Our neighbour (at once/immediately) *suggested* our going/that we should go to the new Chinese restaurant, which she'd heard was excellent.

14 But she *warned* (me) that/She *warned* (me), however, that I'd have to reserve a table.

15 And, eyeing me disapprovingly, she *advised* me to put on a tie.

16 My wife (agreed and) *told/ordered* me to go upstairs and change into something decent.

17 She *forbad(e)* (see 17A) me to go out with her looking as/the way I did.

18 Our neighbour *advised* me to telephone the restaurant first.

19 My wife *told/ordered* me to hurry up, whichever I did first.

20 Suddenly feeling a great need for peace and quiet, I *suggested* both of them going out/that they should both go out instead of me.

Exercise 2

1 *She asked* (me) where *I came* from *and whether/if I was* staying here long.

2 *She asked* (me) *whether/if* this *was* the first time *I'd* been here.

3 *She said she'd* been living here for over a year and quite *liked* the place.

4 But *he said she'd* rather live in London *and asked me whether/if I* wouldn't (rather live there) *too*.

5 *She said I* must find this place rather dull compared with *my* home town.

6 *She asked* (me) what we *could* do this evening if we *decided* to go out.

7 *She said* we could go to the cinema if there *were* any good films on.

8 *She suggested* going to a concert *and asked* (me) if *I liked* music.

9 *She said I* needn't/didn't need to/didn't *have to* decide now, *but could* let her know later.

10 *She asked* (me) *whether/if she should* come round to *my* house or wait for *me* here.

11 *She asked* (me) *whether/if I'd* be ready if *she called* for *me* at six o'clock.

12 *She told me* not *to forget* to bring an umbrella, as it *might* rain.

13 *She said she wished her* car was in order, so *she* could have given *me* a lift.

14 *She said* it *was* being repaired, and *wouldn't* be ready until the end of the week.

15 *She said she wished she* knew more about cars than *she did*.

16 *She said she* could save a lot of money if *she* was able to do the maintenance *herself*.

17 *She said she* had to come here by bus this morning, as *she was* without *her* car.

18 *She asked* (me) *whether/if I* walked or drove to work this morning.

19 *She told me* not *to/She said I* mustn't/wasn't *to* drive on the right here whatever *I did*.

20 *She said that* if *I'd* been to Japan *I'd* know that they *drove* on the left there too.

21 *She asked* (me) *whether/if I thought she'd* like *my* country if *she* visited it.

22 *She asked me to* tell *her* the things *she* should make a point of seeing.

23 *She said* she must/'d *have to* try and save some money so that *she could* visit *me*.

24 *She said she* must/had *to* go now as *she had* to correct some homework.

25 *She told me* not *to/She said I* mustn't/wasn't *to* forget that *I had* some homework to do for tomorrow.

13A

1 I hadn't been . . . four months when *I was taught* the elements of marketing and (was) *made* a sales representative.

2 *I* recently *had* my salary *increased* by thirty per cent. The trouble is that at the same time *I had* my expense allowance *reduced* by nearly half.

3 Denis says *he has been offered* a job in Singapore *by* his firm, but that he won't take it because *he has been promised* a much better job in Japan *by* someone else.

4 *I have been lent* a book on computers and I . . . work. *I had* never *had* them *explained* to me before.

5 Last year *I was overtaxed* and *am* now

owed quite a lot of money. I think that until *I have* it *refunded* to me *I should be paid* interest on it, don't you?

6 *Income tax should be done away with* altogether. If necessary, *value added tax could be put up* by way of compensation. But unfortunately *this Government can* always *be relied on* not to do the right thing.

7 From the way *this Government is being spoken about, it might be thought* that *it will not be voted* back into power at the next election. However, *the result will* probably *be decided* in the Government's favour *by* the proverb ...

8 Over the years *various small, friendly shops have been set up* in this town, but they seldom survive long because *they have* their prices *forced down by* the supermarkets and *are driven* out of business. *It has been suggested* that shop owners should combine in an advertising campaign, but this would probably lead to *them/their being beaten* yet again by the supermarkets, this time ...

9 *Have you* ever *had* your washing *stolen* when ... dry? *I have.* In fact *I have been having* mine *stolen* a bit at a time ...

10 A couple of weeks ago *Peter had* his passport *confiscated. He* won't *have* it *returned* to him now he's been arrested.

11 The latest news is that *he has been charged* with conspiracy, (has been) *refused* bail, and (has been) *jailed. You may be forbidden* any contact ...

12 During the war *we used to have* our letters *opened* and *censored. We were told,* of course, that *we would* never *have* our personal affairs *disclosed* or *discussed by* the censors.

13 *I was* always *having* the pieces I wrote *rejected by* publishers, but now I am glad to say *I am* beginning to *have* them *accepted.*

14 I thought *children were refused* admission to horror films, but the other day *my twelve-year-old niece was allowed in* to see that shocker at the Plaza.

15 *Brenda Pearl was left* a considerable sum of money *by* her father but *she had* quite a lot of it *taken* off her *by* crafty lawyers.

16 *Ken has had* his driving licence *endorsed* again, I'm afraid. The next time *he's caught* for speeding *he'll* probably *be disqualified* from driving for a year.

17 My car broke down yesterday and *had to be towed* to a local garage for repair. *I'll be charged* for the repair, of course, but not for the tow, as *I am covered* for that *by* my membership ...

18 *I was* once *shown* the way to the railway station, but ... pity, because *I am* frequently *asked* it.

19 *I used to have it drummed* into me as a child that ... life. *I was told* wrong.

20 *Martin Luther King was awarded* the Nobel Peace Prize in 1964. *He was assassinated* in 1968.

21 *I was* once *taught* a Finnish song without *being told* what it really meant. In fact *I was played* a nasty trick, because ...

22 *It has been known* for some time that if *the young of domestic animals are fed* penicillin *their growth rate is* significantly *increased.*

13B Exercise 1
1 Willie *has been known to stay up* ...
2 Willie's father *is said to have been* a ...
3 Unfortunately his secretary *is nowhere to be found.*
4 She *is said to have been* last *seen* in ...
5 She *is known* for certain *to have been* at ...
6 She *was found to be* a ...
7 Last night *Ken was stopped* on the motorway and *made to show* his ...
8 He *does not appear/appears not to have been detained.*
9 Both *Helen and Sheila are said to have been* with him ...
10 He *is thought by* some (people) *to be* a ...
11 He *is believed to have had* his licence endorsed twice.
12 Willie's father *is considered* by many (people) *to have been* one ...
13 He *seems to have been ignored by* most of the art critics.
14 He *was said to have insulted* the critics ...
15 Are *such people to be trusted?*
16 The man *was presumed to be waiting* for them outside.
17 He was *nowhere to be seen.*
18 He *should have been made to pay* the extra cost himself.
19 That *kind of paint* is not meant *to be used* on walls.
20 Real craftsmen *are seldom to be found* nowadays.

Exercise 2

1 *She's being considered* for the job.
2 *She may be interviewed* tomorrow.
3 *She won't be told* the result until next week.
4 *She isn't* likely *to be given* the job.
5 *Was she paid* last month?
6 *Is she* usually *paid* by cheque?
7 *She hasn't been paid* anything yet.
8 *She'll be told* what to do.
9 *She should have had* it *explained* to her already.
10 *She was made to look* pretty foolish.
11 *She was being talked about* behind her back.
12 *She's said to have done* her work carelessly.
13 *She was seen running* out of the room.
14 *She'd been insulted.*
15 *She'd* even *had* her hair *pulled.*
16 *She's had* her sabbatical leave *cancelled.*
17 *She's had* her sabbatical leave *cancelled.*
18 *She's going to have* her salary *cut.*
19 *She's going to be made to apologise* to the Principal.
20 *She should have been allowed* the chance to explain herself.

14A

1 *Bang* went the starter's gun and *off* went the runners . . .
2 *Scarcely* had they covered the first lap when . . .
3 *Behind him* at the time was a runner . . .
4 (No change)
5 At . . . last; *second from last* was our friend Ken.
6 The time . . ., so *there were we*, cheering . . .
7 *Around the track* sat the rest of the spectators, silent . . .
8 *Hardly* had we started cheering when *there* came a response from Ken: he . . .!
9 *Well* do I remember Plunger's look . . .
10 *Rarely* have I seen anyone . . .
11 *Hardly* had the thieves got round the corner . . .
12 *Out* they jumped and *off* they ran up the street.
13 Just at that moment *up* drove a couple of police cars.
14 Windows . . . street and *out* popped a lot of heads to watch . . .
15 *At the top of the street* stands a church; *into it* darted one of the fugitives.

16 *Never* had anything like this happened in our street before/*Never* before had . . .
17 *Had* I not seen it . . .
18 (No change)
19 *At the head of the table* sat Lady Blenkinsop, *at the foot* (sat) Sir James.
20 '*Not* since my wedding day have I eaten a dinner . . .
21 In replying . . . he said: '*Only* after thirty years of marriage does a man begin truly . . .'
22 '*Were* I to have another chance,' he said, eyeing his wife, 'I'd . . .'
23 *So* overcome with emotion was the said woman that *down* her cheeks rolled two large tears.
24 *From the middle of the table* came a loud guffaw. 'There goes my son,' thought Sir James. 'Disorderly and disrespectful as usual. *On no account* must he be allowed to make a speech!'
25 Suddenly *there* appeared before Sir James's eyes a vision of his son Toby in twenty years' time, idle . . .
26 '*So* strong are the social pressures to make one smoke that . . .
27 '*Many* a time have I been made tragically aware . . .'
28 *So* amazed was I by what I had heard . . .
29 *Not* for a long time had I heard such nonsense.
30 *Should* you ever hear anyone . . .
31 '*Never, never* shall I trust a man again!' cried Helen.
32 '*Only* by avoiding them altogether can one have peace in this life,' she said.
33 '*Seldom* has a truer word been spoken,' I said. . . .

14B

1 *No sooner* do I come home in the evening *than* I switch . . .
2 *Not only* do I watch it all evening *but* I have it on for breakfast (as well).
3 (No change)
4 *No sooner* had they made the announcement *than* share prices . . .
5 *Not only* did share prices rise *but* the dollar recovered (as well).
6 (No change)
7 *Not only* does Robert's father own half the land in the village *but* he has bought . . .
8 *No sooner* does a hotel in the area come up for sale *than* he buys it.

9 And *no sooner* does he buy it *than* he starts . . .

10 *Not only* did Zena give him the use of her flat *but* she lent him her car (as well).

11 *Little* did she *know* he was . . .

12 (No change)

13 *Not only* may he pinch her car *but* he may ransack her flat (into the bargain).

14 *Little* did we *think* he was . . .

15 *Not only* was it a long way, *but* it was . . .

16 *No sooner* did we get to the hotel *than* we collapsed . . .

17 *Little* did we *know* that there was . . .

18 *No sooner* had we left *than* it started . . .

19 *Not only* was there a bad surface to contend with *but* there was now extensive flooding (as well).

20 *Little* did we *suspect* when we started our holiday that . . .!

---

15 Exercise 1

1	with	16	for
2	about	17	in
3	with	18	to
4	on	19	with
5	from	20	to
6	over	21	of
7	to	22	to
8	on	23	from
9	with	24	of
10	in	25	to
11	of	26	in
12	to	27	about
13	about/of	28	to
14	of	29	of
15	of	30	about

Exercise 2

1	in	16	from
2	for	17	against
3	in/on	18	of
4	of	19	at
5	with	20	in
6	with	21	at
7	for	22	to
8	in	23	on
9	from	24	to
10	to	25	at
11	with	26	for
12	on	27	into
13	in	28	about
14	towards	29	of
15	of	30	in

Exercise 3

1	at	16	in
2	with	17	on
3	to	18	with
4	for	19	with
5	of	20	of
6	of	21	on
7	to	22	for
8	of	23	against /with
9	to	24	to
10	for	25	on
11	with	26	of
12	of	27	on
13	in	28	over
14	on	29	on
15	between	30	on

Exercise 4

1	of	16	to
2	of	17	for
3	with	18	of
4	at	19	on
5	on	20	of
6	in	21	from
7	in	22	of
8	in	23	out of
9	on	24	to
10	of	25	to
11	in	26	from
12	to	27	in
13	on	28	on
14	in	29	for
15	in	30	to

Exercise 5

1	on	16	for
2	in	17	at
3	about	18	into
4	on	19	for
5	in	20	from
6	with	21	in
7	with	22	with
8	of	23	on
9	to /on	24	from
10	for	25	for
11	against	26	on
12	to	27	with
13	of	28	with
14	about	29	in
15	with	30	into

Exercise 6

1	to	4	with
2	with	5	with
3	in	6	to

7	for	19	in
8	into	20	by
9	in	21	into
10	on	22	from
11	in	23	of
12	for	24	in
13	from	25	for
14	in/with	26	to
15	into	27	with
16	to	28	into
17	of	29	by
18	by	30	to

Exercise 7

1	against	16	for
2	on/to	17	for
3	with	18	in
4	of	19	of
5	to	20	to
6	up to	21	to
7	by	22	of
8	on	23	to
9	for	24	to
10	to	25	to
11	of	26	for
12	on	27	against
13	to	28	of
14	at	29	towards
15	of	30	to

Exercise 8

1	for	16	of
2	with	17	with
3	for	18	to
4	to	19	for
5	for	20	to
6	for	21	for
7	with	22	between/among
8	to	23	against/with
9	for	24	to
10	to	25	for
11	for	26	with
12	for	27	for
13	with	28	to
14	for	29	to
15	on / for	30	of

Exercise 9

1	with	8	into
2	towards	9	from
3	of	10	with
4	into	11	against/with
5	of	12	for
6	to	13	of
7	to	14	in

15	in	23	in
16	to	24	from
17	about	25	on
18	in	26	at
19	from	27	in
20	with	28	over
21	with	29	with
22	to	30	of

Exercise 10

1	at	16	of
2	on	17	with
3	for	18	of/about
4	to(wards)	19	with
5	on	20	from
6	for	21	to
7	with	22	from
8	to	23	to
9	for	24	for
10	in	25	in
11	between	26	in
12	with	27	with
13	with	28	for
14	on	29	in
15	about	30	of

16A Exercise 1

1 looked down on ordinary mortals/looked down on them
2 put on a superior air/put one on
3 take people in/take them in
4 take off some of our public figures/take them off
5 gave up her own career/gave it up
6 got through all her money/got through it all
7 put by quite a tidy sum/put it by
8 put up with the man/put up with him
9 letting her husband down/letting him down
10 turned down all offers of help/turned them all down
11 laughed off one outrageous episode after another/laughed them all off
12 make out why she did it/make it out
13 owned up to treating her badly/owned up to it
14 get away with the way he behaved/get away with it
15 running the man down/running him down
16 stick up for the man/stick up for him
17 make up most of these stories/make them up
18 bear out what I've said/bear it out

222

19 takes after her father/takes after him.
20 pointed out the fact/pointed the fact out/pointed it out

12 did not go down well
13 turned down
14 toned down
15 died down

Exercise 2
1   do away with the British monarchy/do away with it
2   look on the monarchy/look on it
3   bring down the Government/bring the Government down/bring it down
4   hold up this Government's legislative programme/hold it up
5   win over all the workers/win them all over
6   let the workers off/let them off
7   wipe out all opposition/wipe it all out
8   take over all the mass media/take them all over
9   try out their new social system/try it out
10 build up a social system/build one up
11 think out a social system/think one out
12 setting about the task of reforming society/setting about it
13 carry out their so-called social reforms/carry them out
14 drawn up a political manifesto/drawn one up
15 set up a republic/set one up
16 worked out how to do it/worked it out
17 getting down to the practical details/getting down to them
18 put up a candidate/put a candidate up/put one up
19 rule out the possibility of their winning a seat or two in Parliament/rule it out
20 look into the matter/look into it

Exercise 3
1   took in
2   check in
3   put in
4   let yourself in for
5   give in
6   join in
7   stand by
8   keep in with
9   falling in with
10 ran into
11 going into/looking into
12 come into
13 taken in
14 run into debt
15 get by
16 put by some of it/put some of it by
17 brought in
18 fell in with/got in with
19 went in for
20 call (in) on/drop in on
21 run in
22 call (in) at/drop in at

Exercise 4
1   fallen off
2   lay off workers/lay workers off
3   broken off
4   put off
5   called off
6   bringing off
7   come off
8   went off
9   gave off
10 laugh off the episode/laugh the episode off
11 get off
12 struck off
13 put a lot of people off
14 make off
15 take him off
16 told him off
17 show off
18 let us off
19 see Christine off
20 cut off
21 wears off

16B Exercise 1
1   done away with
2   get away with
3   brought about
4   takes after
5   set about
6   flew at/went at
7   hanging about
8   driving at/getting at
9   come about
10 died away

Exercise 2
1   runs down
2   look down on
3   handed down
4   let the family down
5   get me down
6   lays down
7   cut down
8   get down to
9   put our past failure down to
10 brought down the Government/brought the Government down
11 put down

Exercise 5
1   getting on for
2   having you on
3   put on
4   put it on
5   coming on
6   look (up)on
7   take on
8   press on
9   pass on the information/pass
    the information on
10 going on
11 went on
12 went on/carried on
13 getting on
14 carry on
15 keep on

Exercise 6
1   worked out
2   were over three hundred pounds out
3   make out
4   put out
5   pointed out
6   thought out
7   cut out
8   bear out

9 have it out
10 wears people out
11 grown out of
12 iron out
13 fall out
14 backed out
15 carry out the scheme/carry the scheme out

16 rule out
17 tried out
18 wiped out
19 gave out the news/gave the news out
20 passed out
21 got out of
22 stood out
23 sticks out

Exercise 7

1 got through/ran through/went through
2 threw her over
3 get the interview over
4 saw through
5 gone/been through
6 was through with
7 made over the property/made the property over
8 blew over

9 got over
10 tide us over
11 thinking over the offer/thinking the offer over
12 talking it over
13 win over the shareholders/win the shareholders over
14 fall through
15 take us over
16 go through with it/see it through

Exercise 8

1 built up the business/built the business up
2 picking up
3 setting up
4 putting up
5 held up
6 drawn up
7 snap them up
8 do them up
9 take up
10 bring up the matter/bring the matter up
11 run up
12 looking up/picking up
13 end up/land up
14 make up for
15 worked up
16 pull up

17 beat up one of the policemen
18 had up
19 put up with
20 look up to
21 is up to
22 stand/stick up for
23 make it up
24 gave up
25 stand/stick up for
26 blew me up
27 size him up
28 was more than up to
29 making up these stories/making these stories up
30 own up to